The public responsibility for higher education and research

Luc Weber and Sjur Bergan (eds)

Council of Europe Publishing

Cover: Graphic Design Workshop of the Council of Europe

Council of Europe Publishing
F-67075 Strasbourg Cedex
http://book.coe.int

ISBN-10: 92-871-5679-4
ISBN-13: 978-92-871-5679-2
© Council of Europe, April 2005
Reprinted January 2006
Printed at the Council of Europe

Table of contents

3

Preface

I take pride in introducing the second volume of the Council of Europe's new Higher Education Series. The Council of Europe's higher education programme has – through its Steering Committee for Higher Education and Research (CDESR) – been addressing key issues of standards, policy and practice for a good number of years. While this work has been highly appreciated by the immediate beneficiaries, our experience has been less widely accessible to a broader public, and it is my fervent hope that this new publications series will help remedy this.

The topic of the publication – the public responsibility for higher education and research – shows the important role the Council of Europe can play in policy development and in putting issues on the agenda. The public responsibility is indeed an issue for all of Europe – and beyond. It is an issue for higher education, but also for the entire education system.

The public responsibility for higher education and research is a cornerstone of the European university heritage. Yet, our societies are changing rapidly, and clinging to old solutions will not further the very values that these solutions were originally designed to protect. The claim on public attention and public funds is growing, but public funds are not, or at least not at the same rate. While public funding of higher education and research is still important, the concept of public responsibility must be understood much more widely. It must also be nuanced by looking more closely at different degrees and levels of public responsibility as well as at the instruments available for exercising such responsibility.

This book is, I believe, an important contribution to what I see as a crucial debate for the future of Europe, and it is highly appropriate that it appears at a time when the Council of Europe is celebrating the fiftieth anniversary of the European Cultural Convention. The book contributes to a highly political debate, and it draws on the strength of the CDESR as a pan-European forum of both academic and government representatives, and with the important addition of the student voice.

European ministers responsible for higher education have twice stated that higher education is a "public good and a public responsibility". The aspect of public responsibility is the most operational part of the statement, but to make it truly operational rather than simply an expression of concern, we must define what public responsibility means in the complex societies that have just crossed the threshold to the twenty-first century. This book aims to do precisely that, and it is therefore important reading for education policy makers and practitioners alike.

The fact that the book is co-edited by Luc Weber, Vice-Chair of the CDESR, and Sjur Bergan, Head of the Council of Europe's Department of Higher Education and History Teaching, is significant, because it illustrates the close co-operation between the elected members of the steering committee and the Secretariat, which is a prominent feature of our higher education programme. I would like to thank the editors, the authors and all members of the CDESR for putting this crucial issue on the European higher education agenda.

GABRIELE MAZZA

Director of School, Out-of-School and Higher Education

A word from the editors

Luc Weber and Sjur Bergan

This book on the public responsibility for higher education and research, the second volume of the new Higher Education Series published by the Council of Europe, is a weighty contribution to the Bologna Process and, more generally, to the reinforcement of the European higher education and research sectors. Due to the globalisation process and to ambitious policies pushed forward in Europe, the European higher education and research sectors are facing a climate of rapidly increasing competition and are at the same time – which is not unusual in the sector – aiming at close co-operation between institutions and countries.

These new developments challenge the traditional provision of higher education and research in Europe and even some of its values, in particular the strong commitment to making higher education equally accessible to all on the basis of merit, whatever their social background, according to the Declaration of Human Rights (1948), and the high confidence in public institutions to provide education, even at the tertiary level, as well as to conduct fundamental research.

The rapid transformation of higher education and research raises many challenges for higher education institutions, in particular:

- the increasing difficulty for the public sector to provide a level of funding sufficient to keep the system internationally competitive;
- the increasing competition within Europe for students, academics and funding;
- the obvious domination of the leading North American institutions and the dazzling ascent of Asian and Oceanian institutions, in particular from China and Australia;
- the fast development of distance and in particular of cross-border education; and
- the rapidly increasing number of private for-profit institutions, in particular in central and eastern Europe.

These developments challenge the way higher education and research are provided, produced and financed in Europe. Obviously, some of the traditional values of higher education institutions could be at risk; it is therefore a responsibility for the European public authorities to promote them without, on the other hand, preventing the sector from implementing the important necessary changes to make Europe a leading Knowledge Society.

The Ministers of Education who met in 1999 in Bologna, where they approved the Bologna Declaration (1999), were conscious of that. They waited, however, until Prague (2001) to support "... the idea that higher education should be considered a

public good and is and will remain a public responsibility (regulations, etc.)".
These concepts of "public responsibility" and "public good" are quite common –
probably even too common; they are broadly accepted and do not raise many questions. However, if we look at them analytically, it is obvious that they merit great
attention, in particular in order to define their nature and scope more precisely.
Even if the nature and scope of the public responsibility for higher education will
differ slightly from one country to another according to their governmental, as
well as political, traditions and sensitivities, it is of utmost importance to higher
education and research that we define what the state should do, and how it should
do it, but also what it should not do. Lack of involvement as well as over-involve-
ment, or badly conceived policies, will harm the sector. In particular, the fast
changing environment requires a reappraisal of the nature and scope of the public
responsibility for higher education and research as well as the instruments for
exercising it. Moreover, the use of the concept of "public good" without defining
it precisely is confusing and could also have negative consequences on the sector
if taken *stricto sensu*.

This preamble explains why the Steering Committee on Higher Education and
Research (CDESR) of the Council of Europe has considered it extremely important to make decision makers at all levels aware of the importance of the question
and, it is hoped, to launch a broad discussion and further work on the subject.

The fourteen contributions assembled in this volume have been commissioned by
a CDESR working party of renowned higher education leaders and scholars having a particular knowledge about and experience of the most relevant aspects of
the topic. Moreover, these contributions were presented and broadly discussed at
a two-day conference which took place in September 2004 at Council of Europe
headquarters in Strasbourg. This favourable succession of events has also made it
possible to commission a general report synthesising the multiple facets of the
question as well as, for the participants, to approve a set of recommendations.

The volume is divided into three parts. Part one examines the context. The first
two contributions, by Sjur Bergan and Luc Weber (the editors), broadly examine
the question of the public responsibility for higher education and research, the former from a political as well as an institutional perspective, and the latter from the
angle of public economics. In Chapter 3, Alain Schoenenberger offers a com-
mented review of the literature on the subject, in particular the economic literature. Aleksander Shishlov concludes the first part with a political reflection on
trends in society and public responsibility.

Part two covers the many facets of public responsibility for higher education and
research. The first four contributions cover specific topics of a fundamental nature.
Pavel Zgaga looks at the public responsibility regarding higher education for a
democratic culture; Paolo Blasi stresses the importance of the contribution of
higher education and research to the Knowledge Society; Roderick Floud looks at
government and higher education approaches to regulation; and Jaak Aaviksoo
raises the question of the public responsibility for research and access to research
results.

The remaining five contributions in this part consider specific topics, all of great importance: the question of equal opportunities by Júlio Pedrosa de Jesús; financing by Carlo Salerno; new trends in higher education by Stephen Adam; preparation for the labour market by Guy Haug; and, last but not least, the public responsibility for information on higher education by Johan Almqvist and Martina Vukasović.

The third part is devoted to the conclusion and suggestions for further developments. The main constitutive element is the synthesis drafted by Eva Egron Polak: "The public responsibility for higher education and research – Conclusions and suggestions". This not only synthesises the main findings of the contributions above as well as the result of the lively discussion during the conference, but also introduces the recommendations adopted by the conference participants.

We must emphasise that a book like this one is the product of a fantastic joint venture. Obviously, the authors must be thanked for their contributions which are the building blocks of this undertaking. Special thanks should also be addressed to the members of the working party, who highlighted the different points to address in order to cover this broad and complex subject as extensively as possible and identified the potential authors. We want also to express our gratitude to the staff of the Higher Education and Research Division of the Directorate of School, Out-of-School and Higher Education of the Council of Europe, in particular to Martina Vukasović, who very successfully ensured the contacts with the authors until the conference, to Josef Huber and Can Kaftancı, who took over in the phase of preparation of the book and to Sophie Ashmore and Mireille Wendling for valuable assistance throughout. We want also to express our gratitude to the language editors, who went through all contributions without betraying the views and intentions of the authors, in particular those – the majority – who are not native English speakers.

LUC WEBER AND SJUR BERGAN

Geneva and Strasbourg, 6 December 2004

References

Bologna Declaration, *The European Higher Education Area. Joint Declaration of the European Ministers of Education,* 19 June 1999.

General Assembly of the United Nations, *Universal Declaration of Human Rights,* Resolution 217 A, 1948.

Prague Declaration, *Toward the European Higher Education Area,* communiqué of the meeting of European ministers in charge of higher education in Prague on 19 May 2001.

The context

Higher education as a "public good and public responsibility": what does it mean?

Sjur Bergan[1]

Introduction

The right to education is fundamental, an integral part of our European heritage values,[2] and one that is included in the European Convention on Human Rights. In European countries, it is, in fact, not only a right but also a legal obligation for certain age-groups, and the average grade school student may well emphasise the aspect of obligation rather than that of right. There is general agreement that public authorities have a duty to provide education for all at basic level, and the interpretation of what basic level means has been expanding. As a result, the length of mandatory schooling has tended to expand over the past couple of generations – but not to the level of higher education.

The situation with regard to higher education, then, is somewhat less clear, even if the concept of public higher education is very strong in Europe. Today, there is a high level of public involvement in higher education in our continent, and this was reflected in the communiqué adopted by the "Bologna" ministers at the Prague Higher Education Summit:

> "As the Bologna Declaration sets out, ministers asserted that building the European Higher Education Area is a condition for enhancing the attractiveness and competitiveness of higher education institutions in Europe. They supported the idea that higher education should be considered a public good and is and will remain a public responsibility (regulations, etc.), and that students are full members of the higher education community."

---

1. This first version of this article was written for the Bologna Conference on the Social Dimension of Higher Education organised by the Greek authorities in Athens in February 2003. The author would like to thank Nuria Sanz, Luc Weber and Lewis Purser for very valuable comments on an earlier draft of this article, none of which absolves the author from final responsibility.
2. The point can be illustrated by two quotes from Sanz and Bergan (2002): "In terms of cultural heritage, the university presents itself as an actor of collective responsibility guaranteeing the sense of certain moral, intellectual and technical values. Freedom of belief, freedom of teaching and the preservation of memory – physical or intellectual – teach values for life and for respect between generations. The project embarked from an attempt at defining a conceptual and contextual framework for the concept of university heritage as well as for considerations deriving from the role of universities as heritage in Europe. In addition, the university appeared as a space for reflection on the delimitation or enlargement of the term "heritage". This programme was inserted into a discussion already underway concerning a heritage that was constantly widening its definition and its basis for social, cultural, economic and symbolic action" (p. 9); and "Heritage is conceived of as an inheritance, as a cultural product and as a political resource. This practice includes more possible kinds of usage, not only those aiming at improving our knowledge of the past, as in the case of history. Rather, heritage conveys contemporary economic, cultural, political or social use" (p. 11).

On the face of it, the statement by the Bologna ministers would seem to reaffirm a well-established European practice. However, we also know something about the context in which the statement was made, which is one of stagnating or even diminishing public budgets combined with increased claims on the public purse, an increase in the provision of private higher education and in higher education with no link to public higher education systems (transnational education) and a general debate on the proper role of public authorities, generally cast as a debate on the role of the state.[3]

This context warrants the question of whether the Prague Communiqué should be seen not primarily as a statement of fact but as an expression of concern. When you need to state the obvious, it is often an indication that it is no longer obvious. The communiqué also provides an opportunity to explore what the ministers' statement could actually mean, as the concept of higher education as a public good is less straightforward than it would seem at face value. In order to do so, I shall seek to outline some questions raised by the statement and then try to identify some common ground before exploring a number of "twilight zones" where the debate deserves to be phrased in shades of grey rather than stark contrasts of black and white. We are at the beginning of a debate, and my ambition is limited to discerning some areas where we might move toward agreement as well as outlining some issues for further discussion.

Some questions

Beyond the question of why ministers felt the need to underline that higher education is a public good and a public responsibility, a number of questions could be asked about the statement. The first one is in what sense the term "public good" is used.

The problem here is that the term is well established in economic theory, where it denotes a good that is freely available to be enjoyed by all. In more technical terms – and that may be a risky undertaking on the part of a non-economist – a public good has been described as non-rival and non-excludable, meaning that one person's consumption of the good does not prevent that of others, and that it is not possible to exclude anyone from enjoying the good (Stieglitz). It follows that public goods are not readily tradable, whereas their opposites – private goods – are essentially sold on the market for exclusive consumption by one person or a group of persons paying for the privilege.

While widespread access to higher education is a cornerstone of higher education policy in most European countries, unrestricted and free access is not a realistic description of the situation: higher education – whether in the form of higher education provision (courses and study programmes) or its outcomes (diplomas and qualifications) can actually be traded and people can be excluded from higher education. In fact, in our societies, concern about the knowledge or qualifications gap

---

3. In this article, I shall prefer the term "public authority" to "state" or "state authorities", as responsibility for higher education is in some countries located at other levels, for example in federal states.

is an indication that exclusion is to some extent the real situation today, and experience from other political regimes past and present shows that undemocratic rulers will go to some length to exclude their subjects – "citizens" is hardly the word to use – from at least the kind of education that may awaken their curiosity and stimulate critical thinking. While these are perhaps extreme examples, the knowledge gap is of great concern also in democratic societies and may well be one of the most important social and economic divides in modern democratic societies. There is also solid evidence that higher education is tradable, hence our concern about the inclusion of higher education in the General Agreement on Trade in Services (GATS) and our distinction between non-profit and for-profit higher education providers. Therefore, higher education is hardly a public good in the economic sense of the term, and it is difficult to envisage policies that would render it so in the foreseeable future.

We are left, then, with an economic term used as a political statement. It is of course not unusual for terms to mean different things in different contexts, or even to change meaning in the course of time,[4] and life is certainly much more than economics. Yet, using a well-established term from one area of knowledge in a different context is not unproblematic, and this shift in usage from the domain of economics to that of a political and social context is perhaps a part of the reason for the confusion. Reality does not always correspond to ideal types, and higher education is probably situated somewhere in between public and private goods, or has elements of both (Quéau, who uses the term "global common good"). In this sense, one is also reminded of the biblical parable of the silver pieces.[5] While the silver pieces were given to individual servants by a demanding master – and were thus eminently private goods – the parable does underline the obligation to put these to good use. This aspect may not be a part of the economic definition of a public good, but it underlines an obligation incumbent on public authorities as well as on individuals: not to let their resources and talents lie idle but to use them in a beneficial way and for the greater good.

The most reasonable interpretation of the term as used in the Prague Communiqué seems to be that good quality higher education should be enjoyed by as many qualified persons as possible on equal terms, and that is a goal that would meet with approval in much of Europe.

If a public good is not marketable, does it also mean it is free of charge? This seems to be a common assumption, and the assumption is reinforced through association with the concept of public service, or rather the French concept of *service public,* which, at least in France, has strong connotations of non-payment. However, even this needs to be nuanced. At least in some countries, services that are regarded as public are in fact performed for a fee, which is normally quite modest. Passports would be one example. More importantly, all goods or services

---

4. The obvious example from English is "gay", which in the space of a generation has gone from describing a mood to describing sexual orientation, and the opposite of which is no longer "sad" but "straight".

5. St Matthew 25, 14-27. I am grateful to Nuria Sanz for reminding me of this parable – as well as of the fact that the Spanish version uses the term *talentos.*

come at a price – the question is, who pays? Even where modest fees are charged, a substantial part of the real cost is borne not by individual users in accordance with their actual use of the service, but by a collective through other payment mechanisms – typically taxes – and where wealth or ability to pay is as likely a criterion as actual use of the service.

However, the ministers do not only refer to public good; they also speak about public responsibility. The next question is, therefore, why the two terms have been coupled. I take the explicit connection between the two as an indication that the ministers are in fact concerned that higher education may not be a public good after all or – more to the point – that higher education may not be accessible on equal terms to all qualified candidates. Public responsibility is in a sense an instrument or a precondition for such a system of higher education, and the more relevant issue for the European Higher Education Area may be to explore the implications of a public responsibility for higher education. I will seek to do so by first outlining some areas on which I believe there is general agreement and then address some points on which opinions are likely to diverge.

Yet another possible question is, what is meant by public?[6] In the widest sense, the public encompasses all members of society and the public sphere encompasses what is done collectively or on behalf of at least a large part of society. For the purpose of this article, however, I will focus on public authorities, as the operationalisation or agent of society.

Some common ground

Higher education framework

Given that there is agreement that public authorities have some kind of responsibility in higher education, this responsibility should at the very minimum extend to the make-up of the education system or, if you prefer, the framework within which higher education is delivered, regardless of by whom.

One important part of the higher education system is the qualifications framework. There is agreement in Europe that public authorities decide the degree structure and its requirements. If this were not to be the case, one of the key goals of the Bologna Process – a three-tier degree structure – would be difficult to implement, as would the goal of transparency. Nor can it easily be argued that public responsibility for the degree structure makes it too rigid, as there is considerable scope for variation within the overall qualifications framework. There seem to be two conflicting tendencies today: on the one hand, study programmes give individual students possibilities to choose combinations that appeal to them for various reasons, whether of personal interest or judgments about career perspectives, and on the other hand there is increasing awareness that this diversity has to be fitted to an overall framework that can be described in a transparent way. These two tendencies can only be combined within a transparent degree structure with a limited

---

6. I am grateful to Birger Hendriks for making this point.

number of levels, but one that allows flexible combinations of credits and courses at each level. Establishing and maintaining this framework is a public responsibility.

Another important element of the higher education framework is quality assurance, where there now seems to be agreement that public authorities are responsible for ensuring that there is adequate provision for transparent quality assurance, whether they themselves carry it out or not. Quality assurance is also an example of how the perceptions of the proper role of public authorities in higher education may change quite rapidly. As late as 1997, when the Council of Europe/Unesco Recognition Convention was adopted, the need for formalised quality assurance was still disputed, and the convention had to circumscribe references to quality assurance by referring to institutions and programmes making up the higher education system of a party. We also had to include separate provisions for parties having a formalised system for the assessment of institutions and programmes and those that did not.[7] Today, the discussion is no longer of whether but of how, and public responsibility for a transparent quality assurance system is one of the cornerstones of the Bologna Process.

Autonomy

University autonomy[8] is another key element of the Bologna Process and would in the first instance seem to have more to do with public authorities keeping out of matters beyond their competence than interfering with them (Magna Charta Observatory, 2002). This is in a certain sense true, but university autonomy is an important part of the higher education framework and can only exist if public authorities make adequate provisions for autonomy in the legal and practical framework for higher education, that is, if public authorities not only ensure laws that guarantee autonomy but also ensure that these laws are implemented. The same is true for higher education governance – balancing concerns of democratic participation, academic competence and stakeholder interests – which has to be implemented at institutional level but which cannot exist without an adequate framework, which again is the responsibility of public authorities.

Equal access

Another point on which there is general agreement and which again concerns the higher education framework rather than case-by-case implementation of the policy is the equal access of all qualified candidates to higher education. Here, the responsibility of public authorities really extends to two aspects of the same policy framework. Firstly, public authorities are responsible for ensuring that qualified candidates are treated equally, that is, that the access process corresponds to the Weberian definition of the much-reviled term "bureaucracy": impartial decisions

---

7. Cf. Section VIII of the convention.
8. It may be argued that institutional autonomy and the freedom of individual academics are at the very least two sides of the coin, possibly separate if related issues, and it may be asked whether universities and non-university higher education institutions should have the same kind of autonomy.

made according to transparent procedures and with predictable outcomes (Weber, 1982, pp. 105-157). In other words, whether you are admitted to higher education should depend solely on your qualifications and not on who assesses your qualifications, at what time your qualification is considered (as long as you apply within the published deadlines), your opinions, beliefs or other characteristics or what favours you might do the person handling your application, generally referred to as corruption.

This is the classical conception of the rule of law,[9] which is essentially that of passively ensuring equal treatment on the basis of the applicant's current situation. However, contemporary European societies would tend to agree on a more activist approach under which public authorities are not only responsible for watching over the equitable application of rules but also ensuring equal opportunities through other means, in this case by taking measures to increase the number of qualified candidates through improving educational opportunities for underprivileged groups. The task, then, is not simply to administer an equitable procedure for qualified candidates, but also to increase the pool of candidates, for example through providing better education opportunities at lower levels of the system. Here, we are rapidly approaching the limits of consensus and the discussion may more appropriately be resumed under the consideration of the "twilight zones".

Higher education subject to general laws

A final example, which is not a minor one, is that higher education is subject to a good number of general laws intended to apply to society at large, and which influence the activities of higher education institutions. Examples include health regulations, for example on hazardous materials in laboratories, accounting practices, salaries or labour regulations, such as the maximum hours an employee can be required – or indeed is allowed – to work per week. Some of these measures are controversial – academic staff do not take lightly to attempts to curtail their working hours – but the principle that public authorities have a right and duty to regulate such matters and apply these regulations also to higher education is hardly at issue.

Absence of public monopoly

The "common ground" includes not only a set of responsibilities for public authorities but also the recognition that in some areas, there is no public monopoly. Here, of course, we are beginning to address the limits of public responsibility. The most obvious of these is that there should be no public monopoly on higher education provision.[10] Higher education institutions may be required to operate within the framework established by public authorities but as long as they do so, it is difficult to argue that they have to be publicly run and financed. To me, the issue

---

9. Possibly more precisely conveyed by the German term *Rechtsstaat* or the Norwegian *rettsstat*.
10. Non-public higher education provision may be non-profit or for-profit; the former seems more readily accepted than the latter, but both forms are a part of the current higher education scene, if not in every country.

is not whether higher education institutions are public or private, but whether they are of good quality, are subject to quality assessment, offer programmes leading to recognised qualifications, offer equal access and ensure academic freedom for staff and students. To paraphrase two dictums of a now outmoded ideology, what matters is not the ownership of the means of education, but whether the cat catches mice.[11]

Secondly, public authorities have no monopoly on defining knowledge or truth. There is no lack of examples from both ends of the political spectrum to show what happens when the attempt is made or, less dramatically, of what happens to the development of research in an environment where, even on an apolitical basis, new and alternative ideas are frowned upon.

Some "twilight zones"

Anything goes in the name of autonomy?

However, there is a caveat to this assertion, and this takes us from the common ground of consensus to the "twilight zones" of controversy. Saying that there is no public monopoly on the definition of truth or the content of teaching is not equivalent to saying that all views are acceptable or that higher education staff may teach anything they want. For one thing, higher education staff also have to abide by laws prohibiting racial discrimination or slurs or incitement to violence and crime. There is, of course, in any society an inherent danger that such laws may be interpreted too narrowly, but as long as they are reasonably interpreted, such laws also clearly serve a noble purpose.

Secondly, higher education staff are required to be competent in their field, and this competence is defined by their peers even if the definition can sometimes be formally approved by public authorities. History teachers who make denial of the Holocaust an element of their courses could probably be prosecuted for breaking laws against inciting ethnic hatred, but they could also be attacked on the grounds of incompetence, since the reality of the Holocaust is not in doubt. Similarly, the medical profession has established criteria for what are academically accepted doctrines and practice, and these would normally be confirmed in legal terms by public authorities. Teaching medical students to treat patients by methods judged to be hazardous would invite disciplinary proceedings. Research is another matter, and the point is perhaps that while seeking new knowledge, and hence a redefinition of truth is acceptable and even laudable, this new knowledge has to be accepted by peers before it becomes a part of the teaching canon. This is nevertheless not an unproblematic point, as is shown in medicine by the case of Semmelweiss, the current debate on human cloning and in more general terms by the tension between teaching and research in sixteenth and seventeenth-century European universities, where teachers often had to lecture according to the

---

11. From Marx and Engels and Deng Xiaoping, respectively.

established canon but disseminated new knowledge through their publications (de Ridder-Symoens, in Sanz and Bergan, 2002, pp. 77-87).

Funding issues

A characteristic element of what I have called the "twilight zone" is that it concerns the details of implementation more than the framework and it concerns what is negotiable in view of a compromise rather than absolute principles. An important part of it is made up of funding issues, the foremost of which is how much funding is reasonable for higher education. The absence of a public monopoly implies that public authorities will not fund all higher education provision, but it is equally clear that public authorities cannot reasonably run away from an obligation to provide substantial funding. That private provision is a part of the higher education system in many countries does not mean that public provision is no longer required. The difficult part is identifying how much public funding is reasonable, and on what conditions.

Public responsibility should extend to funding teaching and research in a wide diversity of academic disciplines, which is something market-driven higher education is unlikely to do. Many disciplines will have low staff and student numbers, but cultural, political, economic or other reasons will dictate that a society have a certain academic activity in these areas, which may concern less widely spoken foreign languages, less studied periods of history, relatively neglected fields of art or areas of mathematics and natural science currently out of vogue. Part of the point is that even areas that seem less important now may suddenly find themselves in the focus of public attention a few years down the road, as when many European countries scrambled to upgrade their meagre knowledge of Arabic language and culture in the wake of the oil crisis in the 1970s. An even stronger reason, however, is that areas that may not be important in numbers may be very important for our cultural identity or as a basis for developing the key concepts on which more applied knowledge is based. These are areas in which our societies need advanced competence, but they may not need large numbers of people with this knowledge.

The fact that public authorities provide significant funding for higher education institutions does not mean, however, that all higher education institutions fulfilling defined minimum quality standards have a claim on the public budget. Firstly, public authorities should have a right to distinguish in funding terms between public institutions, which public authorities fund entirely or substantially, and private ones, for which they provide much less funding or none at all. Secondly, in the same way that public authorities make judgments about the need for higher education institutions and programmes when they decide on the level and distribution of public funding for these institutions, they should be in a position to make similar judgments about public funding for private institutions. A decision that private institutions and programmes are recognised because they are of sufficient quality should not automatically mean they have a right to receive public funds. Needless to say, this is an important point in the context of GATS.

Student support

Student support is another key economic issue where no ready-made answer exists, but which is intimately linked to the public responsibility for making higher education accessible to wider groups and more individuals. The basic principle seems clear: it is a public responsibility that no qualified candidate should have to abstain from higher education because he or she lacks the means to study. This principle, however, raises a number of questions, such as how "qualified candidates" should be defined. Are we talking only about the academically promising ones or also about those who may barely make it through a study programme? Is public responsibility limited to funding some kind of higher education for qualified candidates, or does it extend to giving them access to and funding for the discipline and level of their choice? Is there a free choice of institution or should public student support be given a maximum price tag? Not least, should it be given as scholarships or loans, and if the latter, at market rates or more favourable student rates?

One argument has it that students should bear a substantial part of the cost of their studies because higher education will most likely give them access to more highly paid jobs, so that over a lifetime investment in higher education will pay off in pure economic terms. That may be so, although I suspect it is not true for all academic disciplines in all European countries. Some higher education graduates – lawyers would be an obvious example – may reasonably expect a high financial return on their investment of time and money, whereas others – school teachers would probably be a valid example – would not. An argument in favour of a high level of student support would be that if society believes higher education is vital to its development, and that a country as a whole should have advanced knowledge of a wide area of disciplines, society should also stimulate its members to seek higher education in as many fields as possible. Another argument is that even where there may be lifetime economic gain in pursuing higher education, not all qualified students will actually be in a position to raise the money needed to study in the first place.

If higher education is to be made more widely accessible, a reasonable student support scheme therefore seems to be vital, but there may be a case for designing it in such a way that it caters in particular to less favoured students. This is, however, a difficult discussion that goes well beyond the scope of this article, and it touches on such issues of principle as individual versus group rights and the legal relationship between young adults and their parents.

Direct student support through loans and scholarships is, however, only a part of the discussion. To the extent students do not pay the full cost of their education, they receive public support, and the question is how much such support they should receive or – to phrase it in more controversial terms – whether they should pay study fees. Traditionally, at least in many European countries, public higher education does not charge fees, and the issue is highly charged, even if – or perhaps precisely because – the issue is now being raised in some countries. In considering the issue of fees, it should be kept in mind that higher education is generally considered to be of benefit to the individual, even where it does not demonstrably increase overall lifetime earnings, and that access to higher education is not unbiased, in that young people from families of higher socioeconomic status whose parents have higher education degrees are more likely to take higher education than those of lower socioeconomic status with little or no education traditions in the family. Granted, this argument again raises the question of individual versus group rights, but it should at least serve to illustrate the fact that higher education free of charge to the individual is not an issue to be phrased in black and white.

The point is also illustrated by the opposite possibility: students paying the full cost of their education. Apart from the fact that the full cost of some study programmes would be prohibitive and could cut society off from certain kinds of much-needed competence, this model is also untenable on reasons of principle. While the benefits of higher education may be most immediately felt by those who graduate from it, all members of society benefit to some extent from a high general level of competence in that society. Certainly, the benefits of a medical education are not limited to doctors.

Funds from other sources

If it is recognised that public authorities do not have a monopoly on funding higher education, and indeed that they are unlikely to be able to provide funding at anything like the aspirations of higher education institutions, what is the role of private funding? This is, in my view, not a discussion of whether there should be private funding, but of whether there should be conditions for such funding. Where is the balance between the priorities decided by the governing body of a university and the power of outside funding to modify those priorities? If some academic disciplines will easily attract funding and others not, should a part of external funds be redistributed within the institution through some kind of "internal taxation", or would this be unfair on those who are able to raise money and discourage external sources from contributing because the priorities of those contributors will not be fully respected? Could external funds be used not only to improve the working conditions in certain fields, for example by financing advanced equipment or travel, but also to improve salaries of staff or scholarships for students? In the latter case, access may be improved, but students' choice of academic field may be influenced as much by immediate possibilities for financing their studies as by their own interest in the disciplines or by considerations of future earnings.

This is of course not a new issue: in past centuries, the seminary was often the only possibility for sons of poor families to break out of a cycle of poverty and low status and to satisfy intellectual curiosity, even if they did not all have a burning vocation for the priesthood. Military academies have also been engines for social mobility. However, there are also examples of selection procedures for military training that aim to ensure that control over the armed forces rest with the dominant parts of society (Rouquié, 1987, pp. 84-93).

Funding from private sources is a valuable and much-needed supplement to public finance, but it should be subject to conditions. The precise implementation of this principle, however, implies a delicate balance between ensuring that public and institutional priorities are not unduly skewed through the power of external finance and avoiding setting up rules that would deter potential contributors.

Access policies – How directive and activist?

We considered that the role of public authorities in ensuring equal access to higher education was a part of the consensus, but we also indicated that there were limits to this consensus, and that the degree to which public authorities can direct institutions in their access policies is a part of the "twilight zone", as is the extent to which such policies should be "activist".

If it is recognised that educational opportunities at least to some extent depend on place of residence and socioeconomic or cultural background, public authorities could take steps to ensure favourable access for members of underprivileged groups if these are considered to have the potential to do well in higher education even if they might not satisfy all access requirements at the time of application, or, if access is restricted and competitive, a certain number of qualified candidates from disadvantaged backgrounds may be given preference over better qualified applicants from more classical higher education backgrounds (Council of Europe, 1997 and 1998).

Such measures, often referred to as "positive discrimination" or "affirmative action", are often controversial, as proven by the discussions in many countries about favouring access of women applicants to study programmes in which they are under-represented or measures in favour of ethnic minorities. The latter has frequently been a bone of contention in United States higher education, where the Bakke case is possibly the best-known example since Brown v. the Board of Education,[12] and where the Bush Administration is now seeking to have current practice at the University of Michigan declared unconstitutional on the grounds that it discriminates against members of the majority.[13] In a recent case, Norwegian universities have been directed to review policies favouring qualified women candidates for academic positions, in an attempt to recruit more women in fields where they are under-represented, in particular at the highest levels, because this has been judged unacceptable under the non-discrimination provisions of the European Economic Area.

Ultimately, the main argument in favour of activist public authorities in the domain of access is that the public responsibility for ensuring fair and equitable access to higher education is an important instrument in making higher education something close to a public good. However, exactly where the right balance is to be found between this highly important concern and other policy goals is likely to continue to be a matter of debate.

---

12. In this landmark case from Topeka, Kansas, the US Supreme Court struck a decisive blow against the segregation of US schools.
13. See the *International Herald Tribune*, 17 January 2003, p. 3.

Consequences of quality assurance

As we have seen, a consensus on the need for quality assurance has emerged over the past five years or so. However, this consensus does not – at least not yet – extend to an agreement on what should be the consequences of quality assurance. At one level, while accreditation is in many countries given on the basis of quality assurance, the concept of accreditation is not accepted in all countries. Beyond the concepts, however, there is considerable discussion of what the goals and consequences of quality assurance should be. If an institution or programme receives a negative assessment, should it be closed, should it be given a deadline to bring its house in order but otherwise be left alone, or should a sustained effort be made to turn it into a good quality institution or programme? Most likely, the answer will depend on circumstances. An institution that is seen as important to the development of an underprivileged part of the country is likely to be looked at with more lenience than one that is located in an area where there are many alternatives, and the only study programme in a discipline public authorities consider important is more likely to receive the benefit of the doubt along with an infusion of funds than one that is considered expendable.

Nevertheless, some would go further and reject the notion that a quality assurance process could be linked to decisions concerning funding or licences to operate a given institution or programme. There may be a case for carrying out quality assurance solely with a view to improving existing higher education provision,[14] but in my view it is unreasonable to say that this must in all circumstances be the only purpose of quality assurance. Public funds for higher education are limited, and it would seem unreasonable to spend them on programmes of unsatisfactory quality unless other concerns would dictate a sustained effort to improve those programmes. Likewise, students would be badly served by funding policies that simply aimed to maintain programmes regardless of their quality.

Information

This brings me to my final point in this far from exhaustive overview of the "twilight zone", namely the responsibility of public authorities with regard to information to students, employers, parents and others. We all agree that they should receive correct and comprehensible information provided in good faith (Unesco/Council of Europe, 2001), and that for many kinds of information, this is primarily the responsibility of the education provider. However, what responsibility do public authorities have to oversee the information given by institutions? On the one hand, public authorities should not unduly interfere with academic autonomy and the right of institutions to provide the particular kind of information known as advertising, but on the other hand, public authorities do have some

---

14. The European University Association institutional review programme is intended to support universities and their leaders in their efforts to improve institutional management and, in particular, processes to face change. The emphasis is laid on self-evaluation and allows the institutions to understand their strengths and weaknesses. Such reviews may make specific recommendations to institutional leaders regarding the internal allocation of budgets, but since the evaluation is independent of national or other funding sources there is obviously no link to decisions concerning such funding.

responsibility for ensuring that citizens are not led astray by patently untruthful publicity material.

Again, suggesting an overall rule of thumb is difficult, but I would suggest that public authorities should be responsible for providing information on the higher education system, including its degree structure and on the institutions and programmes that make up the higher education system of a given country,[15] which also implies that the results of quality assurance exercises should be made public and easily accessible. Public authorities should also be able to suggest models for how institutions could provide information, and in some cases they should be able to enforce a specific format for the provision of information. Thus, I am fully in line with the authorities of those countries that have included in their laws an obligation for institutions to provide students with a diploma supplement and/or have made the European Credit Transfer System mandatory. I also believe that public authorities should keep an eye on the overall information provided by institutions operating on their territory and that they should have as much power to act against systematic misinformation by higher education providers as against any other kind of false advertising.[16]

Right to university heritage

Finally, I would suggest that students, staff and society at large have a right to the heritage of universities, that this heritage should be a factor in shaping current policies, and that public authorities share a responsibility for making this right real. As we stated in a different context:

> "The university heritage is not a story of immediate gratification, nor is it one of constant and unfailing success. Its importance is of a different order: the heritage of European universities is one of the most consistent and most important examples of sustainable success and achievement that Europe has ever seen. The university is a part of our heritage, and its future is decided now ... Our reflection on the university heritage coincides with a time when cultural heritage policies are no longer only identified with a typology or with a prescriptive approach to tangible and intangible resources, but are also aimed at valorising problems of heritage policies that also have to do with filiation and affective ties (cultural, sociological, confessional, territorial). From these ties a specific kind of current relationship to the ways of establishing memories can be defined, based on what is lived today" (Sanz and Bergan, 2002, p. 174).

The Bologna Process builds on the heritage of European universities, and the ability to adapt to changing circumstances is very much a part of this heritage. The public responsibility for higher education also includes conserving and building on this heritage and to transmit it to future generations. A medieval scholar might not recognise organised higher education exchange programmes; even if Dom

---

15. In this respect, the European Network of National Information Centres on Academic Recognition and Mobility (ENIC) and the National Academic Recognition Information Centres (NARIC) play an important role.

16. In discussions at the conference for which this article was written, the need for proper guidance to students was strongly emphasised and, I believe, rightly so. However, the main responsibility for guidance would seem to lie with the institutions rather than with public authorities as considered here.

Sancho I of Portugal set up a kind of mobility scholarship scheme as early as the twelfth century (Saraiva, 1978, p. 109), he would be surprised at the range of today's academic disciplines and the fact that academic discourse is no longer in Latin, and he would probably consider the idea of a Socrates Office in Athens as an unnecessary bureaucratisation of philosophy. Yet, the idea of a European Higher Education Area is not only one he could easily identify with, but probably one he would take for granted.

By way of conclusion

As the ambitions for this article were limited to outlining the issues and identifying some areas of consensus as well as for further discussion, the conclusions can hardly be final. They are made up of four elements.

Firstly, I believe public authorities have exclusive responsibility for the framework of higher education, including the degree structure, the institutional framework, the framework for quality assurance and authoritative information on the higher education framework. The framework cannot be left to others.

Secondly, I would maintain that public authorities bear the main responsibility for ensuring equal opportunities in higher education, including access policies and student finance. This is a crucial area in making higher education as much of a public good as possible, and the overall goal for public authorities in this area must be to make sure that any person living in the country[17] be able to make full use of his or her abilities regardless of socioeconomic and cultural background, financial possibilities and previous education opportunities.

Thirdly, I believe public authorities should have an important role in the provision of higher education. While there should be no public monopoly on higher education provision, public authorities should be heavily involved not only in designing the framework but also in the actual running of higher education institutions and programmes, to contribute to good educational opportunities on reasonable conditions and to ensure that higher education encompasses a wide variety of disciplines and levels.

Fourthly, and this point is in part a consequence of the other three, public authorities in my view have an important financial responsibility for higher education. Public funds may and should be supplemented by money from other sources, but these alternative funding sources should never be a pretext for public authorities not to provide substantial public resources.

In thinking about higher education as a public good I was reminded of an illustration in one of the first books I can remember reading. Snorri Sturluson was an Icelander, but he wrote the sagas that have now come to be considered as one of

---

17. To avoid misunderstanding, I deliberately use the more cumbersome formulation "any person living in the country" rather than "citizen", as I believe this obligation extends not only to those who are citizens in the legal, "passport" sense of the term, but to all those who are citizens in the larger sense as members of a given society. For this, residence is a surer guide than cultural or political identity. Besides, at least in some context, "citizen" is now used as the public policy equivalent of "consumer".

the main items of Norwegian literature and the first attempt at writing Norwegian history. In one of his illustrations of Olav Haraldsson's – Saint Olaf's – final battle at Stiklestad on 29 July 1030, Halfdan Egedius showed a steady stream of people bearing arms and moving in the same direction. In the laconic style of the sagas, the caption to this particular drawing simply states that "all paths were filled with people" (Snorri Sturluson, 1964, p. 453). My vision of higher education as a public good is something like this, except that the arms are to be replaced with a desire for learning and that the people on the paths are on their way not to battle – an extreme form of competition – but to higher education institutions and programmes based on competition but even more on co-operation, where they will find a wide variety of offers on terms that will not exclude any qualified candidate, and that will:

– prepare them for the labour market;
– prepare them for life as active citizens in democratic society;
– contribute to their personal growth;
– maintain and develop an advanced knowledge base.

This is no small challenge, but it is vital to our future that we meet it. I am convinced it is one that can be met, and that public authorities bear the main responsibility for meeting it. Public authorities cannot do this alone, and they need to draw on the combined efforts of higher education institutions, students and staff, the private sector, and other members of society. However, the overall responsibility for the exercise and for its success or failure remains in the public domain – which is to say it is a collective responsibility for all of us as citizens of democratic societies.

References

Berlin Communiqué, *Realising the European Higher Education Area*, adopted by European ministers of education on 19 September 2003.

Bologna Declaration, *The European Higher Education Area. Joint Declaration of the European Ministers of Education*, 19 June 1999.

Council of Europe, *Recommendation No. R (97) 1 on private higher education*.

Council of Europe, *Recommendation No. R (98) 3 on access to higher education in Europe*.

Council of Europe/Unesco, *Convention on the Recognition of Qualifications concerning Higher Education in the European Region*, 1997.

Magna Charta Observatory, *Autonomy and responsibility – The university's obligations for the XXI century*. Proceedings of the launch event for the Magna Charta Observatory, 21-22 September 2001 (Bologna 2002: Bononia University Press).

Prague Declaration, *Toward the European Higher Education Area*, communiqué of the meeting of European ministers in charge of higher education in Prague on 19 May 2001.

de Ridder-Symoens, H., "The intellectual heritage of ancient universities in Europe", in Sanz, N. and Bergan, S. (eds), *The heritage of European universities*, pp. 77-87.

Quéau, P., "Global governance and knowledge societies", *Development*, Vol. 45, No. 4, pp. 10-16.

Rouquié, A., *The military and the state in Latin America*, University of California Press, Berkeley and Los Angeles, 1987.

Sanz, N. and Bergan, S. (eds), *The heritage of European universities*, Council of Europe Publishing, Strasbourg, 2002.

Saraiva, J.H., *História concisa de Portugal*, Publicações Europa-America, Lisbon, 1978.

Snorri Sturluson, *Snorres kongesagaer*, Norwegian translation by Anne Holtsmark and Didirk Arup Seip, Gyldendal, Oslo/Stavanger, 1964.

Stiglitz, J.E. "Knowledge as a public good", http://www.worldbank.org/knowledge/chiefecon/articles/undpk2/, first accessed in January 2003.

Unesco/Council of Europe, *Code to Good Practice in the Provision of Transnational Education*, 2001.

Weber, M., *Makt og byråkrati*, Gyldendals Studiefakler, Oslo, 1982, based on the 1922 edition of Max Webers, *Wirtschaft und Gesellschaft*.

Nature and scope of the public responsibility for higher education and research?

Luc Weber

Introduction

Relevance of the theme

At first sight, the topic "public responsibility for higher education and research" might appear a theoretical question of the kind typically cherished by academic thinkers, but without any practical relevance. But I shall argue that, on the contrary, the question is of increasing practical importance for the effectiveness of the higher education and research system. A first and very strong political sign is that the ministers of education stated firmly in their Prague and Berlin communiqués (2001 and 2003) that higher education is a "public responsibility", a principle which was already implicit in the Bologna Declaration (1999). A second, but different concern, shared by university leaders and experts, is that it is crucial to define correctly the nature and scope of the public responsibility for higher education and research and how it is implemented; otherwise this political good intention could act counterproductively. A serious indicator of this potential threat arises from the fact that the ministers of education added in the Prague Communiqué (2001) that higher education "should be considered a 'public good' and is and will remain a public responsibility (regulations, etc.)". This means that the sense given to the expression "public good" is all but insignificant. This is all the more important as we can also hear or read from time to time that higher education and research are a "human right" or a "democratic right", without a precise definition of what is meant by them.

The question of the nature and scope of the public responsibility for higher education and research and, in particular, the interpretation of the notion of "public good" are so important for the effectiveness of the higher education and research system that the Council of Europe, under the initiative of its Steering Committee for Higher Education and Research (CDESR), has decided to organise a conference in the framework of the "Bologna seminars"[18] in order to establish the real nature and scope of the public responsibility for higher education and research and to publish the results in this book.

---

18. Conferences that are a part of the official Bologna work programme. A full list may be found at http://www.bologna-bergen2005.no

Outline

This contribution aims at setting the scene. This essay is strongly inspired by my academic discipline, public economics, and by the stimulating discussions within the working group of the CDESR, who prepared the programme of the conference. The three following topics will be addressed: the public sector's role and policy instruments; the justification for public responsibility for higher education; and the limits of public responsibility for higher education.

Two preliminary remarks are necessary. First, although the ministers of education promoting the Bologna Process intended to create the European Higher Education Area for the first and second cycles, they introduced the doctorate studies (third) cycle as a tenth objective of the Bologna Process in the Berlin Communiqué (2003), in order to bridge the efforts made to create the European Higher Education and Research Areas. Considering the key role played by higher education institutions in fundamental and applied research as well as, more generally, the importance of research for the Knowledge Society and, through it, the economic, social and cultural development of the European nations, this book addresses the question of public responsibility for higher education as well as for research. Due to a lack of space, however, my contribution will refer more specifically to higher education.

Second, the emphasis put in the introduction on the public responsibility for higher education and research neglects the fact that this responsibility has two facets: a public responsibility for higher education and research, as well as a public responsibility of higher education and research institutions, and of their stakeholders, outside and within the institutions, towards society at large. Institutions have first to serve society by educating all those who have the ability to pursue higher education studies, and by developing and applying knowledge contributing to a better society through political, economic, social and cultural development. This public responsibility on the part of higher education and research has various implications, such as, for example, access to higher education independently of social background, the absence of cheating and corruption, the respect of ethical norms in research, in particular in life science research, etc. Although of great importance for society, this facet of public responsibility is not the theme of this book, which is focused specifically on the public responsibility for higher education and research.

The role and policy instruments of the public sector

In any nation, the choice of goods and services produced and consumed, the organisation of their production and the sharing of wealth among individuals and regions is assured by a combination of the three following systems:

– competitive markets, where decisions are strongly decentralised;

– the public sector (or the state), where provision of services is decided in a political process;

– non-profit organisations, serving collective needs (clubs, non-profit associations, foundations), where decisions are made by the members.

History shows that no country can prosper if its economic organisation is based only on one or even two of these systems. The recurring political issue is the right mix and balance between these three systems. Viewed from a more analytical perspective, the system in place for the provision of a good or service depends on the response given to the three following questions:

– who provides it (decides)? A political body, a voluntary non-profit organisation or the market?

– who produces it? The state, a private enterprise or a voluntary non-profit organisation?

– who pays? The state, the beneficiaries or some sponsor?

Surprisingly, the legal status (private or public) is less important.

For education in general and higher education and research in particular, the provision, production, and financing can theoretically be assured either by the state (traditional public universities), by a market process (private for-profit universities) or by private non-profit institutions. Obviously, in the real world, extreme solutions are rare. In particular, public universities benefit increasingly from private funds to finance research, lifelong learning programmes or even traditional teaching programmes (student fees). Public funds are more and more allocated according to "private-like formulae", for example, allocating a given sum per student or, in line with an increasing concern for output, per graduate. Moreover, many universities are quite independent from the state regarding their governance (decision process), the status of their staff or their management, but are nevertheless largely financed by public money. Furthermore, in particular in the United States, many universities, among them most of the best research-intensive universities, are totally independent entities largely financed by private money (student fees, charities/sponsors, return of the endowment funds). These institutions are, in fact, legally and otherwise, private institutions. In Europe, at least some private institutions are, however, quite dependent on public funding, whereas in the United States and possibly also in Europe (at least in the United Kingdom), a good number of public institutions depend to a large extent on private funding. They are nevertheless non-profit organisations, which means that they belong to the category of the voluntary non-profit organisations and not to that of private enterprises. Moreover, these institutions receive considerable public funds on a competitive basis, for example through government research programmes or government student funding (cf. federal student aid in the United States). And even in the extreme case of private for-profit universities, many recognise, apart from extreme liberal thinkers, that the state should keep an eye on them, in other words, it should regulate these institutions. In other words, the state should provide the framework within which these institutions operate and – very possibly – also the quality assurance system to which institutions must submit in order to be able to operate legally.

The lesson which must be drawn from this very succinct recall of the theoretical principles is that various organisational solutions are possible. At one extreme, the state is responsible for everything, that is provision, production and financing and, at the other extreme, there are higher education institutions which are fully private, which means that, in a fully unregulated framework, they produce the service they provide and sell it to their (student) customers with the admitted purpose of making a profit. However, observation of the world's higher education and research systems shows that the majority of institutions are mainly public (provision, production and most of the funding assured by the state) and most of the remaining institutions belong to the voluntary non-profit sector (provision and production by non-profit organisations and the greater part of funding originating from the students or from external private sources). Finally, a small, but growing number of institutions are for-profit organisations or subsidiaries of enterprises (corporate universities), sometimes regulated by the state or an independent accreditation body.

Justification for public responsibility for higher education

In order to clarify and define the nature and scope of the public responsibility for higher education, it is crucial to have clearly in mind that, in organisational terms, any solution, from a totally public to a totally private one, is possible. In other words, the nature of higher education and research does not create strong constraints, which would make some solutions impossible.

Therefore, why have the ministers of education affirmed that higher education is a public responsibility? Is it a purely political argument based on ideology or beliefs, or simply on their own hidden interest in increasing the size of the public sector and consequently their power, or are there tangible elements or arguments justifying a public responsibility for higher education and research? As we shall see, most if not all arguments in favour of a public responsibility for higher education are well established and broadly accepted. However, the fast-changing environment and the political realities and priorities of the time are changing the nature or the relative importance of some of them. Therefore, it is necessary to be aware of these changes before analysing the main arguments in favour of the public responsibility for higher education and research.

The changing environment

If we should describe today's world with only one characteristic, the dominating factor is the increasing competition between people and organisations (public and private) and within them, which is accompanied by a greater interdependence. This is due to a few deep-rooted developments, in particular, globalisation and the rise of the knowledge economy, which are themselves the consequence of various factors. In Europe, this development is complemented by the long-term effort towards a greater economic, political, and, partly also, social integration (Weber, 1999).

Due to this climate of increased competition and to its own dynamic, the higher education and research sector has entered into a period of rapid change: arrival of new providers, increasing differentiation between different types of institutions, challenging of well-established traditions, necessity to become accountable to society at large, challenging of the model of shared governance, etc. Obviously, these events and trends are challenging the idea of public responsibility for higher education and research.

Secure a high level of higher education and research

It is well established that higher education produces a very high private, as well as collective, return on investment. Even the World Bank, which for some time was giving a higher priority to primary education, now recognises that higher education is also extremely important for the development of a country (World Bank, 2002; Salmi, 2003). At the individual level, higher education is the best choice for increased earning over the life cycle and the best "unemployment insurance". At the national level, knowledge is becoming a production factor as important as labour and capital, stimulating growth thanks to the increased qualification of the labour force and to improved products and services, as well as production processes. Moreover, a high level of general and advanced education is improving the cultural level of a society as well as its functioning, thanks to improved values like tolerance and respect of others and to a more rational approach to problems.

If markets for higher education and research functioned perfectly, the equilibrium between demand and supply would correspond to an optimal solution. However, markets for higher education and research are imperfect, which means that they do not produce spontaneously the optimal solution. We shall mention here the two main causes of market failure on the demand side:

– external economies: a positive characteristic of higher education is that it does not benefit only those involved, but also those who abandoned it and who did not return to classes later, just because the general level of education of a nation somehow benefits everyone. In other words, less educated people are better off in a well-educated society than in a society with a mediocre level of education. This is certainly true in terms of the services from which they can benefit (for example, medical services); it is perhaps less obvious in terms of social integration. The same is true with research. Very few private organisations will enter into big investments in basic and/or free research as it is quite uncertain that they will be able to receive a positive return from their investment. These external benefits mean that the collective return on higher education and research investments is greater than the sum of the individual returns. Markets, by definition, are unable to take into account spontaneously these external benefits and will therefore produce a quantity of education which is inferior to the collective interest. This market failure has to be handled by the institution representing the general or collective interest, the state;

– failing information: not every citizen by far is aware of the high individual and collective return of higher education investments. This is clearly the case of young people in their adolescence, families who did not benefit from more than an elementary level of education and many people well installed in a professional activity. The consequence is that their demand for higher education and lifelong learning is inferior to what would be in their long-term interest. Even if the advice from parents, friends or employers can partly compensate for part of this lack of information, it is a responsibility of the state to encourage these groups to increase their demand for education.

These two market failures justify the intervention of the state which can take various forms and importance:

– public funding: this is by far the most important and powerful policy instrument at the disposal of the state to exercise its responsibility. In financing most if not all of the supply of higher education, the state is supplying it at a very low or even at zero price, encouraging many more people to obtain a higher level of education than if they have to pay the market price. The state can also influence the demand of higher education in subsidising the students through grants or loans at a preferential interest rate. For the same reasons, it is also extremely important that the public sector give a high priority to investments in basic and free research. In this respect, the European debate launched in 2000 in Lisbon is crucial for Europe. The long-term competitiveness of Europe will depend directly on its investment in the Knowledge Society through higher education and research, much more than on trying to preserve obsolete structures in a few economic sectors, in particular agriculture, or badly conceived social policies. Even if the market can, in principle, respond to the individual demand for education, the external economies produced by higher education and research mean that by far the main public responsibility is to generously finance higher education and research. This first priority of public policy has to be repeated again and again, in particular in a development phase where the generous social policies put in place in the last fifty years show obvious signs of not being demographically and economically sustainable, with the consequence that they require the appropriation of ever bigger chunks of the public budgets, putting at risk the future development of those countries;

– public influence: the imperfect information identified above is at the origin of a second public responsibility: correcting the decisions made on the basis of insufficient or erroneous information. The public sector can basically act according to two lines of strategies. First, it can act indirectly on demand by decreasing the price of education services, a solution which has been briefly developed above. Second, it can act directly on demand, for example by making primary education compulsory. For higher education, it will do this by implementing various encouragement policies.

Secure a fair distribution of higher education opportunities

The argument raised above about imperfect information was developed in the framework of the optimal quantity of higher education. This is important, but by no means sufficient, as it appears that the lack of information or the existence of erroneous information are not distributed equally among the different classes of society. Obviously, the less educated groups in society – who also tend to be the less well off – are more likely to miss the advantage of education, and in particular of higher education. The facts are there. Despite the efforts made to counteract it, the proportion of people going to higher education institutions is much smaller in low-income families or families living in poorer regions of a country than in well-educated families or more developed regions. This means that there is a strong correlation between the education level of the parents and their children.

Therefore, anyone believing in democratic values, by which every citizen should have an equal position within society, will agree that another extremely important responsibility of the public sector is to make sure that access to higher education is based only on merit, and therefore open to everyone on an equal basis, whatever his or her social origin; in other words, that there is no barrier to access, financial or other.

This responsibility of the public sector has two levels of requirements. At the first level, the state should make sure that there is no financial barrier to access to higher education, or originating from discrimination according to gender, nationality, ethnicity, social class, etc. The measures implemented are financial (free access to higher education, or the attribution of grants or loans at a preferential interest rate) or of a constitutional order to ban discrimination. However, as mentioned above, the proportion of people from disadvantaged families attending higher education institutions remains low in most if not all European countries. This therefore raises the question whether it is not indispensable to take proactive measures. This is the case with affirmative action in the United States in favour of minorities. Such a proactive policy would imply the implementation of active encouragement policies and stronger financial incentive measures.

Secure a quality higher education and research sector

The question of the quality of higher education and research is rapidly gaining in importance and has become an important concern of the public sector and of those involved in higher education and research. I see two reasons for this:

– the increasing struggle for state funds is forcing institutions to manage themselves better and to be more transparent and accountable to their sponsors;

– the increasing competition within the sector; in particular, the creation of numerous private institutions in central and eastern European countries and the fast development of trans-border education (which will be encouraged even more if the GATS negotiations include the education sector) are creating a much greater need for quality control. Also, the impact of European Union (EU) internal market legislation tends to be underestimated and under-studied.

Both the public sector and the higher education system are concerned by this greater need for quality control. In particular, considering the importance of higher education for economic, social and cultural development, a control of the quality of the provision of higher education and research is indispensable. This responsibility calls for a fourth means of action by the state: regulation (next to provision, production and financing). This means that, even if an education or research service is privately provided, produced and financed, the public sector should guarantee that the level of quality is sufficient, or even good.

Basically, the state could be invited to make sure that a few minimum criteria are satisfied, mainly to protect the students as consumers and also to protect the word "university". Depending on the definition given to the terms, some call it licensing (recognition), others accreditation. Considering the difficulty of appreciating the quality of an institution, the public sector should not be too ambitious as the cost of regulation can rapidly become disproportionate and the results arbitrary. As for all human activities, a feasibility of a hundred per cent is impossible, which means that part of the responsibility for judgment should be left with the individual students choosing these institutions.

The question of quality must also be considered in a more ambitious way, that is, to appreciate the quality of an institution, a programme or a department and even to encourage improvement. There is presently a very lively debate between ministries of education, accreditation or quality assurance bodies and the universities represented by the European University Association (EUA) as well as the students, represented by the National Unions of Students in Europe (ESIB), to determine who should be responsible for quality control: the state or independent bodies set up by the state or the universities themselves. The EUA is arguing rightly that institutions should be responsible for their quality assurance, but that their processes should be controlled by an independent body.

The importance of the constitutional and legislative framework

Higher education and research (at least basic research) is a very peculiar type of service in the sense that it aims at producing new knowledge using verifiable processes and to transmit this knowledge, giving justice to different points of view, methodologies and results. As universities are working at the frontier of knowledge, they are best placed to promote the advancement of knowledge and to transmit it; no institution (public or private) is in a better position to do so. This is why it has been recognised for ages that universities should be autonomous from the state, the private sector or from any other organised body, such as churches (see the *Magna Charta Universitatum,* 1998).

This implies that the state has an additional responsibility to set up a constitutional and legal framework securing this autonomy, preventing it from intervening and protecting the sector from other interventions. Although this fundamental rule is very broadly recognised, it has to be repeated permanently as the temptation for the state to intervene is permanent. At present, the pressures arising from financial reductions expose many university systems or individual institutions to the risk of stronger state intervention. This is important as even if the principle of autonomy is recognised, it may well be constrained in a more hidden way because many strings could be attached to the different objects of decision of an institution (students' admission, finance, buildings, programmes, etc.).

Limits to the public responsibility for higher education

I hope I have made a strong case in favour of public responsibility for higher education and research. However, does this mean that there is no limit to state involvement in higher education and research? Does it mean in particular that higher education and research are a "public good" *stricto sensu,* as the ministers of education affirmed in their Prague and Berlin communiqués? Arguing that it is not the case is straightforward. Moreover, it is crucial to realise that it would even be counterproductive for the effectiveness of higher education and research.

Higher education and research are not a "public good" stricto sensu?

As mentioned in the introduction, the answer to the question whether higher education and research are a "public good" depends on the meaning given to this notion. If the ministers have in mind a loose definition with the sole purpose of reinforcing the expression "public responsibility" by repeating it using a different wording, this is acceptable; however, it is confusing as it forces everyone to wonder if the intention is to express two separate objectives or to say the same thing in two different manners.

But the addition of the term "public good" should be looked at with great suspicion if the ministers have in mind that higher education is not only a public responsibility, but also a specific type of good or service, called a "public good". There are at least two lines of argument to prove that higher education and research are not a public good.

For economists, to state that a good or a service in the case of higher education is a "public good" implies that it is "non-rival" and "non-excludable", according to the well-established theory of public expenditure (Samuelson, 1954). The consequence is that it cannot be provided and financed by private organisations; this has to be done by the state. In his survey of the literature included in the present volume, Alain Schoenenberger examines in detail the peculiar characteristics of public goods; I shall therefore not elaborate on them here. He makes it clear that higher education and research are not a public good, and certainly not a pure public good. The best proof is that private institutions can provide and finance higher education and research without difficulty. The only – indeed important – qualification is that higher education and research produce external benefits; therefore, the state has to intervene to avoid under-provision.

The alternative way to define the notion of "public good" is in terms of public administration. Affirming that higher education is a "public good" is a political value judgment that states that this service must be furnished by the public sector, in principle at no charge to the users. In French, the notion of *service public* has a particularly strong political connotation, meaning that it must be provisioned and distributed at no charge by the public sector, and according to the public sector rules. The fact that, in reality, nothing makes it obligatory for higher education and research to be provided and financed by the public sector shows that it is a political view and nothing else.

Moreover, public provision and financing of higher education and research would be quite acceptable if the public sector were able to make and implement decisions perfectly. However, the theory of the public sector has shown that there are not only market failures, but also public shortcomings. Therefore, public policies are not always completely efficient and do not necessarily satisfy entirely the collective needs. If public decisions and their implementation were perfect, state intervention would be justified as soon as a market failure had been identified. However, as it is likely that they are not, the question about the best mix about provision, production, financing and regulation becomes a very complex one in implementing what has been considered a public responsibility. This is true for any domain of public responsibility as well as for higher education and research.

Nor can the statement according to which higher education is a "human right" or a "democratic right" be accepted without being correctly qualified; in particular, it is of the utmost importance to make it clear that the objective of equal opportunity of access applies only to those who have the ability to be successfully enrolled in a higher education programme (General Assembly of the United Nations, 1948; World Conference on Higher Education, 1998). Compared with the individual (human) and the political rights guaranteed by the constitutions of democratic countries, the equal right of access to higher education is restricted on the basis of merit. Neglecting this consideration would imply the absence of selection at the entrance of the higher education sector and, possibly, getting a grade. This would inevitably, as a consequence, lower the average quality of the studies and of the graduates and, paradoxically, be the cause of discrimination against those students capable of study at the higher education level. In other words, democratic values at the level of individual (human) and political rights must be promoted and guaranteed by all means as there is no better way to avoid the domination of one group of people over others and to secure full respect of individuals. However, these notions should not be used, at least *stricto sensu,* in the domain of higher education, where obviously the aptitudes and motivations of individuals to study and obtain a grade differ greatly between individuals, because the provision of higher education is very costly to society (whatever the means of financing) and the quality of graduates very important for social and economic development. We examine below the dangers of considering higher education and research as a "public good" *stricto sensu.* The reader should keep in mind that the same applies while considering higher education as a human or a democratic right.

Dangers of considering higher education and research a "public good" stricto sensu

Europe aims to become the most competitive economy by 2010, thanks to the promotion of the Knowledge Society by way of a strong higher education and research system and in particular to the development of the European Higher Education and Research Areas (Lisbon European Council, Presidency Conclusions, 2000).

These strategic objectives are certainly shared by most if not all of the readers of this book. Therefore, the crucial question is: how do we attain them? More than that, does Europe have any chance of succeeding if it considers that higher education and research is a public good *stricto sensu,* as this implies that the production and financing of higher education and research should be exclusively – or nearly exclusively – the responsibility of the public sector?

Most university leaders and economists would agree that the attainment of this ambitious objective would be greatly hampered if, according to a strict definition of the notion "public good", governments aimed to be even more present in the higher education and research system. Without neglecting the responsibilities of the public sector, it can be argued on the contrary that the public sector should reduce its degree of intervention and that higher education institutions should have an entrepreneurial attitude in order to increase the effectiveness of the sector. The following brief description of some of the inefficiencies and fairness shortcomings of public institutions demonstrates this.

Efficiency shortcomings of public institutions

The overwhelming majority of higher education institutions in Europe are public organisations which, however, receive part of their revenue, in particular research money, from private sources or at least on a competitive basis (research funding bodies). This is the cause of inefficiencies which should be avoided to increase the effectiveness of the system. Whether we like them or not, these facts, in particular economic ones, are working permanently behind the scenes:

– monopoly position: public universities have a quasi-monopoly position in their region as the state will not open and finance more institutions than it considers necessary, and even tends to under-finance the existing ones. Therefore, their students' reservoir is a captive market, their financial support is largely secured and they do not make specific efforts to attract students or to improve. In other words, they deliver less at a higher cost than institutions confronted with competition. The disadvantages of private monopolies have been recognised; why not those of public monopolies?

– weak decision process: the decision structure and process replicate those of a democracy. This is nice in theory as it gives in particular an opportunity to the students to get the feeling of democratic processes in society. The problem is that a university is not a country where no better solution has been found to prevent the domination of one part of the population over the other. Universities are organisations which, as any organisation – public, non-profit, private – must adapt to the rapidly changing environment, while at the same time being responsible towards society. The problem with the decision structures and processes in place is that they are extremely complex and heavy, which makes decisions extremely difficult as they offer too many opportunities to be avoided;

– insufficient autonomy: in most countries, the law attributes a large autonomy to universities. This is often a trap, as many other laws simultaneously restrict this autonomy. In most cases, universities are not allowed to choose their students and to decide about the compensation of their professors. They are often not in charge of their buildings, and suffer from the fact that their budget is totally integrated in the state budget and from not being able to borrow. Moreover, the political authorities (parliament and government) have a great tendency to "micro-manage" them politically. Therefore, it is not too surprising to observe a good correlation between the degree of independence of a university and its reputation in teaching and in particular in research;

– students and teachers are not confronted with the opportunity cost: even if most – but certainly not all – students are spontaneously motivated by their studies, they are not confronted with the sacrifice made by society in their favour as they generally have to pay fees that represent only a small proportion of the cost. They are therefore induced to consume this service up to satiety, unless strict examination rules prevent them from "taking it easy". Raising student fees would make students more responsible, and therefore improve the efficiency of the system. Moreover, no distinction is made between those who are investing in higher education and those who "consume" higher education. If society should certainly encourage investments in higher education, it is not obvious that those who are studying as part of their leisure should also be nearly free of charge. Why should someone pay to go the cinema or visit a museum and not for attending a course without any intention to pass an exam at the end?

– input financing: the state traditionally finances higher education institutions according to the input, in particular the number of students enrolled, staff employed and buildings and equipment required. There is hardly any link with the output of higher education institutions, in particular the number and the quality of the graduates and the quantity and quality of research. Therefore, there is no incentive for the staff to improve. Hence, professors and researchers are responsible and even passionate men and women; but this still does not guarantee that they do all they could to serve their institutions better. Finally, the proportion of university funds based on merit (competitive financing of research) remains relatively small; therefore, incentive is small.

Fairness shortcomings of public institutions

In Europe, it is accepted nearly unanimously that there should be no financial barriers to access to higher education for children from low or medium-income families. This is even by far the main argument in favour of free access to higher education. Unfortunately, this argument in favour of free access is the object of a serious confusion between first the objective of avoiding any financial barrier to access and second the means to satisfy this objective: not charging student fees. This confusion would be without any real importance if it were without practical consequence. Unfortunately, this is not the case. As long as only a proportion of a cohort is going to university and as long as the proportion of children from underprivileged social groups will be clearly smaller that those from middle and upper social groups, the system works regressively. This means that those in the working class paying taxes, even low or moderate ones, are subsidising the studies of children from middle and upper classes, which is certainly not what is desired. This situation is particularly serious in those countries which do not make a great effort to compensate for the cultural barrier unfavourable to extended study in low-income families and/or where the proportion of a cohort going to university is relatively small.

It is obvious that the problem disappears if the great majority of a cohort benefit from any tertiary education. The only way to avoid this reverse income distribution effect is to charge for higher education: as long as the proportion of middle and upper class is larger, they will themselves contribute to cover part of the cost of their studies. In addition to that, in order to avoid any barrier to entry, two accompanying measures should be taken: provide financial support to the low-income students (grants, loans) and put in place policies – even proactive ones – to overcome the cultural barrier.

If the efficiency arguments were in one way or another related to the beneficial advantages of more competition between institutions, staff and students, this last argument is probably more difficult to grasp as it goes against the common sense that free access is favourable to those who are less well off.

Conclusion

The purpose of this contribution was to introduce the topic of this book: public responsibility for higher education and research. This topic is of great relevance for the present and future debates about higher education and research in Europe for two interlinked reasons. First, it is of great importance for the effectiveness of the higher education and research sector, as the main pillar of the Knowledge Society so important for the economic, social and cultural development of Europe, to establish clearly why the public sector has a responsibility with regard to higher education and research, as well as the nature of this responsibility.

The second justification originates from the decision of the ministers of education to add in their Prague and Berlin communiqués that higher education is not only a "public responsibility", but also a "public good". If this added expression has passed unnoticed by the majority of people concerned with higher education and research, it has raised the attention of a few university leaders and scholars of the public sector. How should we interpret the political will of the ministers? Was their intention simply to reinforce the expression "public responsibility" in expressing it a second time using a term which appeared to them stronger or clearer for their communication purpose? Or did they really mean that higher education and research are a special type of service, which means that it can or must be provided only by the public sector at no charge for the beneficiaries?

The many good reasons why higher education should be a public responsibility have, we hope, been established clearly, in particular the external economies, the gaps in information, the necessity to secure and promote quality, as well as the necessity to make higher education open to all those who have the ability, whatever their social origin. The arguments developed can be nuanced and other arguments can be added, but it is difficult to dispute the important public responsibility for higher education and research.

Does this mean that higher education and research are a public good? The response to this question is unambiguous. This notion is acceptable only if it is added to reinforce the concept of public responsibility, although it introduces an element of confusion as the notion of public good is much more ambiguous that the notion of public responsibility.

This paper shows on the contrary that adding the notion of public good is not only ill-founded, but also counterproductive for the effectiveness of the higher education and research sector, if the ministers really wanted to say that higher education is not only a public responsibility, but more than that, is a type of service, which means that it has to be provided by the public sector. First of all, the economic characteristics of higher education and research do not make a public provision at no charge an obligation, although they justify a certain degree of intervention by the public sector, as recalled above. Therefore, the demand for a public provision and production, with no charge for the beneficiaries, is a political value judgment. Moreover, and this seems even more important, to consider that higher education and research are a pure public good provided, produced and put at the disposal of the beneficiaries at no cost would greatly hamper the effectiveness of the system to fulfil the political expectation that Europe should become the most competitive economy in the world thanks to the development of the Knowledge Society. The present system, with a strong involvement of the public sector, has many weaknesses, which means that the improvement of higher education and research requires on the contrary more competition and entrepreneurship.

The conclusion of this contribution is crystal clear: the public sector must be responsible for higher education and research, but higher education and research is not a public good *stricto sensu,* that is a *service public,* as it is considered in the French-speaking countries.

The conclusion of this conclusion is that it would be advisable for Europe to work not only on the scope of public responsibility for higher education and research but also on the means to improve the effectiveness of this sector, as well as promoting equal chance of access independently of social origin (Weber and Duderstadt, 2004).

References

Berlin Communiqué, *Realising the European Higher Education Area,* adopted by European ministers of education on 19 September 2003. Available at: http://www.bologna-bergen2005.no/Docs/00-Main_doc/030919Berlin_Communique.PDF

Bologna Declaration, *The European Higher Education Area. Joint Declaration of the European Ministers of Education,* 19 June 1999. Available at: http://www.bologna-bergen2005.no/Docs/00-Main_doc/990719BOLOGNA_DECLARATION.PDF

General Assembly of the United Nations, *Universal Declaration of Human Rights,* Resolution 217 A, 1948.

Lisbon European Council, *Presidency conclusions,* 2000. Available at: http://www.europarl.eu.int/summits/lis1_en.htm

Magna Charta Universitatum, 1998. Available at: http://www.bologna-bergen2005.no/Docs/00-Main_doc/880918_Magna_Charta_Universitatum.pdf

Prague Declaration, *Toward the European Higher Education Area,* communiqué of the meeting of European ministers in charge of higher education in Prague on 19 May 2001. Available at: http://www.bologna-bergen2005.no/Docs/00-Main_doc/010519PRAGUE_COMMUNIQUE.PDF

Pusser, B., *Higher education, the emerging market, and the public good,* National Academy of Sciences, Washington, 2003.

Salmi, J., "Construction des sociétés du savoir: nouveaux défis pour l'enseignement supérieur", in Breton, G. and Lambert, M. (eds), *Globalisation et universités: nouvel espace nouveaux acteurs,* Editions Unesco/Les Presses de l'Université de Laval, Quebec, 2003, pp. 53-72.

Samuelson, P.A., "The pure theory of public expenditure", *Review of Economics and Statistics,* Vol. 36, 1954, pp. 350-356.

The World Bank, *Constructing knowledge societies: new challenges for tertiary education,* The World Bank, Washington, 2002.

Weber, L.E., *L'Etat, acteur économique,* Economica, Paris, 1997.

Weber, L.E., "Survey of the main challenges facing higher education at the Millennium", in Hirsch, W.Z. and Weber, L.E., *challenges facing higher education at the Millennium,* American Council on Education/Oryx Press, Phoenix, 1999, pp. 3-17.

Weber, L.E. and Duderstadt, J.J., "Challenges and possible strategies for research universities in Europe and the United States", in Weber, L.E., and Duderstadt, J.J. (eds), *Reinventing the research university,* Economica, London, Paris and Geneva, 2004, pp. 239-254.

World Conference on Higher Education, *World Declaration on Higher Education for the Twenty-First Century: Vision and Action,* Unesco, Paris, 1998.

Are higher education and academic research a public good or a public responsibility? A review of the economic literature[19]

Alain M. Schoenenberger

Introduction

Research and education are at the core of the Knowledge Society. Knowledge production and transmission are vital for a modern society and therefore receive increasing attention from policy makers. However, growing demand for state funding does not remain unchallenged as budget constraints push governments to reduce public spending and to increase the efficiency of public policies. The present review of the economic literature on academic research and higher education policy therefore focuses on the question to what extent and in what ways government should intervene in these areas. We shall give an overview of the existing economic literature as well as the available empirical data with regard to efficiency in academic research and higher education policy. Efficiency is, however, not the only concern of public policy. Knowledge production and transmission being at the core of our society and its economic system, redistribution policy and social cohesion considerations also play a crucial role. Equity considerations are important and dealt with alongside efficiency aspects in the vast literature on higher education. We shall accordingly extend our review of the economic literature to present the main results of the literature on the social impact of different policy solutions.

There are a variety of economic aspects of higher education and academic research: education and research consume resources. The economic study of the choices made in allocating resources, which are limited by nature, to various, potentially unlimited needs, plays an important role in policy analysis. Limited public resources to finance higher education and academic research, in the face of other priorities, incite governments and universities to look for private funds. The availability of private funds depends, however, to a great extent on profit considerations (rewards, returns on investment, etc.). The economic analysis of these conditions provides some insight into how private financing can be brought in and what effects it is likely to have on higher education and society. Tight state fund-

19. I would like to thank all members of the Working Party on Public Responsibility for Higher Education and Research for their encouragement and useful comments. My gratitude goes in particular to Beat Estermann who provided valuable research assistance and helped me redraft this literature review. The usual caveats apply.

ing may also mean higher fees for the students, which may negatively influence access to universities.

If education increases skills, competence and income, then education will necessarily affect the distribution of income. Therefore, the issue of access to (higher) educational services, which may be correlated to income, occupies an important place in the equity debate. Often efficiency and equity criteria conflict with each other, and there is no consensus about their relative importance.

In the first section we shall give an account of the theoretical background regarding the debate about the opportunity of public or private provision of goods and services, at the core of which is the notion of "public goods" which generally calls for state provision. While the concept of "public goods" provides the basic foundation for state intervention (and thus public responsibility) within a market economy, there are also concerns about government failures, which are taken up briefly in the concluding remarks, indicating that government provision is not always better than market solutions.

The second section will deal with the nature of higher education and the universities as the main institutions for higher education and academic research. We shall shed some light on the role which universities play in our society and try to give a definition of higher education and academic research in view of the subsequent analysis.

Section three will give an overview of the economic literature dealing with the social and economic impact of higher education, whereas section four presents issues on the provision and finance of higher education. Section five will deal with the question of whether academic research is to be considered as a public good, while section six will address the question of government intervention in research.

Public versus private provision

The opportunity for state intervention in (higher) education can be judged on efficiency grounds. The economic literature differentiates between two types of efficiency: allocative and productive efficiency. The criteria of allocative efficiency require that given resources be allocated between alternative uses in a way that maximises social welfare, that is, taking into account all the positive and negative externalities. According to the criteria of productive (or X-) efficiency, society should produce a given level of output with a minimum of resources, or maximum output for a given level of input. Both types of efficiency are fostered by a competitive environment, which would be favoured by market provision. Market provision, however, is hampered by a number of market failures. These market inefficiencies as well as concerns about equity provide the basis for government intervention.

Theories of market failure

According to standard economic theory, perfect markets exist only in the case of rival consumption and rival production in the absence of externalities and on condition that all economic agents are perfectly informed. The existence of non-rival services, the presence of external effects, which are not dealt with by the markets, and asymmetry of information justify government intervention, such as regulation, government provision, production, and finance. Obviously there are no perfect markets in the real world, and government interventions should be judged in comparison to market outcomes in the absence of state interference.

Public goods

So-called "public goods" cannot be provided at all or not in sufficient quantity by the market because of two characteristics, which are distinct and need not coincide:

– non-rivalness in consumption, that is, the existence of a beneficial consumption externality: according to Samuelson (1954) "collective consumption goods [are goods] which all enjoy in common in the sense that each individual's consumption of such a good leads to no subtraction from any other individual's consumption of that good. Ordinary private consumption goods can be parcelled out among individuals". In his comments on Samuelson's seminal contribution, Margolis questions the existence of collective consumption goods. The facts show that common public services such as education, hospitals and highways, where capacity limitations and congestion arise, are usually rationed. Possibly the only goods which conform to Samuelson's definition are national defence and the traditionally cited lighthouse. According to Musgrave (1969), non-rivalness "does not mean that the same subjective benefit must be derived, or even that precisely the same product quality is available" (for example, the services rendered by a police station, a regional public good, depend on the distance of the consumer from the station). Undoubtedly the feature of non-rivalness is not an absolute but a progressive one (Blaug, 1970). The consequence of non-rivalness of collective consumption goods is the "impossibility of decentralised solution" or in other words that "no decentralised pricing system can serve to determine optimally the(se) levels of collective consumption [for it] is in the selfish interest of each person to give false signals, to pretend to have less interest in a given collective consumption activity than he really has" (Samuelson, 1954);

– non-excludability from consumption: the second characteristic of public goods is non-excludability which hampers the truthful revelation of preferences. Exclusion may not be possible for economic reasons. This is the case where exclusion, which forces the revelation of preferences and thus helps to avoid the need for political mechanisms of preference determination (van den Doel and van Velthoven, 1993), is available only at a high cost compared to the benefits provided by the good. Exclusion may also not be feasible technically, because it is not possible to identify the consumer given the available technology. In a number of cases it is, however, quite easy to prevent other consumers from consuming the public good by denying entry or by charging an entrance fee (bridge, theatre up to the capacity limits). Exclusion can be imposed by the producer, or alternatively the consumer is able to choose the quantity of consumption.

Public goods in Samuelson's sense are pure public goods because they satisfy two conditions simultaneously – consumers cannot be excluded nor can they exclude themselves. It is, however, important to note that the existence of non-rivalness in consumption does not necessarily mean that exclusion is impossible, and the existence of rival consumption does not always mean that exclusion is possible. Public goods can thus be classified according to whether or not producers are able to exclude consumers, and whether or not a consumer himself can choose to consume the goods. The following table presents the typology of pure and impure public goods according to Riker and Ordeshook (1973). The pure public goods introduced by Samuelson are those shown in the bottom right-hand corner. All other public goods are "impure", as in one form or another they come with private as well as public elements, which is for example the case of education (not mentioned in the table).

Table 1. Typology of pure and impure public goods

	Consumer able to choose amount of consumption		Consumer unable to choose amount of consumption	
	Utility increased by consumption	Utility decreased by consumption	Utility increased by consumption	Utility decreased by consumption
Consumer can be excluded from consumption	Recreation area Roads Cable television	Polluted beaches	Civil liberties Fire department	Infectious diseases Military draft
Consumer cannot be excluded from consumption	Lighthouses Knowledge	Airport noise	Public order National defence Pollution or flood control	Air pollution Floods

Source: derived from Riker and Ordeshook, 1973, p. 261.

Merit wants and merit goods

The concept of merit goods has been introduced by Musgrave (1959). He defines it in the following terms: "Such wants are met by services subject to the exclusion principle and are satisfied by the market within effective demand. They become public wants if considered so meritorious that their satisfaction is provided for through the public budget, over and above what is provided by private buyers. The discussion on public goods is based on the assumption that the goods should be supplied in line with individual preferences. Some critics would feel that preferences should be imposed with certain limits by a chosen elite. Society may wish to interfere with individual consumer preferences, be it because its members are better educated, possess greater innate wisdom, or belong to a particular party or sect" (Musgrave, 1969). This concept is somewhat in contradiction to the foundation of welfare theory assuming that each individual is the best judge of his/her own welfare and thus maintaining the view "that all allocation, whether to private or to social goods, is to be made in line with consumer preferences. ... This excludes neither some degree of delegation of decision making (be it to legislators or civil servants), nor implementation through a more or less imperfect mechanism of decision by voting ... but it differs fundamentally from an alternative that postulates some elite or central authority (benevolent or not) which knows best, and imposes its preference on the individual" (Musgrave, 1969). Musgrave suggests two ways out of the contradiction: (a) the imposed choice is justified as an aid to the learning process to obtain the necessary information for a rational choice. The imposed choice would then in the long run be compatible with the objective of an intelligent choice; or (b) merit goods could be explained by interdependent utilities, especially regarding the consumption of basic commodities. Social philosophy may dictate that the freedom to tolerate inequality in the distribution of income and consumption is purchased at the cost of subsidies, which assure equality in the consumption of necessities. The possibility remains of course that choice is to be imposed *per se* (see section on non-economic objectives). As noted by Cullis and Jones (1998), this boils down to two difficult questions, one concerning information and the other rationality. Concerning the latter, Mishan (1981) points out that the value judgment that individuals generally are the best judges of their own welfare could either be a judgment of fact, a judgment of morality (it is appropriate to act as if individuals are the best judges of their own welfare) or a judgment of political expediency (it is politically expedient to act on the assumption that individuals are the best judges of their own welfare). From a public choice perspective – aiming to analyse political phenomena and institutions in economic terms – the problem could be treated on the basis of equal access and the social decision-making process. If one believes that the social decision-making processes are fair, then one would expect that citizens are willing to accept the possibility that at least some policies emerge which will be contrary to their best interest (Littlechild and Wiseman, 1986).

Externalities

Another approach to the classification of impure public goods focuses on spillovers that stem from the provision of the good. Public goods are indeed a special form of consumption externality, since the producer of such goods does not only benefit himself but also benefits others, who can use positive spillovers for free. An externality is present when the utility of an individual depends not only on the goods and services the individual purchases and consumes but also on the activity of some other individual. The same applies to production externalities. The activity of consumption and production may either increase overall welfare (positive externality) or may reduce welfare (negative external effect). The distinct feature of an external effect, which is not compensated for, or internalised, is the interdependence among individuals (or firms in the case of production) that occurs outside the price mechanism.

For example, education may improve an individual's earning potential, but at the same time it may facilitate basic research, creating non-rival and non-excludable knowledge or information, which benefits others in the community. Such development, in terms of culture or technology, may then bear public good characteristics. Recognition of the private-public mix means that goods can be viewed as having private benefits as well as external effects, which bear the characteristics of public goods (Evans, 1970).

Measuring spillover and private benefits is a problem that is tackled in cost-benefit analysis, but the estimation of social benefits is not without significant problems. Most social benefits cannot be measured directly, in the absence of prices and an estimate of the quantities. For instance, the ratio of spillover to private benefits would give an indication of the extent of the externalities, that is, an indicator of the private-public mix and the degree of publicness. Weisbrod (1988) for example tries to use the manner in which goods are financed as an indication of the public-private split of services provided by non-profit organisations. The more public good effects there are, the less may organisations finance themselves through sales, as there are no direct property rights to goods that can be enjoyed on a non-excludable basis. Instead the organisation will to a larger extent rely upon donations, gifts or grants to finance the provision of goods or services. This split may be thought symptomatic of the mix between public good output and private good output. The more an organisation relies upon gifts, grants and donations, the more eligible it may be to benefit from subsidies.

The universities

Universities are the primary producers of higher education and academic research. We shall therefore give a short account of the literature dealing with the universities' role in society and point out their mission as it was defined in 1998 by the World Declaration on Higher Education. This will eventually lead us to a definition of higher education and academic research which will serve as a basis for further analysis.

The universities' role in society

Johnson (1974) distinguishes four functions of universities. First, universities are seen as a symbol and repository of civilisation, defending and contributing to its advancement "through either or both setting standards of taste ... and enabling the rest of the population to increase its productivity, income and command over consumption goods. In this sense a university is a public good, like good weather or pleasant geography". Second, they are a home for research "which is a public good in the strict economic sense, that once produced they can be used by anyone without precluding use by others". Third, universities are an information store, both physically in books and in the embodied form of learned men, and finally, as a clearly recognised function, they are the place where young adults are taught.

Bear (1974) analyses the university (or any other higher education institution) as a multi-product firm. Outputs produced by the university include a variety of components, including:

– increments in human capital which provide a yield appropriable by the individual and a stream of benefits to society as a whole; or, in the words of Attiyeh

(1974), educational and informational output, which refers to "increases in students' knowledge and skills, which increase their productivity and their ability to earn income, and the reporting of students' attributes and educational attainments to students themselves and to prospective employers, which may facilitate more rational choices and hiring decisions";[20]

– entertainment services consumed currently and privately by students during their studies;

– increments in the stock of research, that is, increases in theoretical and empirical knowledge and the creation of new concepts and products which may directly or indirectly increase the economy's productive capacity.

Typically, universities simultaneously produce teaching and research services. Why are those services not produced in separate institutions? Research activity ensures that the teacher is up to date with the latest developments in his field, whereas teaching activity keeps researchers familiar with the basic principles of a discipline which is broader than their specific field of interest. In other words, a positive correlation between the quality of the teaching and productive research activity is expected, as one activity has an external effect on the other.[21] In consequence, the quality of the transfer of technology and knowledge is enhanced. In terms of costs, the same inputs (such as the library or the academic staff) are shared in two production processes, leading to economies of scope. Economies of scope exist when the costs of producing two (or more) outputs jointly is inferior to the sum of the costs of producing them separately. Economies of scope may also exist within the university because of the subject mix in teaching as students need to share a common set of knowledge. On the other hand economies can also be achieved in specialising in one or more disciplines, without necessarily providing tuition in all disciplines (see optimal subject mix, in Johnes, 1993).

By definition, higher education takes place after primary and secondary education. Consequently, teaching and research in universities or similar institutions of higher education is based on the knowledge transmitted from lower levels of education. Historically, our universities have developed from small institutions for the elite of the society, the members of which could afford to study a relatively small number of abstract disciplines (philosophy, mathematics, theology, medicine, etc.) into institutions with a much larger number of students and disciplines. Some disciplines have a higher market value than others in terms of expected earnings, availability of jobs, etc. The mission of the university has changed fundamentally; its prime mission seems to be today to provide a certain level of education that is demanded by the economy, and possibly to fulfil thereby also the aspiration of the majority of the students to an attractive job and comparatively high earnings.

---

20. The second part of the definition is considered by Attiyeh as a separate output, yet the informational output seems to be complementary to and derived from the human capital output.
21. See Barnett (1992) for a critical appraisal of the links between teaching and research activities. Institutions of higher education do not need to conduct research in order to justify the title "institution of higher education". Although research and higher education seem inseparable, that does not mean that either institution or staff are obliged to conduct research. Staff do, however, need time and resources to keep up with their field of study.

According to de Groof et al. (1998), the university discharges three core functions:

– conduct of scholarly and scientific research. The university plays a central and vital part in the education of students, in the training of researchers and in the transmission and preservation of fundamental knowledge; in principle, no particular discipline should be excluded from the support which underpins free, disinterested investigation (compared to applied, and profit-driven research);

– dispensation of learning on a scientific, rational basis, providing high-level academic and scholarly education. The ideal would consist in the transfer of research-generated new knowledge and technique to the minds of students. But how far can "academic education" be distinguished from "education at an academic level" with the advent of "professionally oriented" courses within the university?

– provision of services: rendering expert and specialist services to the wider community (to governments or to the private sector, including the labour market).

World Declaration on Higher Education for the Twenty-First Century: the mission of universities

The World Declaration on Higher Education for the Twenty-First Century adopted in 1998 by the World Conference on Higher Education (Unesco) in Paris provides a mission statement on which all participating countries have agreed. The declaration recalls the principles of the Charter of the United Nations, the Universal Declaration of Human Rights and other universal principles on political, economic, social and cultural rights.

Box 1. World Declaration on Higher Education for the Twenty-First Century

Article 1 of the declaration defines the university's mission to educate, to train and to undertake research:

"(a) educate highly qualified graduates and responsible citizens able to meet the needs of all sectors of human activity, by offering relevant qualifications, including professional training, which combine high-level knowledge and skills, using courses and content continually tailored to the present and future needs of society;

(b) provide opportunities (*espace ouvert*) for higher learning and for learning throughout life, giving to learners an optimal range of choice and a flexibility of entry and exit points within the system, as well as an opportunity for individual development and social mobility in order to educate for citizenship and for active participation in society;

(c) advance, create and disseminate knowledge through research and provide, as part of its service to the community, relevant expertise to assist societies in cultural, social and economic development, promoting and developing scientific and technological research as well as research in the social sciences, the humanities and the creative arts;

(d) help understand, interpret, preserve, enhance, promote and disseminate national and regional, international and historic cultures, in a context of cultural pluralism and diversity;

(e) help protect and enhance societal values by training young people in the values that form the basis of democratic citizenship and by providing critical and detached perspectives to assist in the discussion of strategic options and the reinforcement of humanistic perspectives;

(f) contribute to the development and improvement of education at all levels, including through the training of teachers."

On equity of access, Article 3 stipulates :

"(a) admission to higher education should be based on the merit, capacity, efforts, perseverance and devotion, showed by those seeking access to it ... no discrimination can be accepted in granting access to higher education on grounds of race, gender, language or religion, or economic, cultural or social distinctions, or physical disabilities;

(b) ... access to higher education should remain open to those successfully completing secondary school, or its equivalent, or presenting entry qualifications, as far as possible, at any age and without any discrimination."

The funding of higher education requires both public and private resources. The role of the state remains essential in this regard.

"(c) the diversification of funding sources reflects the support that society provides to higher education and must be further strengthened to ensure the development of higher education, increase its efficiency and maintain its quality and relevance. Public support for higher education and research remains essential to ensure a balanced achievement of educational and social missions."

The principles of the declaration admit private sources of funding, but recognise that public support for higher education and research remains essential. There seems, however, to be a tendency to move away from collective support for higher education given an increasing appeal of the market. Economic competition on a global scale and reduced public financing (in the face of other priorities) could, however, favour the type of skills and disciplines which permit those who acquired them to get the best returns, lower costs and greater profit on the market.

Higher education

Education can be defined as the increase of the stocks of skills, knowledge and understanding possessed either by individuals or by society as a whole. The economics of education concerns the manner in which choices affecting this stock are made, both by individuals who demand education and by the teachers and institutions which supply it. According to Blaug (1976) the birth of the economics of education can be traced back to Theodore Schultz who delivered in 1961 his lecture on investment in human capital to the American Economic Association (Schultz, 1961).[22] This early literature is about the nature and the financing of education services in general, without distinguishing the formal levels of education. It concentrates on the role of education as investment in the future, analysing its rate

22. See also Wiseman (1959) and Becker (1964).

of return compared to alternative investments. However, not only does the return of education provide utility, but education has also a consumption element (the pleasure of learning).

An important argument for state intervention in education is its positive external effects. Although there is a considerable number of positive externalities cited in the literature, it is hard to estimate their practical significance due the fact that the majority of the effects are not measurable and that their link to specific levels of education cannot easily be identified.

In economic terms university education can be regarded "as some mixture of current consumption (i.e. an enjoyable way of passing a few years before assuming adult responsibilities in the economy), the formation of consumption capital (i.e. the development of more sophisticated standards of taste and more discriminatory capacity for choice among consumption alternatives later) and the formation of production capital ("human capital"), i.e. the capacity to contribute more productive services to the economy, and hence to earn more future income, than would be possible in the absence of university education" (Johnson, 1974).

Academic research

Research is aimed at making discoveries or inventions and thus at producing knowledge. Knowledge is a largely non-excludable and a partially non-rival good, and is therefore widely considered to be a public good by the economic literature (Callon, 1994). It is furthermore cumulative, for existing knowledge not only serves as consumption, but also as an intellectual input, spurring the production of new knowledge. Basic or fundamental research aims at producing basic knowledge that allows a fundamental understanding of the laws of nature or society. Applied research and development aims at producing knowledge that facilitates the resolution of practical problems. Tassey (1992, cited in Foray, 2004) distinguishes an additional class of activity consisting in the production of "infratechnology", that is, sets of methods, scientific and engineering databases, models, measurements and quality standards that support and co-ordinate the investigation.

In academic research openness and the free circulation of ideas are the rule. Describing the normative structure of science, Merton (1973) set forth the norms of the "Republic of Science": communalism, universalism, disinterestedness, originality, and scepticism. Science is thereby rooted in the public sphere: the "communal ethos" stresses the co-operative character of research, considering that the accumulation of reliable knowledge is an essentially social process. The universalist norm requires that scientific work and discourse be open to all persons of "competence". The full disclosure of findings and methods form a key aspect of the co-operative, communal programme of inquiry. Full disclosure also procures legitimacy based on "organised scepticism", which demands that all contributions to the stock of reliable knowledge be subjected to trials of replication and verification.

Box 2. The origin of the norms of open science

Throughout the Middle Ages experimental science was a very secretive undertaking and shaped by a political and religious world view which refrained from disclosing to the "vulgar multitude" knowledge that might bring power over material things. The emergence of open science was due to information dissymmetry in the European system of court patronage, which made it difficult for the patrons, who were sponsoring scientific activities, to judge their clients' abilities. They therefore resorted to a system of open communication of findings and peer review, which guaranteed a certain degree of quality control. Based upon this system of open science a new "academic market" emerged later in the nineteenth century among state-funded universities engaging in inter-institutional competition. The particularity of the "academic market" lies in the fact that it uses primary, non-monetary incentives, such as reputation, to steer the allocation of resources. It thus guarantees the quick dissemination of newly created knowledge, without reducing the incentives for doing research.

Although the norm of "openness" in the scientific context has led to considerable social benefits as well as to an acceleration of the research process thanks to rapid replication and swift validation of novel discoveries, the emergence of "openness" is not endogenous to the development of science. The institutions of open science are independent, and in some measure fortuitous, social and political constructs, and as such the result of exogenous social processes. This implies that the institutions of the "Republic of Science" might not resist institutional change if it is brought about without the necessary circumspection.

Source: David, 2004.

Academic science based on the rules of the "Republic of Science" is described by some authors as the first mode of knowledge production. They argue that, since scientific research is becoming more and more application-oriented and is increasingly driven by commercial interests, a new mode of knowledge production ("mode 2") has emerged, which is challenging the norms and practices that have traditionally protected academic openness and autonomy (Gibbons et al., 1994).

The social and economic impact of higher education

Education has an important social and economic impact, as one of its functions is to prepare children and students for the labour market. From an individual perspective, future earnings are therefore a powerful guide, alongside personal and non-economic criteria, for choosing the level of education and the subjects of study. Participation in higher education, however, not only has an impact on the welfare of the individual, but also influences economic growth and the welfare of the nation. On one hand, the existence of private benefits supports the view that education is a private responsibility. On the other hand, the existence of externalities or social returns associated with the educational attainment of individuals may explain collective concern about education justifying government provision and finance. The question is further complicated by equity considerations, as education is an important factor determining social mobility and the distribution of resources within society. Before we address the issue of how and by whom post-secondary education should be financed, we shall therefore give a review of the different contributions relating to the social and economic impact of higher education.

Individual versus social benefits

Estimating the private and social returns on higher education is crucial in answering the question whether higher education is a public good and therefore a public responsibility. The arguments in favour of state provision of education rely on the belief that the market for educational services fails when left to its own devices. According to Blaug (1970), however, "education is not a pure public good because at least some of the economic benefits of education are personal to the educated, and the economist as economist simply has no case to make for state provision of education. His case is one of public subsidy to education and to be sure this is enough to explain state involvement in educational planning".

Whereas human capital theory provides a solid basis for estimating private returns of education, it is widely acknowledged that the benefits of individually acquired education might indeed spill over to other individuals in the same firm, industry, city, region and economy. Channels for such types of externalities include the possibility that educated workers may raise the productivity of their less educated co-workers, that there may be external effects from technical progress or knowledge accumulation, or that an environment with a higher average level of human capital may entail a higher incidence of learning from others. Investment in human capital may also have an external social impact which can in turn have indirect economic effects: for instance, more education has been found to be associated with better public health, better parenting, lower crime, wider political and community participation and greater social cohesion (OECD, 1998). The existence of a linkage between educational achievement and its spillovers is often considered as given a priori by theorists and policy makers, although the difficulties of actually verifying the size and the impact on economic growth and the social returns of education are formidable.

In general, average private and social internal rates of return to education immediately following compulsory schooling are relatively high. This suggests that there are strong incentives for the average student to engage in further education. The excess of private returns over estimated social returns suggests that government policy is set to internalise a substantial part of any externalities that may be associated with post-compulsory education. Furthermore, the large gap between the estimated rates of return of education and the risk-free interest rate on the financial market point to super-normal returns to investment in human capital. This may point to temporary excess demand for higher educated workers, with market forces being expected to eventually drive down the returns to rates that are similar to those on alternative productive assets – though this transition might take a long time.[23] Relatively high returns may in fact indicate under-education, at least until the returns from education have reached the returns of comparable alternative investment in the long run. They could, however, also reflect economic rent related to a scarce resource, namely ability and motivation of individuals, with the internal rates of return for the marginal student being lower than for the average student. If there is a shortage of highly educated persons *per se*, then policy should aim at expanding capacity in post-compulsory education as this would result in high returns at the margin for both individuals and society. On the other hand, if high average rates of return are due to a shortage of abilities, capacity expansion and stronger private incentives to acquire post-compulsory education may not result in high rates of return at the margin for individuals or for society at large.

Private and social returns to education may, however, vary across the different levels of study. Bear (1974), for example, argues that there definitely is a "difference between the public goods generated by primary and secondary education, on the one hand, and higher education, on the other. The principal public benefit of the former is that it enhances the ease of communication in society – that the ability to read, write and perform elementary arithmetic calculations, taken together with the inculcation of a common cultural heritage, permits a member of the society to communicate with others and that such ease of communication is a benefit that cannot be withheld from some subsets of society and granted to others. But once these abilities are reached – and surely this occurs prior to higher education – it is questionable that the ease of communication is enhanced by further education". According to this view higher education would have a lower public to private benefit ratio than say primary and secondary education.

Individual earnings and the labour market (human capital theory)

Human capital theory, founded by Schultz (1960) and Becker (1962), perceives of education as an investment of current resources, including the opportunity cost of the time spent as well as any direct costs incurred by education, in exchange for future, higher earnings. According to the theory, the demand for education derives from the optimal investment decisions of rational individuals who will engage in an additional year of schooling and education as long as its (internal) rate of return – the rate which equates the present values of benefits (earnings) and costs – is superior to market interest rates (opportunity cost of financing).

---

23. Similarly, over-education may also persist in the long run and have an adverse effect on individual productivity. Over-education can be defined in three ways: as a decline in the economic position of educated individuals relative to a historically higher level; as under-fulfilled expectations of the educated with respect to their occupational attainments; or as the possession by workers of greater educational skills than their jobs require (see Tsang et al., 1985).

Box 3. The economic benefit of additional human capital

The pre-tax wage premium earned by tertiary graduates is substantial in all countries for which data were available, but particularly high in the United States, France and the United Kingdom. Investment in upper-secondary education is also associated with significant wage premia over lower-secondary education, especially in the United States and Canada. This wage pattern is broadly the same for both men and women, although education wage premia tend to be somewhat smaller for women. In several countries, the pre-tax education wage premium has tended to rise since the early 1980s, suggesting that the significant expansion in the relative supply of educated workers (reflecting fast increases in post-compulsory school enrolment) has failed to keep up with an even stronger increase in relative demand.

In most countries the earnings of tertiary-educated men and women increase more sharply with age than is the case for less-educated workers.

More education also means a stronger foothold in the labour market and thus lower risk of unemployment. The reduction in risk is particularly large for those investing in upper-secondary education, whereas the gap in unemployment rates between upper-secondary and university-educated workers is comparatively small.

Educated workers are more likely to participate in the labour market, and their active working life is generally longer than that for those with lower educational attainment. With very few exceptions, the participation rate for male graduates of tertiary education is markedly higher than that for upper-secondary graduates.

Progressive income taxation reduces the return on human capital investment. On the other hand, public financial support for education in the form of free or heavily subsidised tuition increases the incentive to invest in education by lowering the cost of investment. Student loans and grants alleviate financing constraints and often involve a significant subsidy element. Finally, the length of study periods influences financial rewards from human capital accumulation.

Source: Blöndal et al., 2002.

The estimation of the return on schooling and education has been the subject of considerable debate in the economic literature (Harmon et al., 2003). Standard multivariate regression analysis for the United Kingdom suggests a return to a year of schooling there of 7-9% for men and 9-11% for women. These figures appear to be at the upper end of returns in Europe, whereas Nordic countries in particular have low average returns. The Harmon survey of the literature concludes that the evidence on private returns to the individual is compelling. Despite some of the subtleties involved in estimating the returns on educational investments, there is an unambiguous positive effect of education on earnings. Moreover, the size of the effect seems large relative to the returns on other investments. One might be tempted to conclude that this high return implies that private returns largely exceed the benefits to society (social returns), so that there is little argument for the taxpayer to subsidise individual study. Partly, however, the relatively high private returns on human capital investment are due to the fact that government typically provides most of the financing of educational services.

In the debate on how higher education should be financed, human capital theory not only serves as an argument in favour of limited government spending, but also accounts for the way demand in education is derived from labour market demand through the individual's anticipation of future income. It therefore also serves as a justification for the shift in government intervention from subsidising institutions to subsidising individuals in order to allow for the allocation of public resources in accordance with market needs.

Positive externalities

In Figure 1 the market demand curve for education is shown as D_p. It reflects the private benefits that students believe they will enjoy as a result of education. These may be viewed as the "private return" on education and they depend in part on the income differential that students expect to receive during their working life as a result of education. If, however, there are other benefits (external benefits) contingent upon education, the social benefits from education will differ from the private benefits. The value of external benefits to others in the community is given by the line E, which shows what the rest of the community would pay for the various levels of education Q_E/t. Adding vertically the values of E to the private demand gives the line MSB. There are positive social benefits from education over and above the private benefits.

According to Cullis and Jones (1998), the external gains that arise from education may include the benefits to others (spillovers) arising for example from: (a) the research undertaken in educational establishments; (b) the cultural environment and the heritage for future generations; (c) the screening device which education provides for the labour market to determine the quality of labour; and (d) the improved decision making of voters and the behaviour of educated citizens, etc.

Blaug (1970) made a comparative list of factors found in the literature (many of which he questions) to distinguish the social rate of return on education from the private rate of return. Some of these factors (such as cultural environment and heritage) have the characteristics of a public good; that is, they can be consumed by one individual in society without reducing the amount available for consumption by others. Indeed, it is for this very reason that it is often supposed that the market will not properly internalise such factors in the decision-making calculus of individuals. In Figure 1 private demand at price P is only q^p, and thus inferior to the socially optimal output q^s (the point at which the marginal social benefit MSB is equal to the marginal cost MC of education).

Figure 1. External effects of education

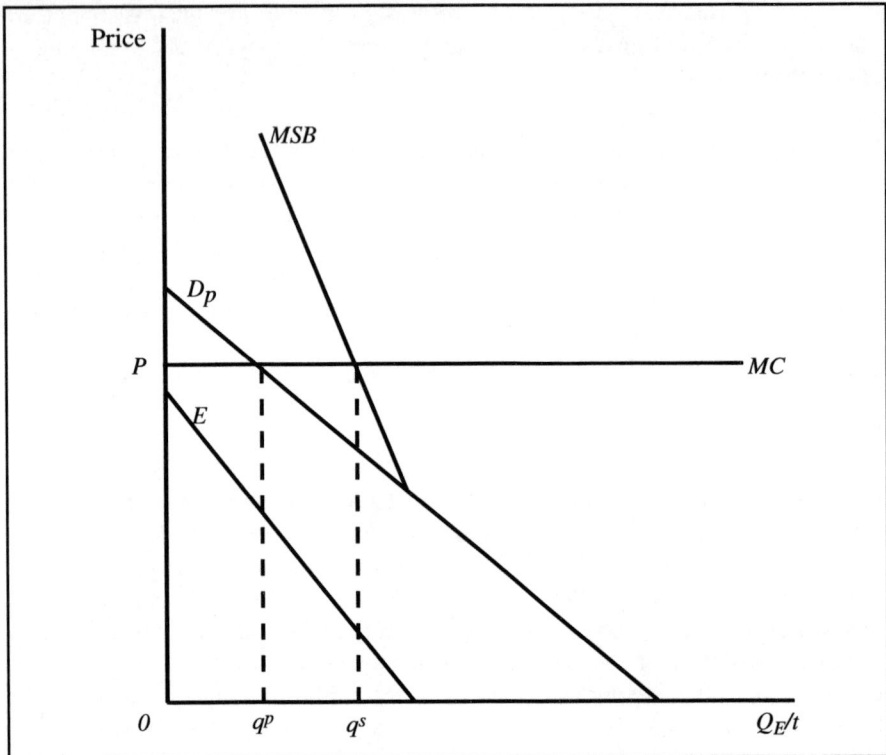

Source: Cullis and Jones, 1998, p. 51.

Signalling hypothesis

Investing in (higher) education, individuals not only raise their productivity in working life, as stated by human capital theory, but education also seems to provide them with a signal to potential employers about their innate productive capabilities and other factors, largely independent of education, as predicted by the "screening" hypothesis (Arrow, 1973). From this point of view, higher wages of those who go longer to school are observed not because education has increased their productivity, but primarily because the schools have identified those individuals who are the most productive, due to their motivations and ambitions. Both screening and human capital views are consistent with the empirical evidence which suggests that earnings are strongly associated with the level of education. There is general agreement that some of the returns to education are the result of increases in skills and some are the result of screening; but there is some disagreement about the relative importance of the two views. Some studies show that wages do not depend closely on the subjects studied; this would suggest that content (skill formation) does not matter much. Weiss (1995), for example, studied low-skilled workers in a manufacturing plant and found that long-run success depended not on any particular skill but on social characteristics like reliability, low level of absenteeism and punctuality. This might be different for very highly skilled labour performing difficult and complex tasks.

The signalling hypothesis may not only explain a part of the private returns to education but also account for social returns, as the identification of capable individuals serves the information of employers on the labour market, thus reducing transaction costs and making the labour market function more efficiently.

Macroeconomic performance

There are several theoretical and empirical approaches to modelling the linkage between human capital and macroeconomic performance (see Box 4 below for an overview). Sianesi and Reenen (2003) conclude their recent literature survey on the macroeconomic return of education with the following statement: "taking the studies as a whole, there is compelling evidence that human capital increases productivity, suggesting that education is productivity-enhancing rather than just a device that individuals use to signal their level of ability to the employer ... Barro-style regression suggests that increasing school enrolment rates by one percentage point leads to an increase in per capita GDP growth of between 1 and 3 percentage points". The results of the "new growth" approaches point to even larger effects which, however, seem to be implausible, severe methodological problems casting doubts on the interpretation of the evidence. Two robust qualitative results are, however, worth mentioning:

– the impact of increases in the various levels of education depend on the country's development. While primary and secondary skills appear to have larger effects in the poorest and intermediate developing countries, it is the tertiary skills that are important for growth in OECD countries;

– human capital has indirect effects as well, for example by stimulating the growth of other productive inputs (physical capital, technology or health), which in turn foster growth and discourage negative factors, such as population growth and infant mortality.

Box 4. Methods for measuring macroeconomic returns of education

Macro growth regressions

Macro growth regressions exploit cross-country variation in factor productivity or growth rates between countries or regions. Empirically, it is often not possible to distinguish between the neoclassical framework which tries to explain the contribution of human capital to the long-run level of per capita output or the "new growth theory" which emphasises the endogenous determination of the long-run growth rate (human capital accumulation producing directly or indirectly new knowledge and technology, generating external effects and/or being co-determined by the growth process). Besides the usual problems relating to the quality and the availability of comparable data, an important methodological problem in estimating the growth equation is the possibility of reverse causality, for education could be, in part at least, the result of (anticipated) economic growth. Most of these analyses group developing and developed countries together, and most regressions are informal ad hoc regressions, sometimes termed "Barro regressions" (Barro, 1997), where the choice of explanatory variables, including educational variables, is largely driven by results presented in the literature and a priori considerations.

Internal rate method

The internal rate method evaluates the private and social profitability of the educational investment. The concentration on private returns may well lead to an underestimation of the full returns to society if education has the characteristics of a public good. Social rates of return include all direct costs of schooling (and not just those borne by the individual) and are calculated on the basis of pre-tax (instead of post-tax) earnings. According to the OECD (1998), social rates of return are consistently found to be lower than private ones. In general, differences between the social and private rates of return in different countries appear to be due exclusively to differences in the direct cost of schooling. The estimated social rates should be regarded as a lower bound of the full returns to education, as all costs of education are well included whereas broader non-employment personal benefits are excluded (social or political gains, lower risk of unemployment, etc.).

Wage regressions

Wage regressions are largely used in calculating the returns to education at the micro level. Their aim is to identify educational externalities by isolating the impact of the average education level of a region on the wage of the individual.

Non-economic effects of education

There is no clear distinction between economic and non-economic objectives. In a narrow sense, economics can be seen as the analysis of choice in allocating resources to (material) needs. From this perspective non-economic effects of education are similar to external effects or social benefits which are not internalised by markets, and constitute public goods. If economics is, however, about the allocation of resources in general, that is, education expenditure, teachers, etc., and human welfare, a whole range of further factors should be included in the analysis. Indeed, a great number of social, political or other factors, which are usually considered as non-economic, might also indirectly influence the performance of the economy. For example, studies have shown that education tends to be correlated with better health, lower crime, political and community participation and social cohesion.

Figure 2 depicts three circles of well-being. Well-being includes economic well-being but also extends to the enjoyment of civil liberties, relative freedom from crime, enjoyment of a clean environment and individual states of mental and physical health. Growth in economic output enlarges the range of human choice (for example, work, leisure or political and cultural activities) rather than serving as a goal in itself. The realisation of human capabilities is vital for a broader notion and measure of human and social development. Human well-being is more than the sum of individual levels of well-being since it relates to individual and societal preferences regarding equality of opportunities, civil liberties, distribution of resources and opportunities for further learning.

Economic well-being – flowing from economic output – is an important component of well-being. However, gross domestic product (GDP) has significant limitations as a measure of economic output. GDP captures current production of those consumption and investment goods and services accounted for in the national accounts but excludes non-market household activity (such as parenting) and activities such as the conservation of natural resources that contribute to future well-being through net additions to the capital stock of society. Aggregate measures of output and income, such as GDP, also fail to reflect social preferences concerning equity goals.

GDP also includes activities which do not contribute to well-being. So-called "social regrettables" arise from outcomes such as pollution, crime and divorce. Social regrettables also comprise outlays and expenditures which do not directly contribute to well-being but are nevertheless deemed to be necessary, such as for example national security.

Figure 2 shows on the input side natural and physical capital as well as human and social capabilities. Human capital stands for the knowledge, skills and health embodied in individuals.[24] The complementary social capital refers to networks as

Figure 2. Inputs to human well-being and their inter-relationship

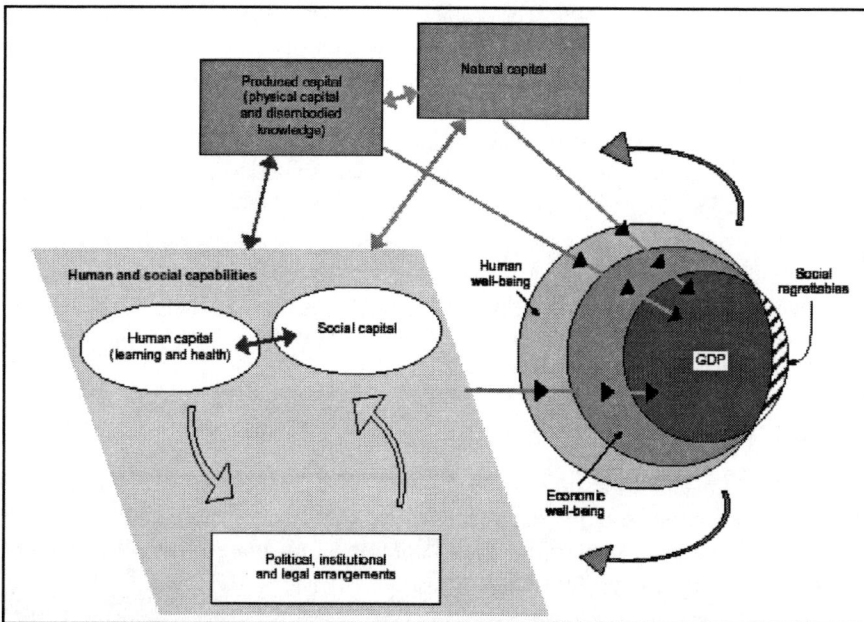

Source: OECD, 2001.

24. OECD (2001) defines human capital as the knowledge, skills and attributes embodied in individuals that facilitate the creation of personal, social and economic well-being.

well as shared norms, values and understandings that facilitate co-operation within or among groups. Education and learning can support habits, skills and values conducive to social co-operation and participation. Good quality institutions, a highly skilled labour force and the prevalence of norms and networks facilitating social co-operation underpin higher levels of investment in physical capital and can potentially enhance strategies to renew the natural environment. Another important input to well-being and economic performance is health, which in turn is linked to age, lifestyle, social status, learning and the extent of social ties and interpersonal support. Indeed, some economists view health as part of human capital.

Furthermore, welfare benefits that are not captured in the models and data of economists may include the immediate consumption benefits and long-term effect on life satisfaction (Temple, 2001). For instance, Blanchflower and Oswald (2000) estimated happiness equations, that is, regressions that relate survey measures of well-being to individual characteristics. The authors find that educational achievements are associated with greater happiness, other things being equal. If individuals' education has positive effects on the well-being of others, self-interested individuals may tend to under-invest in education from a social point of view. Some authors argue that the social (non-economic) benefits are large, possibly larger than direct labour market and macroeconomic effects (Wolfe and Haveman, 2001).

Box 5. Social cohesion and social capital

Closely allied to the concept of social capital is the notion of social cohesion. Defining social cohesion as "the shared values and commitment to a community", Jenson (1998) has identified five important dimensions: belonging, inclusion, participation, recognition and legitimacy. More cohesive societies are more effective in realising collective goals because they are better at protecting and including individuals and groups at risk of exclusion. Ritzen (2001) states: "The objective of social cohesion implies a reconciliation of a system of organisation based on market forces, freedom of opportunity and enterprise, with a commitment to the values of solidarity and mutual support which ensures open access to benefit and protection for all members of society." These understandings of social cohesion describe outcomes or states of social harmony, which are the result of various factors, including human and social capital. Hence, social cohesion is a broader concept than that of social capital.

Access and equity

Blaug (1970) discusses at greater length some of the non-economic objectives of (primary) education. Among the objectives frequently cited are equal educational opportunity and social cohesion. Blaug comments on three different interpretations of educational opportunity:

– equal amounts of education;

– education sufficient to bring everyone to a given standard;

– education sufficient to permit everyone to reach their endowed potential.

The first interpretation has never been put into practice for all levels of education. The second would justify compulsory attendance, but is of no help in making decisions above the minimum prescribed level of education (primary and first level secondary school). Higher education, of a certain standard, requires individual capacities which are not distributed equally among the young population. Typically, only a fraction of the population concerned is enrolled in post-compulsory education (upper-secondary and tertiary education). The implications of the third meaning are quite far-reaching. If the central goal of education were to allow all individuals to develop to their full potential, its realisation would not remove differences between individuals in educational achievement and the associated benefits. Nor would it necessarily mean access for all to the same educational experiences. However, it would imply access to skill development that would enable each individual to develop his or her full potential.

In practice, it will often be unclear whether differences in educational outcomes reflect variation in full potential or differentially effective provisions. Considerations of equity in education therefore address outcomes as well as access (Blöndal et al., 2002). The question is not whether outcomes vary but whether they do so to an extent that is unreasonable and whether the distribution of outcomes is equivalent in groups between which it is not reasonable to expect differences. In post-compulsory education, the equity issue arises in a quite different form because of the extent of individual variation in participation. Two equity issues should be addressed, namely:

- the extent to which the expansion of post-compulsory education has enhanced equality of opportunity in access;

- the distribution of costs and benefits of public spending on post-compulsory education.

Over the past thirty years participation rates in post-compulsory education have increased rapidly. Thus, in OECD countries on average nearly three quarters of the younger cohort aged 25 to 34 have completed upper-secondary education, and one quarter have completed tertiary education. Conversely, among those currently aged 55 to 64, less than half have completed the upper-secondary phase of education, and only one in seven has completed tertiary education. Much of the progress is attributable to women catching up with men – the attainment levels of younger men and women aged 25 to 34 are now very similar. For those aged 55 to 64, only 6% of women (compared to 12% of their male counterparts) have university degrees and 38% have upper-secondary qualifications (compared to 50% of the men);

Evidence from a number of countries suggests that the minority of young people who fail to complete upper-secondary education tend to come from less affluent backgrounds. The participation of young people in tertiary education is highly correlated with the educational attainment of their parents. In many countries, those whose parents have completed some tertiary education are about twice as likely to participate in tertiary education as those whose parents lack upper-secondary education qualifications.

There is a large agreement that family, social and home backgrounds are important in explaining educational achievement. Many studies point to the importance of factors such as the support, aspirations and work habits which parents provide to their children. Bourdieu uses the term "cultural capital" to describe the habits or cultural practices based on knowledge and demeanours learned through exposure to role models in the family and other environments. Cultural capital – which is one dimension of social capital[25] – refers to the resources residing in families which allow individuals to attain a particular social status. It also represents the collection of family-based resources such as parental education levels, social class, and family habits, norms and practices which influence academic success. The higher the expectations of parents (particularly those of the mother), the lower is the probability of dropout.

Bowles and Gintis (2001), reviewing the evidence of the literature published since the publication of their book *Schooling in capitalist America* in 1976, confirm their thesis that "parental economic status is passed on to children in part by means of unequal educational opportunity, but that the economic advantage of the offspring of higher social status families goes considerably beyond the superior education they receive". In other words, "parental income and wealth are strong predictors of the likely economic status of the next generation" (Bowles and Gintis, 2002).

Provision, production and finance of higher education

Governments devote an increasing share of GDP to public education. According to the estimate of Tanzi and Schuknecht (2000), public expenditure in education as a percentage of GDP rose in the developed world from 0.6% around 1870 to 6.1% in the 1990s. Higher education absorbed a constant share of 1.1% between 1970-72 and 1993. The growth of expenditure reflects growing enrolment, including at higher levels of education, and reflects government decisions to finance an increasing share of spending at all levels.

Today, in most developed countries secondary education is free, and higher education institutions are predominantly funded and managed by the government. Students receive free or nearly free education that in theory is available to all according to their academic merit. With universal secondary education and growing enrolment in largely publicly financed universities, education tends to absorb an ever greater share of public resources. Tanzi and Schuknecht note that, despite declining birth rates, there will be pressure for reform in the educational sector to improve its quality and cost effectiveness.

---

25. Social capital refers to the resources gained through social ties, membership of networks and sharing of norms.

Higher education institutions are facing a changing environment and increasing pressures in a number of areas, including the labour market, cost and finance, technology, globalisation, enrolment, etc. Recent developments include:

- increased competition among institutions, including the appearance of for-profit organisations in lucrative areas of higher education;

- use of market or quasi-market mechanisms (students as purchasers of services, supply by university);

- impact of information and communication technologies (e-learning, distance learning, etc.);

- greater transnational mobility and education;

- demand for greater transparency and accountability for efficiency and cost effectiveness as well as quality assurance.

Those changes partly result in income diversification and cost-recovery strategies, which come with specific risks and consequences.

Whereas, due to social benefits as well as efficiency and equity considerations, some state financing is largely admitted by the literature, one of the main questions regarding the provision of education is whether and to what extent educational services in general and higher education (universities) in particular cannot be left to the market. Thereby a distinction needs to be made between production and financing. While there is wide consensus that higher education should in part be financed by the state (and be it only in order to guarantee equal access), this does not necessarily imply that the production cannot take place within private institutions operating in a market environment.

Production versus financing

Musgrave (1969) distinguishes clearly between "public provision" and "public production". Public provision refers to a situation where certain goods are furnished to the consumer free of direct charge and through the budget process. Public provision may take the form of public purchases from private firms, or public production. Public sector provision has two components, namely production and finance.

The arguments in favour of state provision of education rely on the belief that the market for educational services fails when left to its own device. However, Blaug (1970) argues that:

- education is not a pure public good, but a quasi-public good, because of indirect benefits for society, which do not vastly exceed the direct personal benefit;

- arguments about parental ignorance in education, that is, the view that the inability of uneducated parents to appreciate the advantages of schooling and education would allow for state intervention, quickly boil down to philosophical differences about the role of the state (in relation to the family).

67

Positive externalities and consumer ignorance may therefore serve as a ground for state intervention in education, yet both arguments would justify state involvement in education but not necessarily state ownership and state finance.

For Stiglitz (2000), under a system of privately financed education, children might receive an insufficient education as some parents may not be altruistic. There is a wide belief that children's access to primary and secondary education should not depend on their parents' financial liabilities. In consequence, the state should provide the financing for the primary and secondary levels of education (provision could still be private). Concerning higher education, a fundamental difference is that students are able to judge whether the returns to further education warrant further investment. Then, government's role would be to ensure access, so that students have the financial resources to go to universities. So, at present, the government greatly subsidises higher education, in an untargeted way, typically charging in public universities tuition fees which are a fraction of the total cost, giving grants and/or providing loans to students who meet eligibility criteria based on financial capacity or needs, and allowing tax credits or deductions (income tax).

Criteria for the provision and financing of higher education

The four main criteria for the provision and financing of higher education are the maximisation of positive externalities, an access policy which allows for a certain degree of equity, the private finance of private returns, and considerations of market responsiveness.

For Pusser (2003), the most salient question is how the contributions of higher education to the public good can be ensured if non-profit public production gives way to a for-profit market: "The fundamental mission of for-profit market production is to create private benefits for the producers and their customers. The historical mission of non-profit production has been to create both public and private benefits. Non-profit institutions have been centres of public social and political efforts to achieve integration and the equalisation of access to education. It is not at all clear that those goals can be realised through for-profit production ... The adoption of market initiatives may also produce expectations of greater choice, competition, and an increase in the public benefits from higher education."

Empirical data indicate that the beneficiaries of government spending on post-compulsory education tend to come from relatively well-off families and have high income prospects (Blöndal et al., 2002). One reason why the expansion of post-compulsory and higher education has not significantly improved equality of opportunity could be that compulsory education has not succeeded in sufficiently reducing the link between basic educational attainment and children's parental background. This would point to the importance of intervention at an early stage when children's cognitive and non-cognitive abilities are being developed so as to equalise their chances of taking advantage of post-compulsory education. The regressivity of the post-compulsory financing system could be reduced by increasing tuition fees. However, this would reduce the financial gains from investing in tertiary education and might have adverse effects on the access of people from disadvantaged backgrounds to higher education. An accompanying expansion of students' access to loans to finance their education could offset such effects, and the experience of countries that have combined an increase in tuition fees and an increase in student loan facilities suggests that there are no significant adverse effects on participation.

With regard to equity considerations it is often argued that education must not be distributed according to purchasing power, but with reference to differences in capacities to learn ("meritocracy"). However, capacities to learn depend to a large extent on home background and the educational background of the parents, which reintroduces the influence of income. Pure meritocracy therefore requires positive discrimination in favour of children with less than average abilities. Blaug (1970) for example argues that "free" state education is not the only or even the most effective way of equalising educational opportunities. Possibly, the most effective way of dealing with inherent disadvantages of children from low-income families is by direct financial aid in the form of grants, bursaries, scholarships, loans and educational vouchers.

Modes of providing and financing higher education

The main distinction that can be made with regard to financing higher education is the one between public and private funding. Public funding can take place either by financing or subsidising institutions of higher education or in the form of individual subsidies paid directly to students. Private funding can come from students and their families, from philanthropists (endowments or current contributions), or take the form of commercialisation of certain aspects of the institutions or the curricula. Financing higher education in a larger sense does not only cover the maintenance of institutions and the dispensation of education, but also the living expenses of students. In addition, for a cost-benefit analysis, one would also have to take into account the opportunity costs due to earnings foregone by the students engaging in higher education.

While free, merit-based state provision of higher education has been the rule over the past decades in a lot of industrialised countries, budget constraints coupled with increasing participation in education have lately fuelled debates about the shifting of costs from government spending to private finance, especially by students and their families. With regard to the issue of public versus private finance and/or production, Musgrave (1969) notes that:

- private finance by prices and user charges is easily applicable when the good is excludable and rival, whoever, public or private, is responsible for the production;

- public finance by taxation, grants and subsidies is likely to be significant when a good is non-rival and/or is the source of significant externalities (and in the case of redistributive policy);

- private production under competitive markets generally assures X-efficiency and allocative efficiency generated as a result of profit maximisation; private production of a (natural) monopoly is usually subject to regulation;

- public production in the case of rival and excludable goods is more difficult to justify, unless the project is large and indivisible (sunk costs) or private production would confer undue political and economic power to some individuals. Moreover, public production can be justified when it is aimed at exploiting economies of scale so that additional activities can be added with little or no marginal cost. Another, non-economic argument concerns the quality aspects, which are difficult to measure, of some activities that would be lost with private production.

Table 2 offers a synthetic view of types of goods and forms of provision. Categories 1 and 8 are the extremes. Of course, each type of good can be matched with one or more or all forms of provision, and some goods may have more than one characteristic. Most researchers would probably consider education as a quasi-public good (type C), provided that the externalities are significant, or possibly associate it with type F. Therefore, mixed finance would be advisable, coupled with private or public provision. Education services are non-rival up to the limits of the places available in the universities, and they present further characteristics of a public good because of the existence of external effects which benefit society as a whole. Their consumption is in principle excludable.

Table 2. Provision, financing and type of goods

Type of goods	Forms of provision
	Public provision
A. Public (non-rival, non-excludable)	1. Public sector production without user charges
B. Club/toll (non-rival to a congestion limit, excludable)	2. Public sector production with user charges
C. Quasi-public (rival, excludable; significant externalities)	3. Public production with user charges and vouchers or grants to consumers
D. Common pool (rival, exclusion possible or difficult, if absent leading to congestion/exhaustion/extinction)	4. Public contracts to private producers to supply goods and services to the government for user charge or "free" disposal
E. Private (rival, excludable)	5. Public contracts to private producers to supply goods and services to the government for user charge or "free" disposal and grants to producers or consumers with vouchers or grants to cover charges
F. Merit wants (lack of appropriate information and/or complex assessment for the typical consumer)	6. Public/private mixed production with private finance and/or government grants finance
	7. Voluntary, non-profit production with private finance and/or government grants finance
	8. Private sector production with private finance
	Private provision

Sources: Paul, S., "Privatisation and the public sector", *Finance and Development,* Vol. 22, No. 4, 1985, also reproduced in Cullis and Jones (1998, p. 100).

There is a variety of ways to shift costs of higher education away from the state and the public sector or to increase the efficiency of its production by introducing market mechanisms:

– cost-recovery strategy: tuition fees allow students to be charged for their education. Students are willing to pay for their studies provided that their anticipated benefit from additional education exceeds the amount of the total cost. The risk of this strategy is to reduce access for low-income and less advantaged students. Students from low-income backgrounds may respond to higher tuition fees by dropping out or by increasing private sources of income (wages, savings), which can only be a supplement and bears the risk of negatively affecting the students' performance. Well-off students, however, may increase resources from family and friends;

– grant and loan schemes: today, governments typically finance higher education by funding both institutions and students (grants, loans), but this model is not necessarily sustainable because of the fiscal pressure, nor is it fair, as it is regressive. It is frequently argued that public funding may be not only insufficient to develop higher education in the face of increasing enrolment, but also inefficient. Private financing and/or privatisation might be a solution to this problem. Enhanced grant and loan schemes targeted at low-income students could thereby be used to address problems of access. Increased government funding of grants may, however, be in contradiction with a cost-recovery strategy in the face of budget constraints;

– capital market: loans from private markets are generally not available to students because of imperfect capital markets, risk aversion or for cultural reasons. There may indeed be good reasons why individuals do not invest as much in education as they would like to under a market regime (private or public production with private finance), even to the point where private return equals the cost of capital. They may lack access to funds to finance their education. Private lenders are not for the most part willing to lend to finance education, for several reasons.

Because of asymmetric information it is quite hard for the lenders to know the capabilities of the student, his/her ambition and the intended career path, including the uncertainty the student may face (future earnings, unemployment, etc.). Asymmetric information leads to the well-known problem of adverse selection. The premium demanded by the lenders to compensate the risks tends to deter some students with high potential and to attract students with lower potential. The average student will therefore be of lower quality, and the premium would have to be adjusted upwards to reflect the overall deterioration of the students seeking financial help, deterring even more students from taking out loans. Furthermore there may be difficulties in collecting the payments: lenders may have difficulties in locating the students, who tend to be more mobile than less educated persons. Additional difficulties arise from uncertainty with regard to the value of the investment and the capacity to repay, from the illiquid nature of investment in human capital which cannot be sold and from the absence of collaterals, in particular in the case of poorer students.

Nevertheless, some loan models have been proposed or have been operating on a purely private basis in the United States (Lleras, 2004, Chapters 4 and 9). The design of those income-contingent loans (ICL) may vary according to:

– the income on which the estimate of contingent payments and the percentage paid is based;

– the period over which the repayment would be based and the forgiveness conditions, if any;

– the interest rate of the loan;

– the collection method;

– the buyout conditions. In order to take into account the risks of default by life-long low-income earners, third parties or the high-income students could be asked to subsidise them.

Lleras (2004) proposes the introduction of human capital contracts (HCC), "in which students commit part of their future income for a predetermined period of time in exchange for capital for financing (higher) education". This proposal is not new as in its simplest form, Friedman (1955) already suggested creating a financial instrument that would allow investors to buy part of a student's future income, referring to vocational and professional schooling because of the relatively small external effects compared to the private benefits that the individual receives and compared to general education for citizenship (primary and secondary schooling). Recent changes in the financial system in the 1980s and 1990s create new opportunities for HCC, namely the creation of mutual funds and the securisation of assets. The possibility of grouping assets together and selling them in parts fundamentally changes the bilateral relationship between investor and individual in a multilateral relationship. Investors would be clustered into mutual funds and those funds would be invested in a very important number of students assembled through securisation, spreading the risks among the investors and the students.

Some of the difficulties related to financing higher education through the capital market could also be overcome by a government policy providing guarantees for study loans. This would, however, affect the government budget.

Income diversification. Recognising that the students are not the only beneficiaries of institutions of higher education, but that industry equally has an interest in certain aspects of education or in having a privileged access to the students, parts of the institutions or the curriculum can be subjected to commercial contracts. Another way to tap into new financial sources is to encourage alumni to donate to their alma mater. Policy measures to encourage such donations may include tax exemptions.

Voucher systems. A publicly financed and operated system can be inefficient because the students cannot effectively influence operational decisions, except for adopting a strategy of exit (not attending). Allowing for competition by admitting private institutions to the higher education market and thereby increasing the choices of the students could be a policy option. However, private universities are only a part of the solution. Expensive institutions end up being attended by a small elite and cheap universities end up with students that were not admitted to the better public institutions. Another policy option would be to increase the financing of the students rather than institutions: vouchers may increase competition among all accredited public and private institutions (Levin, 1992). For instance, Mixon and McKenzie (1999) have studied management behaviour in private and public universities. They find that the non-transferable property rights (regarding public-owned firms) reduce the incentives to police and detect managerial (in)efficiencies in public universities and that managers therefore face incentives to create internal decision-making processes which increase job security and tenure, along with other non-pecuniary sources of income and utility. The average tenure, for example, of public university presidents is about five years longer than their private counterparts.

In a survey contribution on the so-called emerging market for higher education, Pusser (2003) is, however, rather sceptical about the existence of such a market, arguing that the three fundamental assumptions that shape the prediction of an emerging competitive market-place for higher education are not necessarily valid:

- higher education institutions operate in a market environment;
- lack of institutional efficiency and productivity generates demand for market solutions, and market-like behaviour will increase efficiency and productivity;
- market approaches will produce at least the same quantity and distribution of public and private goods as generated by the present system.

Recent developments

Over the past two decades there have been fundamental changes in the way universities are organised and financed. Increasing participation in higher education has led to growing government spending, which conflicts with budget constraints. Thus there has been considerable pressure to limit government expenditure as well as to improve the cost efficiency of higher education. In a number of countries reforms have been carried out which are aimed at making the university system more efficient by reorganising the way universities operate and interact with government. At the same time there has been a tendency to shift costs from government to students and their families by raising tuition fees. The theoretical basis of this shift is provided by human capital theory, which considers higher education primarily as a private investment.

Organisational reforms

At the core of the present reforms, which are often inspired by new public management (NPM) principles are increased competition among institutions and stronger market-orientation. The relationship between governments and institutions of higher education is being contractualised: universities are given more financial autonomy by means of global budgets, yet as a counterpart they have to commit themselves to fulfilling a certain number of objectives, while a number of quality indicators are used to compare their performance against other universities. The reforms are aimed at setting up a higher education market in which the different institutions compete with each other. This is believed to reduce present inefficiencies in the sector.

There is some debate on whether the universities really have more autonomy in a market system, as is often argued by advocates of the reforms. A number of authors point to the fact that aspects of decentralisation are accompanied by tendencies toward centralisation, especially within systems which prior to the reforms were relatively decentralised. Thus Musselin and Mignot-Gérard (2003) argue that in France, which used to have a highly centralised system of higher education, the reforms aimed at decentralising the system did not lead to a shift of real decision-making power away from the central administration: there is not only extensive regulation reducing the leeway of the universities in conducting their operations, but the central administration continues to intervene in the system by setting specific objectives, the fulfilment of which entitles the universities to extra government financing. Charlier and Mons (2003) note that in Belgium, where the universities used to have a lot of autonomy, the discretionary power of university presidents has decreased in the wake of the standardisation of higher education. The presidents' task increasingly consists in carrying out the orders of the central agency. Deer (2003) in turn notes that the separation of strategic decision making and operational management has allowed the British Government to make budget cuts more easily, delegating the operational aspects to the universities. Deer also points to the increasing centralisation of decision-making processes within the universities and their bureaucratisation due to these changes. Altbach (2003) makes out a certain tendency of uniformisation among universities which see themselves more and more as actors in a global market: in order to be recognised as world-class universities, they are trying to imitate prestigious US universities like Harvard or Berkeley. The question of whether the market-oriented system leads to increased university autonomy or whether it favours the uniformisation of higher education is crucial with regard to the tendency towards increased "client orientation".

Increased autonomy and market orientation of universities combined with budget cuts can lead to growing commercialisation of higher education as the universities seek to tap new sources of finance. Commercialisation may not only touch the way tuition is financed (for instance in the case of study loans from private institutions), but can have an impact on different aspects of university life: thus Shaker and Doherty-Delorme (1999) cite a number of contracts securing exclusive rights for particular brands to be present on campuses in Canada and the United States. In addition they mention a number of university departments and programmes named after large companies. Commercial ties can, however, go further than catering or advertising. Companies directly influence the content of university courses through sponsoring (Bok, 2003) or through special contracts which guarantee them direct influence on the curriculum (Shaker and Doherty-Delorme, 1999). Different authors point to the problem that commercialisation of universities leads to conflicts of interest between the rules and standards of academia and those of private enterprises (Shaker and Doherty-Delorme, 1999; Anderson, 2001; Bok, 2003).

Larger "cost-sharing"

Johnstone (2003) notes that "the burden of higher educational costs worldwide is shifted from governments or taxpayers to students and families". The increasing participation of students and their families in financing higher education is also referred to as "cost sharing".

Measures to increase "client orientation" are supported by the argument that publicly financed and operated systems may be inefficient because the students cannot effectively influence the decisions, except by withdrawing from the system (exit strategy). A solution to this problem consists in introducing a market mechanism to regulate the relationship between universities and their students. This means to increase tuition fees as a contribution of the financing of the education and as an incentive for the students to behave efficiently. Higher tuition charges are based on the assumption that they will induce students and their families, and thus the consumers of higher education, to make more conscious choices, which is thought to increase the efficiency of the education system. Furthermore, diminishing state subsidies for higher education is sometimes seen as a means of reducing the number of long-term students who are remaining in the system only to profit from the benefits related to the status of a student (Johnstone, 2003).

Yet, the students need to have the necessary financial power in order to constitute a demand. An option would be to shift financial resources to students, for example by means of a voucher system, or increases in grants and/or loans. Public financing would then operate through the students instead of subsidising institutions. There are at least two additional reasons which are put forward in favour of increased private funding of higher education. Firstly, according to human capital theory, private benefits of education prevail. Accordingly, government funding should be reduced to cover only the positive externalities of education. Secondly, due to the over-representation of students from high-income families within the higher education system, free provision of higher education is seen as counterproductive from the point of view of equity. Need-based subsidising of low-income students would be a better solution to improve their access to education, while higher-income students would be asked to finance their studies themselves.

The socioeconomic impact of new modes of financing higher education

Increases in tuition fees are often accompanied by loan schemes, which allow the students to borrow the money they need to finance their education. There are a number of studies from countries where "cost sharing" has already been in place for a while (for example, the United States, the United Kingdom, New Zealand and Australia). One concern of these studies is to measure the financial impact on students: Baum and O'Malley (2003), for example, report an increase of the median loan taken out by undergraduates in the United States, from US$9 500 in 1997 to US$16 500 in 2002 (plus 74% in five years). In New Zealand the average annual loan rose from NZ$3 628 in 1992 to NZ$6 135 in 2002, while the cumulative debt rose from an average of NZ$5 525 in 1993-94 to NZ$12 643 in 2001-02 and NZ$13 680 in 2002-03 (NZUSA and NZNO, 2003). Callender (2003) in turn notes that since the British Government has replaced grants by study loans, more and more students are indebted and that the average debt level is increasing. Baum and O'Malley (2003) point to the increasing credit-card debts among students in the United States, the study-loan debt making up only about half of the total student debt burden.

Some studies challenge the assumption that students are well-informed economic actors, able to judge the costs and future returns of education. King and Frishberg (2001) for example find that 78% of the students in the United States underestimate the cost of their debt, especially those with a large debt burden. At the same time, future salaries were overestimated by more than 30% on average. According to another study (Baum and O'Malley, 2003), 54% of the former students participating in the study would borrow less for their studies if they could decide again. Some 34% found that the debt burden causes them more hardship than they had expected, whereas 59% said student loans were worth incurring because of the career opportunities provided.

Other authors have investigated the socioeconomic impact of a system with high tuition fees combined with a loan system. According to Johnstone (2003), empirical research on the effect of both tuition and need-based financial assistance on student enrolment behaviour in the US support the conventional wisdom that net price – that is, the combined effect of tuition fees discounted by financial aid – has little effect on middle and upper-middle income students. However, it can have a measurable discouraging impact on low-income youth, an impact that is only partly offset by increasing need-based aid. An overview of different studies shows that discriminatory effects have been identified mainly in systems where repayment is independent of actual income. In Australia, for example, where repayment is contingent on income, such effects are rare (Chapman and Ryan, 2003a and 2003b). In New Zealand, average repayment time is much longer for women and some ethnic groups (NZUSA and NZNO, 2003; Pearse, 2003). Pearse cites data which suggest that the average projected repayment time is about twice as long for women as for men (twenty-nine years for women compared to fifteen years for men). It takes Maori students 12% longer on average than European origin students to repay their loans, whereas average repayment time for students from other ethnic groups is up to 43% longer. Baum and O'Malley (2003) note in their report of the National Student Loan Survey, conducted by Nellie Mae, the largest private provider of study loans in the United States, that the 2002 data shows for the first time a difference in perception of debt burden between low-income student borrowers and others. Students from low-income backgrounds reported feeling more burdened than the average student borrower. King and Frishberg (2001) show that lower-income students are more likely to have to borrow to pay for college and that they also take larger loans than the average student.

It is also argued that differences in the attitude to debt have an impact on students' decisions whether or not to take out a loan. Reporting on research about the attitude to debt among school-leavers and further education students in the United Kingdom, Callender (2003) points out that students with debt-tolerant attitudes were more likely to participate in higher education than students more reluctant to incur debts. She also identifies the social groups which were the least debt-tolerant: Muslims and Sikhs; black and minority ethnic groups; persons with family responsibilities, especially single parents; older respondents; and those from lower social classes. It is interesting to note that the more debt-averse population comprises the lower social classes and other groups with less than average access to higher education. The findings thus seem to indicate that higher tuition combined with a loan system can have a negative impact on equity. Data from the United States indicate that debt-averse lower-class students frequently opt for relatively cheap low-status community colleges. At the same time there seems to be an increasing tendency among students from well-off families to avoid low-status institutions and to seek access to prestigious universities instead (McPherson and Shapiro, 2000). The authors of the 1998 Nellie Mae report also identify "loan fear" among certain ethnic groups and lower social classes as a reason not to participate in higher education (Baum and Saunders, 1998). Thus, it has to be kept in mind that students from a lower-class background usually have either to borrow higher amounts of money or to attend lower-status colleges, which in itself accounts for a certain degree of social stratification within the higher education system, regardless of any cultural bias against debts.

There are concerns in Australia and New Zealand that higher university fees have an effect on emigration. One study indicates that a large number of indebted medical professionals choose to emigrate to countries where they can earn higher wages, in order to pay back their debt (NZUSA and NZNO, 2003). Pearse (2003) notes that former students choosing to emigrate are likely to have a debt higher than average. More research is needed to investigate the effects of student debt and globalisation on migration and the labour market. Labour market effects should also be analysed with regard to their impact on government's ability to hire qualified professionals. The American Bar Association, for example, estimated that study loan debts keep up to 66% of law students from choosing a public career, because the salaries are too low to pay back the loan within a reasonable time. In fact, overall tuition for legal studies in the United States has more than doubled between 1992 and 2002 (ABA, 2003).

Is research a public good?

The non-excludability, non-rivalness and cumulativeness of knowledge are usually invoked in order to justify public intervention and spending on research. In analogy to the analysis of private and public goods, there are two questions related to the characteristics of research activities, namely: is research a public good? And if so, what are the corrective actions the government should take if the market, left on its own, cannot provide the optimal quantity of research activities?

Research or the production of knowledge as an economic good is non-excludable, in the sense that "it is difficult to make it exclusive or to control it privately" (Foray, 2004). Even if kept secret, information and knowledge escape from entities producing them and can be used freely by rivals, which benefit from positive externalities without financial compensation. In addition, once knowledge is produced, economic agents are not rival users, as there is no need to produce for an additional user a copy of the knowledge. Knowledge is also cumulative as it is likely to spur new ideas and new goods. However, the public characteristics and cumulativeness of knowledge are not absolute, as the access to and the use of knowledge is limited when the costs of accessing, reproducing and transmitting it are high.

Knowledge, and thus research results, may in fact have some of the characteristics of a private good: in the case of trade secrets, for example, or when a company is the only entity capable of appropriating the short-term benefits of newly produced knowledge. Thus, Cohen et al. (2000) find that the key appropriability mechanisms in most industries are secrecy, lead time and complementary capabilities, as opposed to institutional appropriation mechanisms such as patenting. Studying the appropriation mechanisms, Callon (1994) notes that knowledge can to a certain extent be appropriated by choosing a support which does not lend itself readily to dissemination (for instance by not encoding it in text) and argues that, based on the fact that scientific knowledge usually is encoded in a language specific to the field of study, scientific knowledge is only to be considered a non-rival good within a limited community of people who have made the necessary complementary investment to understand it in its context.

Given that research and knowledge have public good characteristics, potential shortcomings in the production and dissemination of knowledge provide a theoretical basis for corrective action by the state.

Nelson (1959) notes that, since the marginal cost of use of knowledge is nil, maximum efficiency in its use implies that there should be no restrictions to its access and that the price of use should be equal to zero. However, producing knowledge and doing research come with a cost, and can even be very costly. In order to achieve maximum efficiency in the allocation of resources to create new knowledge, knowledge should be priced highly enough to cover all the costs of the necessary resources. This dilemma is aggravated by the cumulativeness of knowledge: the more knowledge is likely to spawn the production of new knowledge (and the higher therefore its potential value for society), the more wasteful is the effect of rationing it by price (Foray, 2004).

The positive externalities represent a problem for society in so far as potential producers of knowledge might be discouraged from investing in research if they do not expect to be able to appropriate a sufficient share of the benefits allowing them to gain a comparative advantage. The consequence would be some under-production of knowledge. In addition, since research and development (R&D) spillovers are a key source of productivity growth, secrecy can be seen as a source of economic inefficiency, because it reduces its potential of spurring the production of knowledge (Griliches, 1992). Co-operation as a solution to this dilemma is not likely to be chosen by market agents because each of them would like to reap a competitive advantage and because transaction costs are usually very high.

Nelson (1959) argues that in face of positive externalities, it is crucial for a company investing in R&D to be able to capture a large portion of the externalities. This is especially the case with large, multi-product companies. R&D externalities are therefore a source of economies of scale, putting smaller companies at a disadvantage, which can have negative effects on competition. Later Nelson (1993) notes, however, that size is not in all industries a prerequisite for a company to be a capable innovator. Other aspects which enhance a company's commercial ability to engage in basic research are strong vertical linkages with its suppliers and a constant supply of human capital through a university system responsive to the company's needs. In some sectors, university or public laboratory research also plays an important role in companies being able to innovate.

Government intervention in research

The problem of economic inefficiency due to R&D externalities may be addressed by the state through subsidies, direct government production or the definition of intellectual property rights:

- in the case of state subsidies, society bears (part of) the cost of knowledge production. In return, anything that is produced is the property of society as a whole and cannot be privately controlled;

- direct government production, in turn, is suited to large-scale projects which require a high level of concentration of resources and centralisation of decision making. In this case, knowledge access might not be granted to a wider public (cf. military research);

- by the definition of intellectual property rights, it is intended to facilitate the creation of a market to stimulate private initiative. Access to new knowledge is open, yet its use is restricted by exclusive rights which enable the inventor to set a price for its use. Intellectual property rights generally comprise patents, copyright and registered designs (Foray, 2004).

All three approaches have their own shortcomings.

In the case of public subsidies or private-sector patronage systems, mechanisms of allocating research grants do not lead to the optimal result, due to circuits of positive feedback (reputation increases the probability of receiving a new grant which increases reputation even more) (David, 1994). Assessing the quality of research has in fact been a growing concern in the context of budget restraints and managerial attempts to improve research quality by channelling scarce public resources to the most performing institutions and researchers. Nowotny et al. (2003) have identified three major shortcomings of such output-related funding: distortions are produced by scholars who orient their publishing behaviour according to the indicators, for example by publishing their research in ever smaller bits and thus artificially improving their records. Another problem lies in the disciplinary approach of peer-review, which works as a bias against interdisciplinary research, and a third criticism is that research management mechanisms encourage researchers to adopt an industry-style attitude, which favours the fast delivery of safe and predictable results over the pursuit of new, ground-breaking research, which is more time-consuming.

In public production systems government failures are likely to occur, which reflects the difficulty administrators have in assessing the quality and the relevance of their research. Furthermore, public procurement may create distortions in industrial competitiveness. Also, as David et al. (1999) note, publicly funded contract-specified R&D may substitute for some of the private investment which the firm would otherwise have performed in a competitive bid for a related government procurement contract.

In the case of the private property approach, intellectual property rights determine monopoly prices that create distortions in the market, leading to non-optimal dissemination of knowledge. Furthermore, so-called "hold-up" patents can be used to fend off competitors. Extensive patenting can thus become a substitute for investing in R&D (Bessen and Hunt, 2004a and 2004b). Furthermore, there is much evidence that patent protection does not advance innovation in a substantial way in most industries, pharmaceuticals being an exception (Cohen et al., 2000). Nelson (1959) also points to the fact that there is a large contradiction between the granting of private monopolies to further research and the concept of a free enterprise economy.

Financing research: public or private funding?

In OECD countries, the private business sector spends two thirds to three quarters of total expenditure on R&D: 65% in the EU, 71% in Japan and 73% in the United States (figures for 2002). From 1996 to 2002, the share of the private sector had remained stable for both Japan and the United States, while it had increased by two percentage points in the EU. The rest of R&D expenditure was mainly carried out in the government sector (EU: 13%; United States: 8%; and Japan: 10%, in 2002) or within the higher education system (EU: 21%; United States and Japan: 15%, in 2002) (Eurostat, 2003). While government budgets directed at research as a percentage of GDP had decreased in the EU throughout the 1990s, there has been a slight increase since 2000. The US has seen a similar development at a somewhat higher level, whereas in Japan public R&D budgets have notably risen from a much lower level, thus approaching the level of the EU (Eurostat).

Government spending on research is not limited to the public sector. Governments also subsidise private research and development. Another form of government support of private R&D is tax relief. There are also considerable differences among countries as to the objectives and modes of administering research funds (for example, block grants versus project-related funding for university research). Generalisation across disciplines is also impossible due to the fact that different fields of research face different socioeconomic realities: in some fields (such as pharmaceutics) there is large industry demand for academic research, in some other fields there is considerable demand from the government (for instance, in environmental studies), while demand in certain fields (like literature or philosophy) cannot readily be grasped in economic terms (Bok, 2003).

The economic justification for government support is linked to the presence of two important market failures associated with R&D activities: First, imperfect appropriability conditions imply that the private rate of return to R&D is lower than its social return. Therefore, private sector investment in R&D tends to be below the socially optimal level. Second, risk associated with research requires a high risk premium (Link and Long, 1981). Consequently, smaller companies or new entrants in a particular field have difficulties finding finding appropriate private funding (Guellec and van Pottelsberghe de la Potterie, 1997). However, it is crucial from the economic point of view to know whether public spending on research is a substitute for or a complement to private investment in R&D. There is evidence that public research activity induces industrial R&D spending in some industries (cf. Jaffe, 1989; Jaffe and Traijtenberg, 1996). In a review of thirty-three econometric studies addressing the question of complementarity or substitution, David et al. (1999) note that one third of the cases report that public R&D funding behaves as a substitute for private R&D investment, complementarity thus appears to be somewhat more prevalent.

One approach to deciding whether research should be funded by the public or the private sector is the application of the "public good" criteria, based on the differentiation between "public financed universities and research institutes – dedicated to the creation of new knowledge as a public good – and industry, which [is] to produce marketable goods financed by private capital" (Krull, 2004, p. 34). Already Nelson (1959) had noted, however, that the line between basic and applied research is hard to draw. Forty-five years later, Krull argues that while there had indeed been a dividing line between basic research and industrial innovation until the 1970s or the early 1980s, the borders between the two domains have nowadays lost importance: "especially in biotechnology, the computer sciences, and materials research, innovation has turned into a simultaneous, interactive process. Private investment in publicly funded research laboratories, joint ventures between directors of research institutes and major companies, the outsourcing of long-term research activities by industrial R&D divisions, the establishment of joint professorships for entrepreneurship – these are just a few of the changes occurring at the public-private interface, which require not only new regulatory policies, but also new approaches to the production and distribution of new knowledge" (Krull, 2004, p. 34).

Another instance of how the differences between basic research and industrial innovation are increasingly blurred is the growing "commodification" of knowledge produced as a result of university research: Etzkowitz and Stevens (1998) point to the importance of the Bayh-Dole Act of 1980 allowing US universities to patent the results of research. According to Press and Washburn (2000) this change in legislation has had a huge impact and has boosted university patenting. Thus, results of at least in part publicly funded research do not necessarily remain in the public domain any more (see also Bok, 2003).

Recently, budget constraints have led to increasing commercialisation of research. According to Nowotny et al. (2003) this has taken two main forms: firstly, public funding being insufficient, researchers have increasingly resorted to alternative sources of funding. Secondly, universities and other public research institutions have become more aware of the value of intellectual property generated by their research. Thus, university research is increasingly valued in terms of immediate market return. The economic exploitation of intellectual property challenges the idea of science as a public good. If intellectual property is considered to be a valuable asset, it cannot be given away freely by open publication in peer-reviewed journals. Thus, the commercial orientation of research threatens the institutions of open science (Nowotny et al., 2003).

Anderson (2001) argues that increasing entrepreneurial "academic capitalism" could lead to a loss of research integrity, because conflicts of interest arise between the rules and standards of academia and those of private enterprises. Similarly, Bok (2003) warns that the commercialisation of research, teaching and other university activities might draw the institution away from its core mission.

The increasing market orientation in university research poses yet another problem: strong linkages between academic research and industrial innovation have an influence on the balance between basic and applied research: "basic research is often associated with long-term inquiry, whereas applied research is more likely to address immediate needs and problems" (Etzkowitz and Stevens, 1998). In this view, basic research is the long-range investment that ensures continuity in the expansion of human knowledge; corporate interest in problems of an applied nature shortens the perspective and relevance of research solutions. The very reason that university research has value to the corporate sector is that it takes a broader view of research problems than is typical in corporate research laboratories.

Private property rights or open systems of knowledge production and dissemination

There are two major justifications for the attribution of intellectual property rights (IPR) to those who are producing the knowledge: encouraging research by improving the appropriability of the benefits of innovation and facilitating the circulation of knowledge by encouraging its disclosure and providing a standardised way of publishing it. There are, however, some drawbacks: IPR constitutes a market inefficiency in so far as the price of the good will be above the marginal cost of its production (Dixon and Greenhalgh, 2002), in other words as the value to society of an additional unit of knowledge is greater than its marginal production cost, expanding that knowledge would increase the welfare of society. Another negative aspect is the transaction costs which are generated by patenting: registration procedures and costs of enforcement. These may, however, be outweighed by the role which IPR play in promoting the codification and dissemination of knowledge. While the overall social usefulness of the patent system was already called into question half a century ago by Fritz Machlup and Edith T. Penrose (Machlup and Penrose, 1950; Penrose, 1951; Machlup, 1958), there is growing concern nowadays that the patent system has in fact become an unnecessary burden for society (Foray, 2004).

Collective organisation of knowledge production is not confined to the public sector. There are also other forms of organisation which are neither private nor controlled by the public sector, such as for example user groups or other collective actions. For such forms of public, but not government-administered ownership and production, the term "comedy of the commons" was coined – as opposed to the tragedy of the commons with regard to traditional common property, such as community grazing land or common fishing grounds, which typically fall prey to overuse. Rose (1986) argues that a comedy of the commons arises where open access to a resource leads to scale returns – greater social value with greater use of the resource. Arrow (1971) points to the potential of collective action to compensate for market and state failures. Bowles and Gintis (2002) point out that community governance is not a substitute for effective government, but rather a complement. They stress the importance of an appropriate legal and governmental environment for their functioning. Institutionalising open systems of knowledge production and dissemination (an example of which is open science as incorporated by Merton's "Republic of Science") is today seen as a promising alternative to maintaining a burdensome patent system (Foray, 2004).

Concluding remarks

The theory of market failure has largely been applied to higher education and the university. Markets are unsatisfactory when benefits are non-rival and/or non-excludable, property rights are not assigned, transactions are costly and information is limited. However, in some sense, no markets are perfect, and this would always justify some forms of government intervention. Implicitly, imperfect markets are compared to perfect state interventions and allocations, which are as fictional as is the competitive ideal. Government failures may well occur and be very large depending on the institutional organisation and the political system. Wolf (1987) points out many deficiencies of public sector activities: for example on the demand side the short time horizon of the elected politicians, the separation of the costs and benefits of decision – either on the micro level favouring special interests or on the macro level through the redistribution of income –, the bias of individual preference for increased public sector activities (that is, lower tolerance for the shortcoming of markets), or even biased information provided by self-interested members of the public sector. Non-market supply may be criticised also on several grounds as public sector output is produced under near monopoly conditions and cannot be rejected, governmental output is often produced in an inefficient manner (Niskanen, 1971), notably by bureaucrats, and government interventions often come with unintended costs and large unanticipated side-effects. There is no doubt that a great deal of government output is not well defined and its measurement is complex and difficult. The relationship between input and output is vague, uncertain or even unknown, and government output, services in general, is not produced mechanically. All these factors may contribute to explaining growing government interventions and an increasing (relative) size of government.

The comparison of public sector and market activities is made with reference to the neoclassical firm and economics which are the dominant ones. A fundamental value judgment is that it is individual preferences that should matter; there is no superior organisation of society which is more than the sum of its individual members. In traditional public finance literature, the theory of market failures can be viewed either as a description of the responsibilities of the state – which of course falls short of reality considering the large number of government activities which could be performed at least as well if not much better by the (imperfect) market, or as a normative proposition where government should act – being of course aware that today's governments also provide and finance largely private goods and services. Blankart (2001) maintains that market failures may indeed explain part of the activities of the state, but that they constitute neither a necessary nor a sufficient condition for political decisions and actions. Market failures may be a reason for political decisions, but collective decisions are also taken for other reasons.

Economic analysis privileges the efficiency criteria over equity considerations. In traditional public finance and economic theory, equity is an exogenous notion that is defined by the political system (Blankart, 2001). The recent alternative approach tries to define equity and distributional justice endogenously by two economic motives: individuals are willing to contract a collective insurance which compensates possible income losses in the future, and redistribution may also prevent social unrest and revolution. Equity and justice may be defined by rules determined beforehand by consensus and written down in constitutions and specific laws. Whatever approach is chosen, equity matters to society, and society's legitimate pursuit of economic efficiency must take it, as well as other "non-economic" factors into account, when deciding on the financing, provision and regulation of higher education The ability to empirically measure the non-economic contributions of higher education is weak. Economic analysis and theory put forward some convincing arguments in favour of at least government regulations, if not financing and provision of higher education. However, they cannot deliver a definitive answer to the question as to what extent higher education and academic research is a public responsibility. The consensus around the role of higher education as service to society is more likely to be achieved through political and policy debate.

The fundamental arguments for public provision coupled with public funding are that this offers the greatest influence over the institution and its activities and that it is the organisational type best suited to the rapid expansion of higher education. Public supply also provides the most direct mechanism for the production of public goods and benefits that would not be produced if consumer demand were insufficient to generate private non-profit or for-profit provision or if private provision led to an undersupply of those goods and benefits. Faith in the market and its potential role in reforming the provision of higher education is based on a fundamental tenet of market ideology, that competition creates efficiencies, productivity gains and cost savings. However, there is so far very little empirical evidence to support this efficiency effect. In addition, contemporary literature on the need to adapt to changing demands through market solutions does not sufficiently account for the evolution of the non-profit institution as the dominant form for the provision of post-secondary education. Nor does contemporary research sufficiently explore the relative inability of market-based, consumer-driven systems to produce opportunities for universal access and the redress of social inequalities. There is also a great deal of uncertainty over how competition would affect educational quality.

References

Akerlof, G.A. and Kranton, R.E., "Identity and schooling: some lessons for the economics of education", *Journal of Economic Literature,* December 2002.

Alesina, A., Baqir, R. and Easterly, W., "Public goods and ethnic divisions", *Quarterly Journal of Economics,* November 1999.

Altbach, P.G., "The costs and benefits of world-class universities", *International Higher Education,* Fall 2003.

American Bar Association, *Lifting the burden: law student debt as a barrier to public service,* final report of the ABA Commission on Loan Repayment and Forgiveness, American Bar Association, Chicago, 2003.

Anderson, M.S., "The complex relations between the academy and industry: views from the literature", *Journal of Higher Education,* Vol. 72, 2001.

Arrow, K.J., "Political and economic evaluation of social effects and externalities", in Intriligator, M.D. (ed.), *Frontiers of quantitative economics,* North Holland, Amsterdam, 1971, pp. 3-23.

Arrow, K.J., "Higher education as a filter", *Journal of Public Economics,* 1973.

Asplund, R. and Telhado Pereira, P. (eds), *Returns to human capital in Europe. A literature review,* Taloustieto Oy, Helsinki, 1999.

Attiyeh, R., "Surveys of the issues", in *Efficiency in universities: the La Paz Papers,* Heriot-Watt University and Stanford University/Elsevier Scientific Publishing Company, 1974.

Banque mondiale, *L'enseignement supérieur, les leçons de l'expérience,* Washington, 1995.

Barnett, R., "Linking teaching and research: a critical inquiry", *Journal of Higher Education,* Vol. 63, No. 6, 1992.

Barro, R.J., *Determinants of economic growth. A cross-country empirical study,* MIT Press, Cambridge, 1997.

Baum, S. and O'Malley, M., *College on credit: how borrowers perceive their education debt.* Results of the 2002 National Student Loan Survey. Final report of the National Student Loan Survey, Nellie Mae Corporation, Braintree, MA, 2003.

Baum, S. and Saunders, D., *Life after debt: results of the National Student Loan Survey.* Final report of the National Student Loan Survey, Nellie Mae Corporation, Braintree, MA, 1998.

Bear, D., "The university as a multi-product firm", in *Efficiency in universities: the La Paz Papers,* Heriot-Watt University and Standford University Elsevier Scientific Publishing Company, 1974.

Becker, G.S., "Investment in human capital: a theoretical analysis", *Journal of Political Economy,* October 1962.

Becker, G.S., *Human capital. A theoretical and empirical analysis, with special reference to education,* Chicago University Press, Chicago, 1993.

Bessen, J. and Hunt, R.M., *An empirical look at software patents,* Working Paper No. 03-17/R, 2004a.

Bessen, J. and Hunt, R.M., *A reply to Hahn and Wallsten,* 2004b.

Blanchflower, D. and Oswald, A., "Well-being over time in Britain and the USA", *Journal of Public Economics,* forthcoming.

Blankart, C., *Öffentliche Finanzen in der Demokratie*, 4th edition Verlag Vahlen, Munich, 2001.

Blaug, M., *An introduction to the economics of education* (1970), Gregg Revivals, Aldershot, 1991.

Blöndal, S., Field, S. and Girouard, N., "Investment in human capital through upper-secondary and tertiary education", *OECD Economic Studies,* 2002.

Bok, D., *Universities in the marketplace. The commercialisation of higher education.* Princeton University Press, Princeton, 2003.

Bourdieu, P., "Les trois états du capital culturel", *Actes de la Recherche en Sciences Sociales,* No. 30, 1979.

Bourdieu, P. and Passeron, J.-C., *La reproduction. Eléments pour une théorie du système d'enseignement (Reproduction in education, society and culture,* Sage, London), Editions de Minuit, Paris, 1970.

Bowles, S. and Gintis, H., "Schooling in capitalist America revisited", *Mimeo,* November 2001.

Bowles, S. and Gintis, H., "The inheritance of inequality", *Journal of Economic Perspectives,* Vol. 16, No. 3, summer 2002.

Bowles, S. and Gintis, H., "Social capital and community governance", *Economic Journal,* Vol. 112, No. 483, November 2002.

Cacoualt, O., *Sociologie de l'éducation,* La Découverte and Syros, Paris, 2003.

Callender, C., *Attitudes to debt: school leavers and further education students' attitudes to debt and their impact on participation in higher education.* A report for Universities UK and HEFCE, South Bank University, 2003.

Callon, M., "Is science a public good?", *Science, Technology, and Human Values,* Vol. 19, No. 4, 1994.

Chapman, C. and Ryan, C., *The access implication of income contingent charges for higher education: lessons from Australia,* Discussion Paper No. 463, Australian National University, Centre for Economic Policy Research, 2003a.

Chapman, C. and Ryan, C., *Higher education financing and student access: a review of the literature,* Economics Programme, Research School of Social Sciences, Australian National University, 2003b.

Charlier, J.-E. and Mons, F., "Gérer des universités en Belgique francophone", *Sciences de la Société*, No. 58: "Les universités à l'heure de la gouvernance", February 2003.

Cohen, W.M., Nelson, R.R. and Walsh, J.P., *Protecting their intellectual assets: appropriability conditions and why US manufacturing firms patent (or not)*, National Bureau of Economic Research Working Paper No. 7552, 2000.

Cullis, J.G. and Jones, P.R., *Public finance and public choice*, Oxford University Press, Oxford, 1998.

Dasgupta, P. and Serageldin, I., *Social capital. A multifaceted perspective*, The World Bank, Washington, 2000.

David, P.A., "Positive feedbacks and research productivity in science: reopening another black box", in Grandstrand, O., *Economics of technology*, Elsevier Science, 1994, pp. 65-89.

David, P.A., "From keeping 'Nature's secrets' to the institutionalisation of 'Open Science'", in Gosh, R.A. (ed.), *CODE: collaborative ownership and the digital economy*, MIT Press, Cambridge, MA, 2004 (forthcoming).

David, P.A., Hall, B.H. and Toole, A.A., *Is public R&D a complement or substitute for private R&D? A review of the econometric evidence*, Working paper prepared for a special issue of *Research Policy* on technology policy issues, forthcoming in the year 2000 under the guest-editorship of Albert N. Link, 1999.

Deer, C., "Changements politiques et évolution des pratiques de gouvernance universitaire en Angleterre", *Sciences de la Société*, No. 58: "Les universités à l'heure de la gouvernance", February 2003.

Derek, B., *Universities in the marketplace. The commercialisation of higher education*, Princeton University Press, Princeton, 2003.

Dixon, P. and Greenhalgh, C., *The economics of intellectual property: a review to identify themes for future research*, 2002.

Etzkowitz, H. and Stevens, A.J., "Inching toward industrial policy: the university's role in government iniatives to assist small, innovative companies in the US", in Etzkowitz, H., Webster, A. and Healey, P. (eds), *Capitalising knowledge: new intersections of industry and academia*, State University of New York Press, Albany, 1998.

Eurostat, *Statistics on science and technology in Europe*, Part 1, European Communities, Luxembourg, 2003.

Evans, A.W., "Private goods, externality, public goods", *Scottish Journal of Political Economy*, 1970.

Foray, D., *Economics of knowledge*, MIT Press, Cambridge, MA and London, 1994.

French, N.J., *External funding and university autonomy*, report on a NSU-NUAS-IMHE seminar, University of Oslo, June 2003.

Friedman, M., "The role of government in education", in *Economics and the public interest,* Rutgers University Press, New Jersey, 1955.

Friedman, M., "The role of government in education", in Friedman, M., *Capitalism and freedom* (Chapter VI), University of Chicago Press, Chicago, 1962.

Garratt, R. and Marshall J.M., "Public finance of private goods: the case of higher education", *Journal of Political Economy,* June 1994.

Gibbons, M., Limoges, C., Nowotny, H., Schwartzman, S., Scott, P. and Trow, M., *The new production of knowledge,* Sage, London, 1994.

Griliches, Z., "The search for R&D spillovers", *Scandinavian Journal of Economics,* Vol. 94, No. 3, 1992, Supplement, pp. 529-547.

de Groof, J., Neave, G. and Svec, J., *Democracy and governance in higher education,* Kluwer Law International, The Hague, London, 1998.

Guellec, D. and van Pottelsberghe de la Potterie, B., "Does government support stimulate private R&D?", *OECD Economic Studies,* No. 29, 1997/II.

Hagendijk, R.P., "The public understanding of science and public participation in regulated worlds", *Minerva,* Vol. 42, Kluwer Academic Publishers, 2004, pp. 41-59.

Hansen, W.L. and Weisbrod, B.A., *Benefits, costs, and finance of higher education,* Markham Publishing Company, Chicago, 1969.

Harmon, C. and Oosterbeek, H.W., "The returns to education: microeconomics", *Journal of Economic Surveys,* April, 2003.

Helliwell, J.F., *The contribution of human and social capital to sustained economic growth and well-being,* International Symposium Report, Human Resources Development Canada and OECD, 2001.

Jaffe, A., and Traitenberg, M., *Flows of knowledge from universities and federal labs: modeling the flow of patent citations over time and across institutional and geographic boundaries,* NBER Working Paper No. 5712, 1996.

Jaffe, A.B., "Real effects of academic research", *American Economic Review,* Vol. 79, No. 5, December 1989.

Jenson, J., *Mapping social cohesion: the state of Canadian research,* Canadian Policy Research Networks Study, 1998.

Johnes, G., *The economics of education,* Macmillan, London, 1993.

Johnson, H.G. "The university and the social welfare: a taxonomic exercise", in *Efficiency in universities: the La Paz Papers,* Heriot-Watt University and Stanford University/Elsevier Scientific Publishing Company, 1974.

Johnstone, D.B., *Cost sharing in higher education: tuition, financial assistance, and accessibility in comparative perspective,* International Comparative Higher

Education Finance and Accessibility Project, State University of New York, Buffalo, 2003.

King, T. and Frishberg, I., *Big loans, bigger problems: a report on the sticker shock of student loans,* State Pirgs Higher Education Project, Washington, DC, 2001.

Krueger, A. and Lindahl, M., "Education for growth", *Journal of Economic Literature,* December 2001.

Krull, W., "Towards a research policy for the new Europe: changes and challenges for public and private funders", *Minerva,* Vol. 42, Kluwer Academic Publishers, 2004, pp. 29-39.

Larédo, P. and Mustar, P., "Public sector research: a growing role in innovation systems", *Minerva,* Vol. 42, Kluwer Academic Publishers, 2004, pp. 29-39.

Laval, C., *L'école n'est pas une entreprise. Le néo-libéralisme à l'assaut de l'enseignement public,* La Découverte and Syros, Paris, 2003.

Leslie, L. and Brinkman, P., *The economic value of higher education,* Macmillan, New York, 1989.

Levin, H.M., "Market approaches to education: vouchers and school choice", *Economics of Education Review,* Vol. 11, No. 4, 1992.

Levin, H.M., "Raising school productivity: an X-efficiency approach", *Economics of Education Review,* Vol. 16, No. 3, 1997.

Levin, H.M. and Jacks, D., *Privatising education: can the marketplace deliver choice, efficiency, equity, and social cohesion?,* Westview Press, Boulder and Oxford, 2001.

Link, A.N. and Long, J.E., "The simple economics of basic scientific research: a test of Nelson's Diversification Hypothesis", *Journal of Industrial Economics,* Vol. 30, 1981, pp. 105-109.

Littlechild, S.C. and Wiseman J., "The political economy of restriction of choice", *Public Choice,* 1986.

Lleras, M.P., *Investing in human capital. A capital markets approach to student funding,* Cambridge University Press, Cambridge, 2004.

Lumsden, K., "Efficiency in universities", in *Efficiency in universities: the La Paz Papers,* Heriot-Watt University and Stanford University/Elsevier Scientific Publishing Company, 1974.

Machlup, F., *An economic review of the patent system,* Study No. 15 of the Committee on Judiciary, Subcommittee on Patents, 85th Congress, SD Session, 1958.

Machlup, F. and Penrose, E., "The patent controversy in the nineteenth century", *Journal of Economic History,* Vol. 10, No. 1, 1950, pp. 1-29.

Margolis; J. "A comment on the pure theory of public expenditure", *Review of Economics and Statistics,* 1954.

McPherson, M. and Shapiro, M.O., "Financing lifelong learning: trends and patterns of participation and financing in US higher education", *Higher Education Management,* Vol. 12, No. 2, 2000.

Merton, R.K., "The normative structure of science", in Storer, N.W. (ed.), *The sociology of science: theoretical and empirical investigations,* University of Chicago Press, Chicago, 1973, pp. 267-278.

Mishan, E.J., *Introduction of normative economics,* Oxford University Press, Oxford, 1981.

Mixon, F.G. and McKenzie, R.W., "Managerial tenure under private and government ownership: the case of higher education", *Economics of Education Review,* Vol. 18, 1999.

Musgrave, R.A., *The theory of public finance,* McGraw-Hill, New York, 1958.

Musgrave, R.A., "Provision for social goods", in Margolis, J. and Guitton, H., *Public economics,* Macmillan, London, 1969.

Musselin, C. and Mignot-Gérard, S., "L'autonomie, pas à pas", *Sciences de la Société,* No. 58: "Les universités à l'heure de la gouvernance", February 2003.

Nelson, R.R., "The simple economics of basic scientific research", *Journal of Political Economy,* Vol. 67, No. 3, 1959, pp. 297-306.

Nelson, R.R., "A retrospective", in Nelson, R.R. (ed.), *National innovation systems: a comparative analysis,* Oxford University Press, New York and Oxford, 1993.

New Zealand, *Student Loan Scheme,* Annual Report, Ministry of Education/Inland Revenue/Ministry of Social Development, New Zealand, September 2003.

Niskanen, W.A., *Bureaucracy and representative government,* Aldine-Atherton, New York, 1971.

Nowotny, H., Scott, P. and Gibbons, M., "'Mode 2' revisited: the new production of knowledge", *Minerva,* Vol. 41, Kluwer Academic Publishers, 2003, pp. 179-194.

NZUSA and NZNO, *The impact of student debt on nurses: an investigation,* New Zealand University Students' Association and New Zealand Nurses Organisation, 2003.

OECD, *Returns to investment in human capital,* Centre for Educational Research and Innovation, OECD, Paris, 1998.

OECD, *The well-being of nations. The role of human and social capital,* OECD, Paris, 2001.

Pearse, H., *The social and economic impact of student debt,* Research Paper, Council of Postgraduate Associations Incorporated, March 2003.

Penrose, E., *The economics of the international patent system,* John Hopkins University Press, Baltimore, 1951.

Press, E. and Washburn, J., "The kept university", *Atlantic Monthly,* March 2000, pp. 39-54.

Psacharopoulos, G. and Patrinos, H.A., *Returns to investment in education: a further update,* World Bank Policy Research, Washington, 2002.

Pusser, B., *Higher education, the emerging market and the public good,* report of a workshop, National Academic Press, 2002.

Ricker, W.H. and Ordeshook, P.C., *An introduction to positive political theory,* Prentice Hall, Englewood Cliffs, 1973.

Ritzen, J., "Social cohesion, public policy, and economic growth: implications for OECD countries", in Helliwell, J.F. (ed.), *The contribution of human and social capital to sustained economic growth and well-being: international symposium report,* Human Resources Development Canada and OECD, 2001.

Rose, C., "The comedy of the Commons: custom, commerce and inherently public property", *University of Chicago Law Review,* Vol. 53, No. 3, 1986, pp. 711-781.

Samuelson, P.A., "The pure theory of public expenditure", *Review of Economics and Statistics,* 1954.

Schultz, T.W., "Capital formation by education", *Journal of Political Economy,* 1960.

Shaker, E. and Doherty-Delorme, D., "Private money, private agendas", *Higher Education Ltd,* Vol. 1, No. 4, 1999.

Sianesi, B. and Van Reenen, J., "The returns to education: macroeconomics", *Journal of Economic Surveys,* 2003.

Stiglitz, J.E., "Education", Chapter 16 in *Economics of the public sector,* W.W. Norton and Company, New York, 2000.

Tanzi, V. and Schuknecht, L., *Public spending in the 20th century, a global perspective.* Cambridge University Press, Cambridge, 2000.

Temple, J., "Growth effects of education and social capital in the OECD countries", *OECD Economic Studies,* 2001.

Tsang, M.C. and Levin, H.M., "The economics of overeducation", *Economics of Education Review,* Vol. 4, No. 2, 1985.

Unesco, *World Declaration on Higher Education for the Twenty-First Century: Vision and Action,* Unesco, Paris, 1998.

Van Den Doel, H. and Van Velthoven, B., *Democracy and welfare economics,* Cambridge University Press, Cambridge, 1993.

Weisbrod, B.A., "Education and investment in human capital", *Journal of Political Economy,* Vol. 70, No. 5, October 1962.

Weisbrod, B.A., *The non-profit economy,* Harvard University Press, Cambridge, 1988.

Weiss, A., "Human capital versus signalling explanations of wages", *Journal of Economic Perspectives,* Vol. 9, No. 4, 1995.

West, E.G., "Private versus public education: a classical economic dispute", *Journal of Political Economy,* October 1964.

Wiseman, J., "The economics of education", *Scottish Journal of Political Economy,* 1959.

Wolf, Jr., C., "Market and non-market failures: comparison and assessment", *Journal of Public Policy,* Vol. 7, No. 1, 1987.

Wolfe, B.L., "External benefits of education", in Carnoy, M. (ed.), *International Encyclopaedia of Economics of Education,* Elsevier Science, New York, 1995.

Wolfe, B.L. and Haveman, R., "Accounting for the social and non-market benefits of education", in Helliwell, J.F. (ed.), *The contribution of human and social capital to sustained economic growth and well-being: international symposium report,* Human Resources Development Canada and OECD, 2001.

Wolff, L. and de Moura Castro, C., *Public and private education for Latin America: that is the (false) question,* Inter-American Development Bank, Washington, 2001.

The context – Trends in society and reflections on public responsibility in higher education

Aleksander Shishlov

It has become almost commonplace to speak about the knowledge-based economy and the Knowledge Society when discussing twenty-first-century perspectives and it is hard to find a politician or a government denying the importance of education and in particular higher education for the development of the national economy and national society. But the reflections on public responsibility in higher education in terms of real politics and life practice is a much more complex and contradictory issue. The changing balance between the level of governmental regulations and private initiative, between degrees of personal and social responsibilities is the real point for discussion. We need to find optimal solutions for each particular case. The aim of this presentation is not to cover in detail all trends and reflections on public responsibility but to propose a framework which can be used for the discussion of public responsibility in higher education and to illustrate it with some practical examples.

The past decades have demonstrated a complex trend in the development of public responsibilities: a development towards extended public responsibilities on the one hand and, on the other hand, an increased emphasis on private economic activity and deregulation of important sectors of society. This trend covers such areas as education, public health, arrangements for consumer protection and social security, as well as public standards for the environment, business accountability and some other areas where one can see considerable public involvement. At the same time there are opposite trends against the extension of public activity in telecommunications, transport, public provision of a number of services (such as electricity, garbage collection) and public monopolies (for instance, broadcasting).

The term "public responsibility" may be considered in different contexts – firstly as the responsibility of public authorities of different levels (national, regional or local) and secondly as the responsibility of public non-governmental bodies or other kinds of institution which may be responsible for some public functions by law, by agreement with the government or by tradition or historical background. In this article I am mostly going to discuss the responsibilities of public authorities (legislative, executive, and local government).

Public demand and public responsibility

The degree of public involvement and the limits of public responsibility are definitely influenced by the demands of society. Thus the analysis of public attitudes seems to be of great importance.

Speaking about public responsibilities it seems reasonable to begin with public expectations and public demands concerning higher education (in the last case I mean "society" by the word "public").

Higher education in the contemporary world is considered not only as a public good but in a more concrete sense as a key value for the overall majority of the population. This trend seems to be universal. But the question is how much we are ready to pay for this value from public and private funds.

The Russian case is quite interesting in this sense because of the fast transition from an entirely state-controlled, regulated and funded system of higher education towards a diversified educational system.

The recent research on public opinion conducted by Dr Yablonskene from the Moscow School of Social and Economic Sciences[26] clearly shows that society's demands on the education system are in transition from the so-called industrial period of higher education towards general higher education and specialised higher education. Higher education is considered by 58% of respondents to be a necessary precondition for success in life and only 27% believe that a lower level of education is sufficient. Other research conducted by the Higher School of Economics[27] shows the same trend and the fact that the respondents' attitude towards higher education correlates slightly with family income, place of living and level of education. Even among those who do not have more than secondary education the number of respondents considering higher education to be important for success in life is more than 50%. More than 60% of the families are ready to pay for their children to get higher education.

This public demand for higher education coexists with the understanding that there is great labour market demand for qualified workers and that it is much easier to find work with solid education credentials.

On the other hand, it is important to realise that the demand for higher education may be formed not only by the influence of such factors as the requirements of the labour market or the educational aspirations of individuals. It may also be affected by other external circumstances like for example conscription: it is wellknown that many young people in Russia enter universities rather to avoid military service than to get professional knowledge.

After the collapse of the Soviet Union where higher education had only state budget funding the share of students who pay tuition fees for their higher education is increasing rapidly each year. The total number of students in Russia studying free

26. "The materials of a complex sociological research project on people's attitude towards educational reforms in the Russian Federation, Moscow School of Social and Economic Sciences, Moscow, 2003. Original reference in Russian: "å‡ÚÂ‹Ë‡Î° ÍÓÏÔÎÂÍÒÌÓ„Ó ÒÓˆËÓÎÓ„Ë˜ÂÒÍÓ„Ó ËÒÒÎÂ‰Ó‚ÌËﬂ Ó‚‹Ë ÏÚÓ‡‚‹ÌËﬂ êÓÒÒËÈÒÍÓÈ îÂ‰Â‡ˆ‹ËË ÔÓ ,ÓÔˆÓÒÏ Ó^Â‹ÍË ÓÒÚÛÓﬁÌËﬂ ÒËÒÚÂ‡° Ó•‡‡ÁÓ,‡ÌËﬂ, ÓÚÍÓ^ÂËﬂ ‡ÒÚÂ‚ÌËﬂ Í Ó‡‡‡Ï ÏÓ‰ÂÏÍÂ‡‡^ËË ÒËÒÚÂÏ° Ó•‡ÁÓ,‡ÌËﬂ Ë ÓÚ‹ÂÏ Ì˚ Ï‡Ó˜‡,ÌÂÌﬂ Â˜ ‹Â‡ÎÂ‡‡^ËË" , åÓÒÍÓ,ÓÍ‡ﬂ ¯ÍÓˆ ÒÓ˜ËˆﬁˆÌ˚°˚‚ Ë ˜ÍÓÌÓÏË˜ÂÒÍÂ˚ Ï‡Û˚ ÁÍ‰‚Â‚ËË Ï‡•Ó‰ÍÓ,Ó ˆÓÁÂËÒÙ,‡ ÔÒÍÂ è‡‡^,ËÚ‡Î˚ÓÚ,Á‡ÓÓÚËÒÍÓÈÓÈ Ì‡‰Â‡‡^ËË (å˚ëﬁˆ Äˆ¨), åÓÓÍ,‡, 2003.
27. *Monitoring of economy of education,* Vol. 2, 2004, Higher School of Economics, Moscow.

of charge, that is, funded with state, regional and municipal money, increased from 2.426 million in 1995/1996 to 2.919 million in 2002/2003, while the number of students who pay tuition fees rose almost ten times from 0.364 to 3.027 million during the same period.

Now about 59% of Russian students pay for their studies including 54% of those studying at state-owned universities and higher education institutions.

According to the estimation of the Russian Economics of Transition Institute, the general state budget expenditure for education in Russia was halved in terms of comparative figures from 1991 to 1999. The public expenditure for education as a percentage of GDP in Russia in 2000 was as low as 2.9%. This fact together with the figures cited above shows that public demand for higher education and the public policy in this area were not well tuned.

This may be explained partly by the fact that unfortunately the polls show that education is not at the top of the priority list for the general public, and this is the case not only for Russia. So the fact that real governmental policy often does not give priority to education is hardly a surprise.

One of the consequences of continuing under-funding of higher education and the growing public demand for higher education is the growth of corruption. The polls show that respondents consider corruption to be the main problem of the contemporary Russian higher education system – mostly corruption at the stage of access to higher education but also corruption during studies. This example demonstrates the potential danger of poor co-ordination between public social demand and public governmental responsibilities.

In a wider context I suppose that the place of education on the scale of political governmental priorities is a good test of the political wisdom and foresight of political leaders.

International background for public responsibility in higher education

Raised in the recent years, the discussion on public responsibilities in higher education has definitely been stimulated by the globalisation process and the increase of international trade as well as the development of a more international labour market and a knowledge-based economy and society.

Some of the internationally recognised principles for the distribution of public responsibilities in higher education were clearly expressed in the Convention on the Recognition of Qualifications concerning Higher Education in the European Region, which was elaborated by the Council of Europe and Unesco and adopted in Lisbon on 11 April 1997. The convention has now (January 2005) been ratified by forty countries and signed by a further eight.

The convention set up some basic guidelines for public responsibility in higher education:

– holders of qualifications issued in one party shall have adequate access to an assessment of these qualifications in another party;

– no discrimination shall be made in this respect on any ground such as the applicant's gender, race, colour, disability, language, religion, political opinion, national, ethnic or social origin;

– each party shall recognise qualifications – whether for access to higher education, for periods of study or for higher education degrees – as similar to the corresponding qualifications in its own system unless it can show that there are substantial differences between its own qualifications and the qualifications for which recognition is sought;

– recognition of a higher education qualification issued in another party shall give access to further higher education studies on the same conditions as candidates from the country in which recognition is sought, and may facilitate access to the labour market;

– all parties shall develop procedures to assess whether refugees and displaced persons fulfil the relevant requirements for access to higher education or to employment activities, even in cases in which the qualifications cannot be proven through documentary evidence;

– all parties shall provide information on the institutions and programmes they consider as belonging to their higher education systems.

All parties shall encourage their higher education institutions to issue the Diploma Supplement, which aims to describe the qualification in an easily understandable way, to their students in order to facilitate recognition.[28] The Bologna Process, which aims to establish a European Higher Education Area by 2010, is another cornerstone of the discussion of public responsibility.

The joint understanding of what is public responsibility in higher education is developing with each conference of the ministers of the member states. Fixing the objectives for the creation of the European Higher Education Area, the founders of the Bologna Process agreed to a joint approach to some areas of public responsibility like adoption of a system of easily readable and comparable degrees, adoption of a system essentially based on two main cycles, undergraduate and graduate, establishment of a system of credits, promotion of mobility for students, teachers, researchers and administrative staff, and promotion of European co-operation in quality assurance.[29]

---

28. The Diploma Supplement aims to explain a given qualifications and its place in the education system to which it belongs in such a way as to facilitate the assessment of the qualification by informed foreigners; cf. http://www.cepes.ro/hed/recogn/groups/diploma

29. *The European Higher Education Area. Joint Declaration of the European Ministers of Education,* Bologna, 19 June 1999.

This approach was further developed in the Prague Communiqué (2001)[30] where ministers supported the idea that higher education should be considered a public good and is and should remain a public responsibility (in terms of regulations, etc.). The Prague conference also underlined that students are full members of the higher education community – certainly the full membership of students should be guaranteed by corresponding legal regulations.

At the Berlin conference (2003) the next step was taken and ministers agreed that by 2005 national quality assurance systems should include in particular the definition of the responsibilities of the bodies and institutions involved, and a system of accreditation, certification or comparable procedures.[31] They encouraged the member states to elaborate a framework of comparable and compatible qualifications in terms of workload, level, learning outcomes, competencies and profile. They also decided to elaborate a joint "overarching" qualifications framework for the European Higher Education Area.

It seems especially important that the Berlin conference emphasised the role of students.

The new objective was set that every student graduating as from 2005 should receive the Diploma Supplement issued in one of the widely spoken European languages automatically and free of charge.

The conference acknowledged that students are full partners in higher education governance and called on institutions and student organisations to identify ways of increasing actual student involvement in higher education governance.

Finally, I would like to recall that the Berlin conference stressed the need for appropriate studying and living conditions for students, so that they can successfully complete their studies within the appropriate period of time without obstacles related to their social and economic background.

It is evident that all these intentions may only be realised provided that the corresponding expansion of public responsibility is achieved including new or amended legal regulations and sufficient financial support. That also means that a certain minimum level of public responsibility at state level must be acknowledged in every member state of the Bologna Process.

But, on the other hand, higher education is a very specific area where national and historical features play an important role. The educational system is one of the key aspects of national and cultural identity so it is hard to expect universal understanding of the distribution of public responsibility among all the member states.

So while the common European principles of public responsibility for higher education are being established by international documents, they are being developed in a more detailed way by national laws and other legal acts and implemented

---

30. *Towards the European Higher Education Area*, communiqué of the meeting of European ministers in charge of Higher Education in Prague on 19 May 2001.
31. *Realising the European Higher Education Area*, communiqué of the Conference of Ministers responsible for Higher Education in Berlin on 19 September 2003.

through governmental policy. The key elements of such a policy are the distribution of public responsibilities between the levels of governance, and the financial policy providing the educational system with adequate resources both through direct budget funding and by creating favourable conditions for private investment in education.

Public responsibility: laws and funding

Generally speaking, we may consider several types of public responsibility in any area – legal, financial or moral.

The first and most important is the legal framework for a particular activity.

The second is the real governmental policy in a particular area including the allocation of financial and other resources.

And the third one is what is hard to formalise – a kind of moral public support for a particular activity – but it seems important because of the sense of social status and public respect. It may be realised through a great variety of forms from state rewards to public statements issued by the head of state to support professional leaders and their activity. The concrete model of the level or the size and the distribution of public responsibilities between the tiers of the governance may vary. But I suppose there is a universal principle of distribution: money follows responsibilities. The distribution of public responsibilities between the levels of government must correspond to the distribution of the resources, including tax collection.

The ratio between educational expenditure and the gross domestic product or consolidated national budget expenditures is a quite informative indicator of the national implementation of public responsibility for education.[32] But such indicators mostly reflect direct public expenditure and do not reflect the whole range of public responsibility, for instance tax breaks for educational donors, etc.

The role of public authorities in the development of the education system is not only to provide it with direct funding but also to stimulate private investment in education by means of tax breaks and tax reductions, educational loans, cross-sector partnership programmes, etc.

As it is widely acknowledged that the quality of higher education is at the heart of the setting up of the European Higher Education Area, and as national assurance systems must be improved significantly by 2005, it seems important to discuss the division of public responsibility in this area between governmental and non-governmental (for instance, professional) bodies.

Both governmental and non-governmental systems have their advantages and weaknesses. I would say that professional quality assessment may certainly be influenced by corporate solidarity while governmental assessment may be more

---

32. One can find the corresponding comparative data in OECD indicators published in *Education at a glance* latest editions and official Unesco publications.

affected by corruption. But generally speaking, non-governmental quality assessment seems more effective.

Independent expertise legally regulated by governments with the participation of employers' associations would probably be the most proper form of distribution of public responsibility in this area. In any case this is a point for the general regulation through national law.

In the context of quality assurance development I would also like to draw attention to the success criteria for the education institutions. I think this will become an important issue in setting up the European Higher Education Area because the institutions are sensitive to their position in the market. The procedures of university ratings already exist. For instance, one of the criteria in use is to measure the proportion of the university graduates who have obtained a professional position in accordance with their specific qualifications. But is it a proper criterion for measuring the success of a university? I suppose that the laws of the market and the laws of quality are not always the same, especially in education.

The real implementation of public responsibilities, even those embedded in national law, is influenced by the political priorities of governments, which also depend on public opinion and particularly on the position and the activity of the professional education community.

In this respect I may give as an example the recent transformation of the Russian laws on education which was made on the government's proposal. Until now there was a particular paragraph in the national law on education establishing state guarantees as to the priority of education in governmental policy. For instance there were certain tax breaks for universities and some legal mechanisms of social support for students and higher school teachers. There was an explicit governmental legal responsibility to allocate a certain share of the national budget to educational expenses. Now, after new amendments have been adopted, these regulations have been abolished. It means that public responsibility, at state level, for education is diminishing, but paradoxically at the same time the level of independence and responsibility of state education institutions is diminishing. And I suppose one of the reasons that such serious changes have been adopted is the weakness of the professional education community, which did not oppose the government's plans effectively.

By the way, the declared reason to adopt the amendments mentioned above was not to decrease the general level of public responsibility in education but to make the division of responsibilities between the levels of governance more clear, which is definitely essential. But the problem of the transfer of responsibilities from the government, in case it reduces its mandate for some reason, may be resolved successfully only if the corresponding resources are provided.

Governmental public responsibility may be exercised by different levels of government (national, regional and local) depending on the country. For instance, in the United States the majority of public universities are run by the states (or regions, in European terms) while in Russia the overall majority of public education institutions are run by the federal government (only 1.35% of total budget expenditure for higher education comes from regional budgets and 1.7% from municipalities). In OECD countries there are only six countries where regional governments provide more than 50% of tertiary education funds (Belgium, Canada, Germany, Spain, Switzerland and the United States). Some countries like Denmark, Finland and the United States have a substantial proportion of local funding. But I suppose the distribution of funding does correspond to the distribution of budget income (like taxes) more than to the distribution of educational policy decisions.

Certainly the general legal approach to public responsibility is determined by national laws and governmental regulations. But the real implementation may vary in different regions and municipalities. The regional and local authorities may establish special privileges for education institutions like local tax breaks (for instance for property tax) and may allocate more public contracts to local institutions and universities, encouraging them to play a more active role in regional and municipal development (look at the British strategy: *The future of higher education* published by the Secretary of State for Education and Skills in January 2003). I suppose that regions and municipalities may also have a significant impact on the development of higher education through providing supplementary support, especially for students.

Student support seems very important for providing equal access to higher education for all qualified candidates, particularly for those from disadvantaged backgrounds. There is a wide variety of supporting instruments which reflect public responsibility enabling equal access to higher education including loans, stipends, providing student hostels, etc., and many of them can be operated by different levels of government.

The regional differences in access to higher education may be very significant depending on regional development and regional policy.

Addressing once again the Russian experience we may see that the expenditure for tertiary education varies in different regions from more than 35% (Moscow, Saint Petersburg, Tomsk region) to less than 10% of the total public expenditure for education; while the average level in Russia is 21.9%, the average level for countries covered by OECD's *Education at a glance* and *World education indicators* programmes is 20.7% and the level for the first group of OECD countries having the highest incomes is 22.7%.

The existing regional and social distinctions in access to higher education are another argument for the expansion of public responsibility and using education as a social lift to create a more homogeneous and tolerant society.

Public responsibility: obligatory and optional

Some kinds of function should definitely be the subject of public responsibility. For some functions, it would be desirable for them to be the object of public responsibility and some functions may become a public responsibility or not depending on circumstances.

Speaking of particular areas of public responsibility for higher education, I would like to recall the classification proposed by Sjur Bergan at the Bologna Conference on the Social Dimension of Higher Education (February 2003). In his presentation "Higher education as a 'public good and public responsibility': what does it mean?", he proposed a very useful framework for a discussion of the responsibility of public authorities for higher education dividing the areas of public responsibility into four groups:

- exclusive responsibility for the framework of higher education, including the degree structure, the institutional framework, the framework for quality assurance and authoritative information on the higher education framework;
- main responsibility for ensuring equal opportunities in higher education, including access policies and student support;
- important role in the provision of higher education. While there should be no public monopoly on higher education provision, public authorities should be heavily involved not only in designing the framework but also in the actual running of higher education institutions and programmes, to contribute to good educational opportunities on reasonable conditions;
- important financial responsibility for higher education. Public funds may and should be supplemented by money from other sources, but these alternative funding sources should never be a pretext for public authorities not to provide substantial public resources.

We may argue about the content of these groups and about the degree of public involvement in some particular activity but the classification of different types of public responsibilities into groups of exclusive, predominant and supplementary responsibilities seems quite helpful.

My personal view is that when society expands its obligatory mandate for responsibility in higher education (not by detailed state regulation, because government failure is a reality as well as market failure, but mainly by creating the framework and infrastructure) and provides the optional part of responsibility with an adequate amount of resources and stimulating legal mechanisms there will be a long-term positive effect. This is because the mission of higher education not only satisfies labour market requirements but develops active citizenship and participation in democratic society. Higher education is one of the crucial factors in the development of a more effective economy and a more tolerant world.

The concept of developing public responsibility for higher education is already a concern for the leaders of the professional education community and ministers of education. But this is not enough. To succeed, it should become a real political concern and commitment for the governing elite at both national and international levels because this would make the world more secure and wealthy.

The many facets
of public responsibility
for higher education
and research

Higher education for a democratic culture – The public responsibility

Pavel Zgaga

Introduction: multiple roles of higher education

It would be interesting to make a detailed survey of how the role (that is, the function; the position in society, etc.) of higher education is perceived in contemporary societies. I guess that the prevailing perception could be characterised by key words like "training in concrete skills", "income", "employment", "economy", etc. More facts than values? If it were true then it would not be merely a reflection of the affluent society as some people usually complain. Indeed, partly it could be a reflection of anyone's position on the (global) labour market of today, that is, a reflection of a hard everyday life. On the other hand, we should not forget that it could also be partly a product of the modern concept of science, that is, a product of the discourse upon "objectivity" and "truth", cleaned of any "subjective presumption".

However, if we asked respondents in an interview more about their perceptions, we would get a new set of keywords, probably like this: "to train in concrete skills to empower an individual", "enhancing quality of life", "employment" and "economy" versus "society" and "cohesion", etc. Now, we should not forget that asking (or calling for arguments) has always been an important characteristic of education and scholarship and an important method of searching for truth as well. Actually, searching for truth is not only about discovering facts but it is also about searching for values if we only remember Socrates and reach traditions established upon his ideas.

Higher education has had a multiple role in society: it has been an agent of scientific, technological, economic, etc., development; at the same time it has been also a place of individual shaping and cultural development in the broadest sense, and last but not least, a site of citizenship and democratic culture. It is impossible to separate these dimensions one from another. What constitutes higher education is precisely the totality of its proved multiple role.

Higher education, responsibility and democracy

In this context, it is not difficult to grasp the relationship between "higher education" and "(public) responsibility". It is obvious that there should be always some kind of responsibility for higher education (financing, legal framework, respecting autonomy, etc.) from the society and/or its organisations if we expect "results", that is, an effective performance of its multiple role. Similarly, there should always be some kind of responsibility on the part of higher education: not only with regard to its concrete performance (accountability; public funds, etc.) but also with regard to, for example, the ethical dimension of the search for truth, etc. Yet, how to understand the relationship between "higher education" and "democracy" in this context?

Today, the field of democratic culture is probably the most appropriate place where public responsibility for higher education and public responsibility of higher education can meet one another. This is the point where universities and other higher education institutions could make important contributions based upon epistemological grounds (for example, criticism and rational reasoning, etc.), upon specific fields of studies (social studies, history, education, etc.) or upon their "inner" or institutional practice of democratic culture (for instance, in terms of institutional governance, student involvement, relations to the environment, etc.). This is also the point where public authorities should strive to provide good conditions (legislation, financing, etc.), on one hand, that is to enable institutions to cope successfully with these challenges but also, on the other hand, to enable not only the transfer and dissemination of technologically and economically important results but also the transfer and dissemination of results which could make an important contribution to strengthening democratic culture in modern societies at large.

Contemporary discussions of democracy and related issues show deep shifts in the traditional concepts as we know from the twentieth century. In this context, the idea of education for democratic citizenship was born and has received more and more attention as well as importance.[1] Analysing the arguments from these discussions Kelly (1995; p. 182) synthesises two streams of interpretation of the increased contemporary burgeoning interest in "education for citizenship": (1) "extensive changes which have been occurring in the social fabric of western societies in recent years"; and (2) "citizenship is coming to be regarded as a possible source of cures for what are seen as the ills that are increasingly besetting modern society"[2]. On the other side, Audigier ascertains that the terms "citizen" or "citizenship" have changed and have entered new contexts; even more, he states an increasing concern for the citizenship and citizenship education in recent times: "the affirmation and extension of the term 'citizenship' are recent developments" (Audigier, 2000, p. 5).[3]

---

1. See for example, EDC pages www.coe.int/T/E/Cultural%5FCo%2Doperation/education/E%2ED%2EC/
2. See further (p. 183): "At one extreme the view has been expressed that, since those changes in the fabric of society which we noted earlier, allied to those intellectual changes subsumed under the term postmodernism, have led to a fragmentation of culture and of society, and a corresponding loss of any serious idea of common interests, to seek for some unifying concept such as citizenship is to take on a lost cause (Wexler, 1990). As we have seen, however, to adopt such a view is to see democracy too as a lost cause. At the other extreme there have been those who have recognised the significance of these changes, and have acknowledged the tensions they are creating, but have accepted a concept of citizenship as providing a new unifying factor (Heater, 1990; Gilbert, 1992)."
3. See further (pp. 6-7): "The relatively recent (re)emergence of the term 'citizen' would thus be a way of going back to the question of 'living together', a question which had more or less been forgotten in democratic states for some decades, but is now arising very acutely again under the pressure of various factors: exclusion of a growing proportion of the population, extension of the globalisation of economies and cultures, the latter disseminated through the international media, calling into question of the political references of the past two centuries in Europe, such as the Nation-state, and the more recent social dimension of Welfare state, risks of ethnic fragmentation and the growth of exclusive specificities, challenges to the basic values of our societies, the phenomena of racism and xenophobia, etc."

Now, is the idea of a democratic culture and its relation to (higher) education a (post)modern one divorced from any tradition and heritage?

Historical roots

It is always shocking when we find in ancient authors clear ideas which we have strictly considered only as modern or postmodern concepts. Thus, Aristotle says in *The politics* (1337a11) "just as there must also be preparatory training for all skills and capacities, and a process of preliminary habituation to the work of each profession, it is obvious that there must also be training for the activities of virtue". Furthermore, he states in the continuation of the same paragraph: "But since there is but one aim for the entire state, it follows that education must be one and the same for all, and that the responsibility for it must be a public one, not the private affair which it now is."

Thus, he opened a discussion which is, after two and a half millennia, only more complex, intensive and important than it was at the beginning. On the one hand, (higher) education today is the most reliable tool for promotion of any individual in modern societies and an issue of utmost privacy. On the other hand, the role and function of (higher) education has never been reduced to this dimension only; it has also always been providing "training for the activities of virtue" in the broadest sense: economic wealth but also cultural development, better technological support but also better health care, etc. Last but not least, critical thinking and democratic awareness have always been more or less directly connected with (higher) education. These are substantial reasons why the responsibility for it must be a public one.

However, it is not easy to define "the activities of virtue" which should be taught; it is not even easy to define "public" and "responsibility" in more depth. Ethics and social and political philosophy have always had a lot of work in defining these ideas. The great experiences of the past – not always only of the far past – prove that (higher) education could be also involved as a mechanism of ideologically secured social reproduction: it has always happened when the unrelenting supreme virtue and the unquestioned hegemon put in the shade and/or eliminate the constant rational dispute over human virtue(s) and social relationship(s). The dispute over truth and virtue, in fact, has been an important part of academic traditions and at least indirectly also an intellectual source of democratic culture.

Democracy and culture

Do (post)modern times split off circumstances which had been interlacing academia and science into "external" power structures, ideology and myth? Has the eternal devil finally been beaten down? This could be a dangerous question, conserving not the content but the form of understanding which, in fact, belongs to the suspected – and supposedly beaten – discourse.[4] Living in deeply changed

---

4. "While universities do in my view have a democratic mission, we should not fall into the trap of thinking this is because academia is inherently democratic. It is, unfortunately, not difficult to think of examples where both institutions and individual academics have been profoundly undemocratic and where they have contributed to man's inhumanity to man" (Bergan, 2003, pp. 39-40).

social circumstances we may cheerfully today split off inhumanities, stamping down the human dignity, etc. of the past but we should not forget the past – for the sake of our present and future. It has not happened only once that an important political change (processes of 1990) or technological change (communication technologies) and "the progress" achieved have made only a step towards encountering new problems; sooner or later, it has usually become clear that any historical step or achievement should be observed and treated in as complex a way as possible.

In this way, "developments throughout the 1990s underlined that institutions and laws are necessary but not sufficient preconditions for a functioning democracy, and that democratic society can only function if it is built on democratic culture" (Bergan, 2003, p. 6). Experiences from central and eastern Europe show that many higher education institutions have been profoundly reformed on the basis of new legislation adopted soon after political changes but a longer period of time has been needed for "the reconciliation". More importantly, new issues have grown up during this period, quite often exceeding the initial problem. Of course, other examples from other countries could also be found to prove a common and rather a simple truth: not only that rooting new legal norms in the everyday functioning of institutions is a process but also that legal norms and institutions depend on people's everyday practice, their culture. Yet, the distinctive feature of (higher) education is that it encompasses a process of transferring and changing culture patterns.

We encounter a particular paradox today which is far from being a characteristic only of higher education; it refers to our societies at large: as formal possibilities for people (students) to engage and participate in society and (higher education) institutions are broader, so fewer people are taking them up. Participation in the national parliamentary elections (or, as we could learn this year, the election to the European Parliament) in almost all countries could seem only shocking from the point of view of brave fighters for democracy from our past, and students' participation in the election of their representatives at universities could seem even more shocking compared with the student rebellions of 1968. In a recent survey on student participation in the governance of higher education in Europe, Annika Persson reports: "The average percentage of students participating in the election of student representatives to university bodies or student organisations varies greatly between countries, regions, institutions and levels of governance. The bracket most frequently indicated is that between 16 and 30 percent, followed by the interval just below (0 to 15 percent)" (Persson, 2003, p. 9).

Democracy, culture and indifference

Reflecting these processes, can we discuss culture in this context also as a culture of democratic indifference, perhaps as a culture of indifference to democracy? More or less, we are all aware of this paradoxical fact but it is really very difficult to establish a sound argument to overcome the modern liberal attitude that it is totally up to an individual to practice his/her civil rights, or not. Sharing this attitude, however, it should be clear that we cannot remain indifferent (cf. Kelly: "the ills that are increasingly besetting modern society", 1995, p. 182). It seems obvious that this could be a point where we encounter serious new problems; and these problems are related to (higher) education as well.

Here, we should make a reference to the results of an interesting recent project realised in the framework of the Council of Europe's activities: the Plantan Report. The project confirmed and gave much new evidence that formal provision for shared governance and protection of faculty and student rights at our universities are often at odds with actual practices. It is proved again that "formal institutional structures and arrangements are a necessary, but *not sufficient* condition for ... greater democratic participation; ... the promotion of aims and objectives of instilling notions of civic responsibility within students; ... understanding the nature and extent of a university's interaction with its surrounding community; and ... curricular change and altering the management functions within the university" (Plantan, 2002, pp. 12-13).

The report demonstrates that participation in the governance of our universities is not what might be hoped for and expected, that students mostly do not know enough about their rights and that faculty often do not find reasons and do not know arguments to connect higher education and democracy.[5] The scale of the problem is rather a complex one. One of Plantan's important conclusions which we find at the end of the report is that "this suggests that the promotion of democratic values and civil responsibility is not merely a pedagogical question, but must also be addressed structurally in terms of the organisation and practice of university governance" (Plantan, 2002, p. 49).

If we consider today the promotion of democratic values and civil responsibility as a pedagogical question in the traditional sense, that is, for instance, as "imparting" values and feeling for responsibility (indoctrinating),[6] there would not be much of a chance to convince either students or faculty. We support Plantan's statement that the issue is not merely a pedagogical one and that it is intertwined with the organisation and practice of university governance: in today's culture, democratic values and feeling for responsibility cannot be "imparted" but one should get a certain knowledge and skills as well as empowerment or chances to practise them independently in the everyday life of the institution (university) and broader societal environment.

However, we believe that the complex scale of the problem is even broader and encompasses – besides pedagogy and governance – also epistemology. If there is a certain reservation or contest or refusal from faculty today of the idea that universities must stimulate democracy among students than there are at least two

---

5. "As a corollary to the previous point, most university administrators and faculty considered institutional responses to promoting democratic values and civic engagement as an infringement upon or a dilution of the university's primary educational mission, such as the training of specialists and technicians and other professionals. ... Faculty surveyed constantly contested the idea that universities must stimulate democracy among students" (Plantan, 2002, pp. 13 and 47).

6. Latin *in* (into) and *doctrinare* (teach). Reflecting these relations, universities would probably get interesting new initiatives from reinventing the practice of "teach-in" as developed in the 1960s and 1970s.

levels of explanation: (a) various but always unpleasant experiences of "imparting" practices as well as jealous guarding of freedom of teaching and research, and (b) the epistemological grounds of university teaching and research, that is, disinterested scholarship.

Democratic society, communicative society

This seems to be one of the central points in discussing the relationship between higher education and democracy in modern times. Traditionally, university teaching and academic life in general has been developed as a kind of meritocracy, as the power of knowledge. Yet, the idea and the reality of the university have undergone deep changes, influenced by society at large, politics, economy and culture. As I tried to argue in another paper, "democracy at the university cannot be justified by the *power of knowledge*. This may also be true for the principles of the autonomy of the university and academic freedom ... Its foundation can only be a *communicative society,* a community of researchers, a community of learners, in which the participants are free and equal according to the principle of communication without domination. In this sense I recommend the differentiation between the *power of knowledge* (as power which is an argument and not an intersubjective relation; but it can really be conditional on it one way or another, for instance when the authority of the argument is transferred to the authority of the teacher) and *power as structuring real social or political relations*" (Zgaga, 2004).

In other words, democracy at the university of today cannot be an "imposed" or "imparted" value. It would be against epistemological grounds and scientific discourse as well as against the norms of modern democratic societies. In particular, I would like to stress that not only norms of modern democratic societies but also the epistemology of the age of modern communicative society argue for the same option: democracy is not an extrinsic supplement to (higher) education but it is its complex inner value.

Higher education at various stages of its historical development contributed to science, culture and society at large; in their searching for the lost European university identity, contemporary authors recognise this contribution as an extraordinary potential. However, they also warn that we are living in new times and that answers from these former stages – despite their incontestable importance – cannot contribute actively to coping with modern problems. The university needs a new identity to reactivate this potential.

During its millennium the university has found itself in crisis not only once. It was such a case at the dawn of modernity when Humboldt conceived the new formula (university as a unity of knowledge; teaching through research; corporative organisation) which proved its strength and influenced European countries and the world for two centuries. However, "occasionally viewed with nostalgia, the Humboldt model could never be redesigned to meet contemporary needs" (Renaut, 2002, p. 125). As the university before Humboldt's invention was challenged by fragmentation and loss of its societal influence it is today challenged by new fragmentation and loss: pressuring demands of the economy, increasing specialisation, postmodern absence of an entire concept of human knowledge. In parallel, this process appears under new circumstances of European integration, increased economic, educational, scientific and cultural co-operation, global communication and interdependence. In searching for the new university identity in this new context, Alain Renaut proposes an interesting approach: "that the unity which constitutes the aims and purposes of the university since its invention by Europe could be reinterpreted today as being that of a culture".[7] Renaut refers here to a European citizenship; it seems self-evident to us that this statement subsumes also the notion of a democratic culture.

Opening the "social dimension" in higher education policy

Today, there is an obvious and indispensable role which education in general and higher education in particular can play in developing and maintaining a democratic culture. This role is connected also to the issues of higher education policy as we can also see in important recent documents adopted at the national and international level. The challenges of the time have put higher education in the middle of global competition processes; new problems encountered in this way prove that its position in a local and/or global culture of co-operation is now even more important. European countries have become aware that the potential of their universities – as European universities – depends more and more on their increased co-operation as well as on the transparency and compatibility of national higher education systems. A reform of higher education structures is an obvious result of this awareness; however, it is not only observed instrumentally but in relation to shared basic values as well. Under the circumstances of the late 1990s, a document as important as the Bologna Declaration (1999) stated as follows: "The importance of education and educational co-operation in the development and strengthening of stable, peaceful and democratic societies is universally acknowledged as paramount, the more so in view of the situation in South East Europe."

In this perspective, we can continue reading the Prague Communiqué (2001): while reflecting on the future Europe as built upon a knowledge-based society and economy, education is considered necessary not only "to face the challenges of competitiveness and the use of new technologies" but also "to improve social cohesion, equal opportunities and the quality of life". This is the place which is closely linked with the term "social dimension" (rather vague but since 2001 probably one of the most quoted terms in Bologna discussions) invented in Prague, where ministers "reaffirmed the need, recalled by students, to take account of the social dimension in the Bologna Process".

---

7. See further: "If Europe, as is often repeated these days, is not to be confined to the euro, one way of enhancing the existing economic and financial union and making it less soulless could be for our universities to make a genuine contribution to the establishment of a common European culture." The next paragraph ends with an important and inspiring question: "has the time not come to include in at least the first phases of higher education the cultural requirements necessary to create a European citizenship?" (p. 126).

On the same track, the Berlin Communiqué (2003) reaffirmed "the importance of the social dimension of the Bologna Process. The need to increase competitiveness must be balanced with the objective of improving the social characteristics of the European Higher Education Area, aiming at strengthening social cohesion and reducing social and gender inequalities both at national and at European level. In that context, Ministers reaffirm their position that higher education is a public good and a public responsibility. They emphasise that in international academic co-operation and exchanges, academic values should prevail".

These quotations from recent strategic documents could be also taken as proof that higher education for democratic culture is (or is becoming) a public responsibility. The forthcoming Bergen Conference of European Ministers for Higher Education (May 2005) and the European Year of Citizenship through Education (2005), proclaimed by the Committee of Ministers of the Council of Europe, bring new challenges in this context; we would only expect productive responses.

References

Aristotle, *The politics,* translation by Sinclair, T.A. (1962), Penguin Books, London, 1992.

Audigier, F. (2000), *Basic concepts and core competencies for education for democratic citizenship,* DGIV/EDU/CIT (2000) 23, available at: http://www.coe.int

Bergan, S. (2003), "The responsible university", *Cuadernos Europeos de Deusto,* No. 29, 2003, pp. 31-62.

Berlin Communiqué, *Realising the European Higher Education Area,* adopted by European ministers of education on 19 September 2003.

Bologna Declaration, *The European Higher Education Area. Joint Declaration of the European Ministers of Education,* 19 June 1999.

Kelly, A.V. (1995). *Education and democracy. Principles and practice,* Paul Chapman, London, 1995.

Persson, A., "Student participation in the governance of higher education in Europe. A Council of Europe survey", in *Report 2003. Bologna follow-up seminar on student participation in governance in higher education,* Oslo, 12-14 June 2003, Ministry of Education and Research, Oslo, 2003, pp. 1-50.

Plantan, F., *Universities as sites of citizenship and civic responsibility. Final general report – February 2002,* CDESR, Strasbourg, 2002.

Prague Declaration, *Toward the European Higher Education Area,* communiqué of the meeting of European ministers in charge of higher education, Prague, 19 May 2001.

Renaut, A., "The role of universities in developing a democratic European culture", in Sanz, N. and Bergan, S. (eds), *The heritage of European universities,* Council of Europe, Strasbourg, 2002, pp. 119-127.

"Remembrance and citizenship: from places to project", symposium organised jointly by the Council of Europe and the European Cultural Centre of Delphi (Delphi, 25-27 September 1998). Final report prepared by the Directorate of Education, Culture and Sport. CDCC/Delphes (98) 3, available at: http://www.coe.int

Zgaga, P., "Knowledge and power: university, transition and democracy", in Fisher, R. (ed.), *The idea of education,* Learning Solutions, Oxford, 2004, available at: http://www.see-educoop.net/education_in/pdf/knowledge-and-power-slo-enl-t07.pdf.

The contribution of higher education and research to the Knowledge Society

Paolo Blasi

The history

The evolution of society over the past three centuries has been amazing and has proceeded by many steps: from the agricultural society to the first industrialisation, the second industrialisation, the post-industrial society, the information society, and, lastly, the Knowledge Society.

The interacting context for people has changed dramatically. From the village, to the region, to the nation, to the continent, to the whole world, this characterises the Knowledge Society and the globalisation phenomena.

In the agricultural society, the larger part of the population (up to 80% or 90%) lived and worked in the countryside or in small villages. Most of them could not read or write, they were taught by their relatives how to cope with the problems connected to cultivation and rearing livestock, and learned on the job. Few people went to school and only very few reached a higher education level.

During the seventeenth and eighteenth centuries the development of science and technology produced the industrial revolution, with fewer and fewer people involved in the hard work of agriculture and more and more people leaving the countryside to live in big cities and to work in manufacturing industries. The industrial work required workers able to read and write and therefore primary education soon became compulsory in all the industrialised countries. The French Revolution produced the new concepts of national state and citizenship.

The organisation of society changed and new professions developed to tackle the new needs of the population. Higher education institutions, and in particular universities, provided professional skills and training, and educated the leaders of the new society. Universities also became the institutional places for producing knowledge through research activities.

Nevertheless, in Europe up to the mid-twentieth century, only a few per cent of young people attended university courses to obtain a professional degree.

After the Second World War the fast and widespread development of scientific knowledge and impressive technological innovations produced a new displacement of people from the countryside to the cities and the new manufacturing industries asked for more and more educated workers. Therefore, in Europe the compulsory period of studies of five years changed and shifted first to eight, then to ten or twelve years. In the 1960s and 1970s the number of students attending university courses was growing, reaching in some countries, like the United States, 50% of the age cohort and in Europe about 20% to 30%.

The development of ICT (information and communication technology) and the great progress in transport – such as high-speed trains, cheap cars, larger and faster airplanes – greatly improved the mobility of people, goods, news, and ideas, giving rise to what we today call globalisation.

The information society has in fact been characterised by the spread of information that can bring news about the whole world to each person, every day.

These developments have deeply affected the geopolitical situation of the world and extended the complexity of society. Today we talk of Asia, Europe, North America, etc., more than of single nations. Events like the Olympic Games, world championships as well as regional wars like those in Kosovo or in Iraq are followed on television by billions of people all around the world.

In the developed countries only a few per cent of people are still involved in agriculture and only between 10% and 20% in industry. More and more are in fact engaged in the so-called "third sector" which includes all the services like national health services, teaching, research, transport, information and communication, sport and leisure activities, etc.

The Knowledge Society

The incoming Knowledge Society (a society in which the way information is exploited is crucial) puts on the table new problems and asks for new solutions.

Land and natural resources have become less important; on the other hand human resources are crucial and strategic for the future of each country, thus making investment in education and research the most fruitful.

Through the media (television, newspapers, Internet, etc.) people share every day what happens in every part of the world and often the dramatic events prevail in this information.

Therefore, those who still live in developing countries in poor conditions, becoming aware of their low level of living, ask for a better living environment and expect to reach the living standard of more evolved countries in a short time.

At the same time, people belonging to given cultures and religions get in touch with people of different cultures and religions and the problem of how to manage a multicultural society arises.

The degree of development of one country is measured as the percentage of growth in GNP (gross national product) and also as life expectation for the new generations. In fact, the economic parameters are often the only ones taken into account. On the other hand, the limits of world resources do not allow the six billion people living today in our world to consume the average resources per person that are used in the United States.

Other problems such as air pollution, the availability of drinking water, waste management, etc., can be faced and solved only at global level through global collaboration.

The wisdom society

These are the reasons why the information society is becoming the Knowledge Society and the Knowledge Society should evolve into the "wisdom society" in order to face properly the new world situation. This asks for a deep change of mind and behaviour primarily in developed countries. For example, I think that it is no longer reasonable to measure the degree of development of a country only through the growth of GNP. To preserve the level of quality of life reached by developed countries it is necessary that other people improve their living conditions faster to reduce the gap between rich and poor countries. We can maintain our better conditions, but because of the limited resources in the world, we should at the same time reduce energy consumption, pollution, waste production, etc.

In other words, to measure the degree of comprehensive development for a country we have to introduce other non-economic parameters such as the degree of education, the efficiency of the public health systems and of the public transport system, the impact on the environment, etc.

An award should be granted to the countries that increase such parameters using less energy, producing less waste and keeping their GNP stable.

Education of the person in all his/her dimensions

Knowledge is an aware utilisation of information; wisdom means to behave according to shared knowledge in order to enhance the well-being of everybody in the awareness that personal actions have a social consequence, and that today each part of the world is connected to the others.

The concept of knowledge is not only the scientific one which refers specifically to the natural world. It also concerns the artistic and humanistic world, and last but not least the spiritual and metaphysical world. In particular, the spiritual and humanistic dimensions of the human being play a major role in giving meaning to human life and contribute a lot to improving the quality of life.

If we want to contribute to realising a "wisdom society" in which there is wise use of knowledge, it is necessary to develop in each person, in a well-balanced way, the different dimensions of his/her being, namely the knowledge and economic dimensions together with the creative and spiritual dimensions.

Each person should be aware of his/her responsibility to fully exploit his/her own potentialities and at the same time to act as a member of society. In other words, everyone has to recover consciousness of the social impact of his/her actions.

If these are the real frames and the most likely perspectives of our society, it is very important to educate and train people to live and act properly in this new, dynamic, and more and more complex society in the global context.

119

The role of higher education

Universities, colleges, higher education institutions and research centres therefore have to play a crucial role.

As for the Information and Knowledge Society, twelve years of school have been considered necessary; to shift from the knowledge to the wisdom society it is very important to extend opportunities for higher education as much as possible, both providing university courses and/or post baccalaureate courses to the largest possible number of young people (from 50% to 70% of the age cohort) and providing the opportunity to resume education many times during the life of an individual (lifelong learning).

The Bologna Process was set up to provide a new common frame of teaching and learning for the European universities in order to proceed from elite institutions to mass higher education institutions. The main objective is to raise and widen the level of education for as many people as possible.

The wisdom society is a continuous learning society: every person has to act at the same time as learner and teacher in every context, therefore everybody must be taught how to learn and how to communicate; this should be the task not only of primary and secondary schools, but in particular the goal of higher education.

In a Knowledge Society as well as in a wisdom society, knowledge is expected to be disseminated quickly and easily. This may create a tension between the needed knowledge certification and the needed knowledge diffusion. Many examples can be given: the knowledge of nuclear energy production and safety, the knowledge of the risks in the diffusion of genetically modified organisms, or on the propagation of electromagnetic fields.

Thus, how to facilitate and accelerate knowledge dissemination without impairing knowledge certification?

Certainly more and well-educated people are necessary although this cannot be sufficient. Therefore, we have to extend higher education (through different channels and ways) to almost everybody.

Higher education organisation

Higher education should, in my opinion, be supported mainly by public funds, because of the general needs that it has to fulfil and also to guarantee more independence to education and research. On the other hand, I judge positively the payment of some fees by the students (between 20% and 50% of the real costs) as they thus become more aware of the value of acquiring new knowledge and professional skills and therefore they feel compelled to make a stronger commitment to their studies.

Of course the principle that the students should contribute to the costs of their studies is a very conflictual issue which needs to be reconciled with the possibility of access for everybody. Different solutions are possible with good results, provided they are coherent with the particular context.

The Bologna Process is developing in Europe with different trends but toward the same goal. A problem is still there: how to implement teaching and learning for the most talented people in order to exploit their potentiality to the full? This is in their own interest but also in the interests of the whole society. In other words, how can we fulfil both the needs of mass education and the necessity to prepare good leaders? This can be done by differentiating between mass and elite institutions or by organising in the universities special support and opportunities for the best students, but both solutions can also be applied together.

The goals of higher education today

Other problems have to be solved by higher education institutions. For example, what kind of competences should be developed by higher education, considering the fact that society is in fast evolution and that we have to provide young people with competences that must not become obsolete too fast?

Higher education should, in my opinion, be focused on developing primarily the "core competences", the skills necessary to live in a complex, very interacting, and continuously changing society. Some of these "core competences" are: the ability to learn, listen, interact, communicate, be active and proactive, solve problems, understand other cultures and religions, etc. This implies, for example, the ability to manage the information and communication technologies, to speak and understand other languages, to be aware of one's own cultural identity.

Curricula and teaching methods need to be changed and shaped for the new objectives. A greater flexibility in curricula is necessary, as well as more personalised interactions between students and teachers. A multidisciplinary approach to problems should also be encouraged.

Moreover, education must not remain a theoretical learning exercise; rather the transfer of knowledge must be integrated with practical experience. Traineeships in working contexts are the unavoidable means to educate young students to act, to be proactive and to learn how to evaluate themselves. The new young generations in Europe come from families where the parents have been more engaged in realising themselves than in educating their children; they live in a continent where traditional values have become weaker and many people are opportunists and consumers.

When they enter the university they seek to discover the meaning of their life: they dream of meeting the right person to create a real family, they hope to find a good job after graduation, and they would also like to contribute to changing the society they know into a better one.

Universities have to take into account all these expectations and hopes and provide their young students with suitable opportunities and new means in order to facilitate their search for the meaning of life. Young students have to learn how to distinguish what is more important from what is trivial for their life.

Universities should also present to the students models of behaviour, how to build up their own personality and how to strengthen their own independence.

Research and innovation

A word which synthesises well the need for new approaches, new solutions and new educational targets is "innovation". It is necessary to innovate in every field: technology, social sciences, politics, organisation, etc. To innovate, we have to develop research activities in all these fields, and we have to train more and more people to have an active role in research, in research transfer and in exploitation of research results.

At the Lisbon meeting (March 2000), the European Union leaders committed themselves to "make Europe the world's leading knowledge-based economy by 2010". To reach this goal, Europe has to support more effective basic research and its follow-up in industry and society.

Intensive research universities are the main agents for basic research; they have the capability to be dynamic and effective engines for the development of the Knowledge Society and economy, and a magnet for international talents.

Europe must invest more money in basic research, which is the source of creation of new knowledge and of most innovation in society. A clear and acceptable balance should be reached between the pursuit of knowledge for its own sake and the demand for basic research aimed at a tangible return to the economy and society at large.

Research and higher education

Framework programmes, new funds for basic research distributed by a European Research Council (ERC) and structural funds can provide an adequate support to the building of a European Research Area (ERA). The Bologna Process, the mobility programmes (Socrates, Tempus, etc.), the creation of university networks and bilateral collaboration are important tools for creating the European Higher Education Area (EHEA). The EHEA and the ERA must be integrated to optimise their contribution to the Knowledge Society.

Research not only provides the necessary background for innovation but also creates a suitable environment for education, as was pointed out by the Berlin Communiqué in which the third cycle (doctorate level) was explicitly included among the priorities of the Bologna Process.

The Knowledge Society not only needs excellence and top-rate research but also depends on a larger number of highly educated people who, while not engaged in active research, have sufficient knowledge to make good use of the latest research results.

To learn "core competences" and to be trained in employability skills, more and more students should have the opportunity to undertake traineeships in research groups and in other working environments, not only at doctoral level but also at graduate and undergraduate level.

As higher education and research are becoming more and more strategic activities for a new kind of development for our Knowledge Society (my dream is to see the dawn of a wisdom society), the governments should proportionally increase their investment in research and higher education institutions.

Universities seem to be the most suitable institutions for developing integrated activities of higher education, research, and innovation, and therefore they should be the main recipients of new public and private funds devoted to development.

On the other hand, to optimise the exploitation of public and private funds given to universities it is necessary to enlarge the universities' autonomy, to introduce both internal and external evaluation procedures, and to improve the social responsibility awareness of teachers, researchers and students. The European University Association is strongly committed to these challenges, and state governments as well as the European Commission and Parliament have to act in this direction.

Funding research

The governments at single-state and European level have responsibility for the allocation of public funds and therefore they have to provide incentives for and support the transfer of research results from laboratories to society. This can be done in different ways: certainly the most effective is through the mobility of the people involved, from labs to industry and society and vice versa. Again this can be enhanced if bureaucratic obstacles are removed: the mobility of researchers should not have negative consequences on their careers and in particular on social benefits such as health care and future pensions. This requires new legislation at European level that overcomes the current rules of single states.

Due to the limitation of public funds for research, also in case they are increased as everybody asks for, the problem of setting priorities is ever present. In my opinion, the public funds for research should be divided into three categories: the first should be devoted to fertilising free research, and allocated according to the quality of researchers. The second should be devoted to basic research and allocated to the large fields evaluated as more important for society's growth (for example: natural sciences, humanities, social sciences, etc.). The third should be devoted to applied and finalised research, taking into account the actual needs of society (for example: energy production, health care, communication, transport, environment preservation, etc.).

In a democratic country the allocation of research funds between these categories must be the responsibility of the government and parliament. Then the allocation of each part should be decided by the scientific and academic community for the first two categories; for the third, the academic and scientific community can decide jointly with industry and other productive agents.

Conclusion

The wisdom society should be characterised by greater institutional autonomy, more personal responsibility and fewer rules: governments must facilitate and fund more research in humanities and social sciences to educate people to manage scientific achievements and technological development properly at personal and global levels, in order to foster personal and social growth.

Finally, I am also convinced that to improve personal responsibility based on shared strong values it is better to trust the role of faiths and religions as traditional regulators of good personal behaviour than to try to control the growing complexity of society and personal actions only by augmenting the number of laws and rules approved by parliaments or governments.

Government and higher education: the approach to regulation

Roderick Floud

Introduction

Throughout Europe, the relationship between government and higher education is changing. In many countries, universities are gaining greater autonomy from the state. In some, there has been a rapid growth of private institutions – some run for-profit – while, in others, previously state-funded institutions are being allowed or encouraged to charge fees to students and to seek funds from the provision of services to business and industry. In both eastern and western Europe, research activity that was previously separate from universities is being integrated with them in a variety of ways, while at the same time many governments are seeking to concentrate research funding within a subset of universities. Finally, although education as a whole, and university education within it, is not within the competence of the European Union, the creation of a Single Market has inevitable consequences for universities, who are also engaged, with the active support or even direction of governments, in harmonising their activities under the auspices of the Bologna Process.

Some of this change is specific to higher education, but much of it – perhaps more than is usually recognised within universities – is paralleled by similar developments in other public services. In many countries, governments are seeking to devolve responsibility for activities which were previously carried out by the state. Even when such devolution stops short of the wholesale privatisation which was characteristic, for example, of the United Kingdom under the governments of Margaret Thatcher, there are many examples of governments establishing separate agencies to carry out specific functions or introducing market mechanisms or quasi-markets within public services. Some have introduced, for example, distinctions between purchasers and providers which operate within public services while there have also been experiments in giving direct purchasing ability, for example through vouchers, to consumers of those services.

The roots of these changes are difficult to disentangle. Some of them, for example in the former communist countries, represent reactions to previous regimes. Others, in western Europe, stem from attitudes expressed within ideas of "new public management"; these assume that the methods of private industry are more efficient than those of state control and therefore seek to import those methods into public services. In some cases, as in the private finance initiatives (PFI) and public-private partnerships (PPP) introduced in the UK, the provision of services such as hospitals, schools and railways has been contracted to private companies on the basis – not always justified in practice – that they will share the risk of investment and run the activity more efficiently than the state or local government.

However, for whatever reasons such changes in organisation or governance are introduced, governments are rarely willing to disengage completely. Whether because of bureaucratic inertia or because of a genuine public wish that the state should retain oversight, a decline in direct control is almost always accompanied by a rise in regulation. This often takes the form of the state setting targets for agencies and monitoring, sometimes in great detail, the work of the agencies to discover whether the targets have been met. This rise in regulation from one direction – regulation of activity previously provided by the state – is paralleled by the rise in regulation of activities which were not previously provided by the state or which were left entirely to the market. This may take the form of setting rules for the conduct of business or the information which must be supplied to customers and the wider public.

Within this wider context, this paper considers approaches to regulation in higher education. The focus is initially on the United Kingdom, partly for reasons of space but also because the universities of the UK have recently experienced a rise in regulation of teaching quality, research and other activities which has been seen as a model – although perhaps one to be avoided – by other European countries. A brief history of higher education in the UK is then placed in the context of the growth of the "regulatory state." This growth is then related to changes in the regulatory and funding systems for higher education. The paper then attempts to establish, within a framework developed by Julian Le Grand (2003), which can be potentially applied to higher education in the rest of Europe as well as in the UK, the extent and nature of regulation which will produce the most effective higher education system.

The paper assumes that there is a public responsibility for the provision, regulation and quality of higher education. While private universities, including some for-profit institutions, exist in a number of countries, they are in a small minority when compared with non-profit universities controlled or financed by governments. In a "Knowledge Society" it is a matter of great importance to governments that the qualifications which are awarded to graduates, the predominant knowledge workers, should be properly awarded on the basis of a thorough academic and vocational training. This applies both within countries and in the case of cross-border provision which has developed in recent years and may develop further in future. Governments have, I believe, a responsibility to ensure that higher education maintains and enhances its standards.

The structure of UK higher education: a brief history

The universities (and other higher education institutions) of the UK are unlike the majority of universities in other European countries or in the United States in one major respect. They are all formally private institutions, though established as charities serving a public benefit. The earliest foundations, at Oxford and

Cambridge, both dating from the Middle Ages, were joined later by a number of Scottish universities and then, in the first half of the nineteenth century, by the University of Durham and by colleges of what became the University of London. Further universities were founded in the other major cities of the UK in the second half of the nineteenth century, some initially offering degrees of the University of London but later becoming independent institutions. There was then a burst of university expansion in the late 1960s, following the report of a committee chaired by Lord Robbins, with the foundation of the so-called "plate-glass" universities, often in small country towns. These, and their predecessors, were established by Royal Charter, not by legislation. All were expected to undertake research as well as teaching and, from early in the twentieth century, all received funds to undertake teaching and research from government through a University Grants Committee.

The late 1960s also saw the establishment by the government of polytechnics, as the alternative sector of UK higher education, across what became known as "the binary line." The polytechnics – like the state schools – were under the control of local government and were intended to provide technological and vocational education for the benefit of their local communities; they did not initially award their own degrees, but rather those of a Council for National Academic Awards (CNAA), and they were subject to national inspection by inspectors from the government Department of Education. Although they were also subject to national control in terms of the subjects which they could offer, their curricula gradually widened and they began to award larger and larger numbers of masters and Ph.D. degrees. They did not, however, receive substantial funding to undertake research.

Under Margaret Thatcher as Prime Minister, the UK Government in the 1980s sought to reduce the influence and control of local government. One aspect of this policy was the decision, enacted in 1988, to remove the polytechnics from local authority control, to establish them by legislation as independent institutions – formally higher education corporations – and to establish a Polytechnics and Colleges Funding Council to provide them with funds. This decision was then followed, in 1992, by the end of the binary line, when the polytechnics were allowed to take the title of university and a unified Universities Funding Council was established. Finally, the devolution of responsibility for higher education to Scotland, Wales and Northern Ireland, by the Labour government after 1997, led to the establishment of separate Higher Education Funding Councils for those countries and for England.

Throughout these changes, the universities retained formal independence from the state, although in practice they received the bulk of their funding, for either teaching or research, from the state. They were, however, free to seek and receive other funds, for example from private business for carrying out contract research, and they could – subject to various constraints at different times – charge student fees. The state did not – except in relation to the polytechnics for a relatively brief period – control the subjects offered. It did not control the admission of students, the subjects they were taught, how those subjects were taught or the award of degrees; nor did it control research by academic staff. The state did of course limit the funds provided, which exerted at different times implicit or explicit controls on student numbers, but it also provided – almost entirely to the pre-1992 universities – research funds which could be spent on any topic at the choice of the university. Until very recently, therefore, the extent of formal state regulation of higher education in the UK remained very limited.

Regulation: the wider context

The recent growth of state regulation of higher education in the UK has to be seen in a wider context than that of the universities themselves. Part of this context is indeed global – the growth everywhere of student numbers and the strains that this has put on the funding of university systems – but this is considered by other contributors. In the UK, the proximate causes of the growth of regulation lie in the major changes in government and the workings of the economy which have occurred since the 1970s. Even to those who have lived through them, it is often difficult to comprehend how fundamental those changes have been.

The most visible outcome of the Conservative governments which, initially under Prime Minister Margaret Thatcher, ruled Britain from 1980 to 1997 was the end of the experiment with state ownership of the major industries which had begun during and after the Second World War.[8] In a short time, all those industries, together with a great deal of the stock of social housing, were transferred to private ownership. This transfer was ideologically motivated – driven by the belief that private ownership and the operation of the market was inherently more efficient than public control – and was abetted by the view, not always wellfounded, that the nationalised industries were badly managed and a drag on national economic performance (Hannah, 2004). The drive to privatisation went further, as local governments were forced to employ private industries in such activities as refuse collection and the running of sports facilities, although this was never extended to such areas as personal social services. By 1997, however, only the National Health Service and state education survived as "industries" financed and managed by central government.[9]

Even within the services and activities which remained as the province of central or local government, attempts were made to create quasi-markets, which would import the benefits of competition and choice, or to introduce into the public services the methods of what came to be called the "new public management"[10]. This was based on the belief that the management methods of private industry were either inherently superior to those of the public services or, at the least, that civil and local government "servants" – as they used to be called – could benefit from adopting some of those methods. Thus activities previously undertaken by

---

8. State ownership, in the sense of the public ownership of the utilities – roads, water, gas, electricity, public transport and others – was actually much older, since many of these activities had been developed under the control or ownership of local government in the late nineteenth century or even before.
9. There were a number of other small exceptions, such as the air traffic control system and some parts of the nuclear power industry.
10. The origins of the new public management lay in the United States, but for a brief description of its implementation in Britain, see Moran, 2003, pp. 126-131.

government departments were hived off to independent or quasi-independent agencies and previously monolithic departments were broken up into smaller units which could be more easily and more efficiently managed. In general, governments sought, not always successfully, to make a distinction between the work of policy formation and planning, on the one hand, and administration on the other; the latter was set apart from the direct control of politicians whose role was that of "light-touch" regulation and policy-setting.

Even full-blown privatisation, however, spawned – probably to the surprise of many Thatcherites – a plethora of regulatory bodies, few of which existed before 1980. It was apparent, even to the most fervent enemies of the nationalised industries, that it would not be sufficient merely to sell them off, if the result was merely the creation of private monopolies. These would, if uncontrolled, exploit their monopoly power to the detriment of consumers. Although valiant attempts were made to create real competition within the privatised industries, it was often difficult to achieve this within the so-called "natural monopolies" such as the supply of water or sewage disposal; even in areas apparently more open to competition, it was transparently inefficient to encourage numerous telephone or electricity companies to dig up the streets, each to supply their own wire to each house, and substitutes for unbridled competition had to be found. They were found in bodies successively named OFGAS, OFWAT, OFCOM, etc., with OF standing for Office for the Regulation of ... In many cases, these were given powers by legislation to control prices and the quality of service.

The development of regulation of the former nationalised industries intersected with the development of regulation of areas of economic and social activity which had not previously been thought to require similar regulation. This development – of great importance in the context of higher education – is less easy to explain than the creation of regulatory bodies for monopolies and quasi-monopolies, but it is possible to discern a number of strands which seem to have become woven together since about the middle of the 1980s. These were an attack on the professions, a decline in trust in government and "authority", the "rise of the audit society", and an emphasis on the rights of the individual consumer.

The work of professionals – engineers, doctors, lawyers, accountants, bankers – has traditionally been, in the UK, self-regulated, in the sense that groups of professionals themselves established the conditions for entering the profession and determined what was, and was not, acceptable behaviour. This was often done in conjunction with the universities, since in many cases the possession of a degree in a relevant subject was sufficient to gain entry, at least to a training programme which would provide experience of work in the profession concerned. In some but not all cases, the self-regulatory bodies – composed of the senior members of the profession – were given statutory powers to control entry and standards and, if necessary, to expel an errant member from the profession. This was justified – as in the case of architects or engineers – on the grounds of protecting the public, but the power lay firmly with the profession itself.

Both Conservative and Labour governments, since the 1980s, evinced considerable distrust, bordering at times on hostility, towards groups of professionals, who were seen as promoting their own self-interest at the expense of the public. At times, this hostility sprang from the successful resistance of professional groups, such as lawyers or doctors, to proposed reforms affecting the courts or medical services. This resistance was expressed on grounds of principle – the defence of the freedom of the individual, for example – by the professionals, but perceived by government as stemming from the wish to retain lucrative privileges. More generally, it was argued that the system of self-regulation – for example in the stock market or in insurance – had failed to protect the public from the predations of fraudulent or incompetent professionals, often shielded or inadequately punished by other professionals who might, *sotto voce,* be saying "There but for the grace of God go I." The combination of such fears and a succession of scandals in which members of the public, or pensioners, lost money, resulted, in the financial services sector for example, in a move from self-regulation and the creation instead of the Financial Services Authority, there to protect the public and to lay down and enforce professional standards.

This attack on the professions was, however, only a part of what a number of commentators, in particular Onora O'Neill, have identified as a breakdown of trust, on the part of the public, of government and authority in general (O'Neill, 2002). This has been ascribed to a variety of factors. There were doubts over the quality of scientific advice – as in the case of "mad-cow disease" or BSE – or genetically modified foods. The press treatment of various scandals, in both the public and private sectors, fostered cynicism about politicians and businessmen, who were seen as constantly covering up mistakes and "spinning" stories to put themselves in a better light; there was certainly nothing new about such press activity, but it seemed to cause a deeper crisis of confidence than in previous years (O'Hara, 2004). More speculatively, the development of the Internet made it much easier than ever before to gain the information needed to question the judgment of professionals; doctors who had hitherto been used to unquestioning deference from patients found themselves challenged by printouts from Internet sites.

This general decline of trust in authority was accompanied by a crisis of confidence – and self-confidence – in what Moran has called "club government". This is a description of the "oligarchic, informal and secretive" (Moran, 2003, p. 4) system by which, Moran argues, Britain was ruled for much of the twentieth century, though it was itself a legacy of the political and financial systems, and the self-regulatory systems, established at the end of the industrial revolution. Moran sees this "club rule" as "an attempt to practise oligarchy under conditions of formal democracy" in which the real decisions were taken by self-perpetuating elites sheltering behind such constitutional mystifications as "royal prerogative"; its instruments were a plethora of quasi-non-governmental organisations (quangos), committees staffed by members of "the great and the good" who believed implicitly that they were acting for the public good but were in practice contemptuous of the public whom they professed to serve. The membership of this amorphous, but undoubtedly powerful, group, which spanned all the political parties, became known as "the establishment". The system by which they, and the civil service, worked was captured perfectly and hilariously by the television series *Yes, minister.*

In the aftermath of Thatcherism, Moran argues, and particularly after the election of the Labour government in 1997, this system of club government came under increasing attack. It faced demands for the replacement of implicit understandings by codified rules, for "evidence-based policy" to replace the whims of politicians. These challenges intersected with arguments for the new public management and led to the establishment of agencies, separated from government departments, to carry out executive and administrative functions. The result was a major reorganisation of almost every aspect of government and of the regulatory and self-regulatory regime which had existed for much of the previous century. Even where a state regulatory system had existed, as for example in the inspection of schools, the old, cosy, system was replaced by an adversarial approach, backed up by legislation to impose on teachers a national curriculum, which had not hitherto existed in British schools. All this was seen, by the professions being regulated, as an attack on their professionalism and on their status and a complete breakdown of trust. Onora O'Neill puts their feelings perfectly (2002, p. 43):

> "Like many of us, I live and work among professionals and public servants. And those whom I know seek to serve the public conscientiously – and mostly to pretty good effect. Addenbrooke's for example, is an outstanding hospital; the University of Cambridge and many surrounding research institutions do distinguished work; Cambridgeshire schools, social services and police have good reputations. Yet during the last fifteen years we have all found our reputations and performance doubted, as have millions of other public sector workers and professionals. We increasingly hear that we are no longer trusted."

One outcome of this crisis of confidence in the work and role of professionals, politicians and civil servants was an increasing demand for measurement of activity as a means by which they could be "held accountable" for their actions. It felt to many public bodies that they were being buried beneath a mountain of targets, many of them apparently incompatible or contradictory, and constantly challenged to account for their behaviour by an army of accountants. This is the third aspect of the changes that have taken place; Michael Power has well described it in *The audit society: rituals of verification* (1997). Fuelled by demands for the measurement of performance, justified in terms of accounting for the use of public money, auditors and accountants have demanded, or been willingly given, the right to audit and inspect many aspects of the work of the public services, far outside the original competence of accountants in the field of finance. Internal audit services, which hitherto had been concerned with such matters as financial controls, have found themselves expected to pronounce on the performance of an organisation against a whole range of qualitative as well as quantitative targets.

The latest manifestation of this audit society is the current emphasis on "risk management." This entails listing all the risks, financial and otherwise, facing an organisation and then similarly listing the actions which will be taken to mitigate those risks. The risks range, in the case of a university, from a fire burning down a building through the fraudulent behaviour of the director of finance to inadequate library provision or poor teaching quality. The latter is included because of what is known as "reputational risk": the risk that one's reputation will be damaged by complaints about the behaviour of a teacher. Like all such fashions, risk management can be guyed: one vice-chancellor has referred to his risk register as "excellent for propping open the fire doors". Any sensible person or organisation will of course try to foresee and avoid risk – we do it all the time when driving a car or walking down the street – but there is a danger in excessive formalism; it may, in fact, discourage initiative and entrepreneurial behaviour, just when such behaviour is being urged on universities and other public agencies. Crucially, in the context of an argument about lack of trust and need for regulation, risk management and the audit society represent a means by which professionals are challenged to explain and justify what they do.

The final strand in the web of arguments for regulation lies in the wish to enhance the power of the ordinary consumer. This leads, in the name of creating the informed consumer or customer, to the demand for the increased provision of information on the basis of which a choice can be made. In addition, since it is crucial that the information should be in a form which the consumer can understand, the demand for more information is coupled with the demand for the systemisation of information. Information must be provided, in other words, in a form which allows a consumer or customer to compare the services offered by two or more producers; they must therefore be forced to produce information in a comparable form. At its extreme, this lies behind the demand for information in a form which can lead to the compilation of "league tables", such as those produced by government and the press in the UK to compare the performance of schools, hospitals, local authorities and universities. As with the attack on "club culture" and the rise of the audit society, this movement for greater information seeks to demystify and to reduce the power of professionals over the ordinary person, be he or she a student, patient or taxpayer.

Moran (2003) locates the rise of regulation in a framework of major constitutional and ideological change, linked to globalisation, the end of imperialism, the impact of Europeanisation on British political culture and the major constitutional changes which have occurred in the UK since 1997. Such a wide-ranging explanation is eschewed by O'Neill and by Power, but all three agree that behind the rise in regulation lies a decline in trust and in deference to professionals and the old political order. One aspect of that old order, as Moran (2003, p. 11) emphasises, is the role in the UK of the elite universities. What has been the impact of these trends on the regulation of them and the remainder of the UK higher education system?

The regulation of higher education in the UK: recent trends

It is not an exaggeration to say that, until the 1970s, the UK university system was hardly regulated at all. Universities received their funds from the state, through the University Grants Committee, without any real oversight of their activities; it was assumed – in a manifestation of Moran's "club culture" – that the academics and university leaders, who were very much members of the club,[11] would undertake excellent teaching and research and would therefore be worthy recipients of large sums of public money. Universities decided whom to admit as students, academics decided what and how to teach, research was a matter of personal choice and the award of degrees was a matter for each university – moderated only by an external examiner whose role was to ensure that degrees in one university were of the same standard as in others. It was implicitly assumed that all universities applied the same standards, even if it was also assumed that there was a greater concentration of excellence in teaching and research in the two ancient universities of Oxford and Cambridge, where indeed most academics at other universities had received their own undergraduate education.[12]

In one sense, the lack of regulation still persists; universities are autonomous institutions, free to award their own degrees and to undertake whatever teaching and research they please. In many other senses, however, there has been a major extension of state regulation over their activities. This affects, in different forms, their teaching, their research, their admission of students and their links with business and industry.

Space does not permit a full description of the development of the system of quality assurance of teaching and learning in UK higher education. However, that development really falls into two main phases. The first, which is familiar in the context of other European countries and is still a major issue within the Bologna Process today, was dominated by the issue of who should control the system; the second has been, and to some extent still is, dominated by the issue of what should be assessed and assured, how this should be done and what information should be provided.

From the outset, the universities were determined that, as autonomous institutions exercising powers granted by a Royal Charter – one of the "mystifications" mentioned by Moran (2003) – they should devise their own procedures of internal quality control and also be in control of any system of external quality assessment. The government and the funding councils[13] were equally determined, on the basis of the higher education laws and because of their responsibility for the proper use of public money, that they should control the assessment of teaching for which the government was paying. After a period in which two systems operated side by

---

11. This was often literally true in the sense that most vice-chancellors, like many heads of government departments, senior lawyers and bishops, were members of *The Athenaeum,* a men's club in the west end of London.

12. More formal regulation was applied to the other side of the binary line, the polytechnics, where courses and standards had to be approved by the Council for National Academic Awards and where teachers were inspected, as in primary and secondary schools, by Her Majesty's Inspectorate, a branch of the Department for Education. However, the tendency throughout the life of the polytechnics was to reduce the extent of central regulation and to transfer responsibility for academic standards to the polytechnics themselves. The role of the inspectorate was similarly removed when the polytechnics became independent of local authorities in 1989.

13. This term is used generically to represent the various bodies, the University Grants Committee, the Universities Funding Council, the Polytechnics and Colleges Funding Council and the current Higher Education Funding Councils for England, Scotland and Wales, who have been concerned with this issue.

side, to the confusion of almost everyone involved, a compromise was reached; the Quality Assurance Agency, established as an independent body by the universities and colleges, would be contracted by the funding councils to carry out assessment processes. The result is a somewhat peculiar system of state regulation carried out through a self-regulatory agency.

The disputes which led to this compromise were confined to a small part of the university community but the second phase, about assessment methods, has involved a much wider group. It would be tedious to rehearse the details, but essentially scrutiny began by concentrating on the adequacy of the processes of quality assurance in each institution. This was succeeded by a formal system, known as Teaching Quality Assessment (TQA), in which ultimately every teaching department, in every university or college, was visited by a team of assessors (drawn from current and former academic staff); the visit normally lasted a week and resulted in a grade of 1-4 on each of six aspects of provision.[14] Despite the fact that these aspects – such as curriculum development, care of students and teaching quality – were all difficult to measure or compare, it was easy to see the results as marks out of a total of twenty-four and this led immediately to their incorporation in newspaper league tables.

The system as a whole was very unpopular, both with academic staff and, perhaps less strongly, with university managements. It was undoubtedly intrusive – a challenge to professional autonomy in an area where it had previously been assumed that each academic knew exactly how to do his or her job – and the requirements for evidence were enormous. Complaints about this were somewhat inconsistent, since the need for evidence was partly driven by the need to ensure that the judgments which were made were fair and defensible. However, partly because of the volume of evidence, the costs were very considerable. Various estimates were made, depending on how much time was taken up in preparation, but the consensus was that TQA cost about £200 million per year over five years, or £1 billion pounds to survey every department in every university and college. This equated to about 1.5% of the total turnover of British universities, but a much higher proportion of the grant for teaching. In more than 98% of departments assessed, the judgment was that teaching and provision for students was satisfactory or better.

Debate raged throughout the process of TQA about whether it was effective and efficient and about whether the benefits justified the costs. Taking the process as a whole, there is no doubt that the work of the Quality Assurance Agency has, over a period of two decades, greatly enhanced the importance of good teaching within the university system and encouraged academics to take their teaching seriously. Until the system began, academics in the old universities – the position was significantly different in the polytechnics under the tutelage of the Council for National Academic Affairs and the inspectorate – were largely free to devise their own syllabi and to teach as they pleased. There was normally a process of approval of a new course, but this was often cursory and confined to a brief look by a com-

---

14. This describes the system as it was finally applied; there were earlier variants.

mittee at a reading list. Most importantly, it was unheard of for anyone to seek to inspect anyone else's teaching; even a senior professor or head of department would not, as it would have been described, infringe academic freedom by sitting in a lecture audience of a junior member of staff. During the late 1960s, a number of universities introduced brief introductory sessions, for newly appointed academics, in how to teach, but these were often voluntary; it was essentially assumed that, if you could write a few good research articles, you were worthy of appointment as a university teacher and could then be left to get on with the job. Only if your teaching was utterly incompetent would there be any, usually mild, attempt to rectify the situation.

This situation has now changed radically, although it is not possible to ascribe this entirely to the work of the Quality Assurance Agency; there were other strong pressures, as the universities expanded in the 1980s and 1990s, to improve the quality of university teaching and the information provided to students. For whatever reason, however, it is now a requirement that course organisers or teachers on each course should specify the contents of the course, the requirements for undertaking it and the outcomes – in terms of the factual material and techniques which will be acquired – which a student can expect from taking it. This information has to be accompanied by a course booklet which contains reading lists, lists of assignments and assessments, and other material such as regulations and advice on such issues as plagiarism. Every course has also to be located within the framework of course descriptors set out by the Quality Assurance Agency. All this has certainly increased the rigour with which courses are designed, although at the cost of a considerable amount of extra bureaucracy within universities.

A further development represents a radical change from the old tradition that an academic's teaching was his – or rarely her – business alone. Almost certainly as a result of the Teaching Quality Assessments, it has now become customary for academics to assess each other's teaching and for mentors to be assigned to new members of staff. Most universities now require all new staff to undertake a formal course, normally of at least a year, in university teaching, which is assessed and accredited in the same way as the other courses of the university; from 2006 (in this case at the insistence of the government) all new university teachers will have to pass such a course. In general, therefore, what were presumably the desired outcomes of the whole assessment process – an improvement in the quality of teaching and learning in UK universities – has probably been achieved.

These have all been positive outcomes of the work of the Quality Assurance Agency, but they were bought at a price, perhaps of £200 million a year. The QAA also made itself very unpopular with a number of academics, perhaps particularly from elite universities who objected to the assessment regime, and with a number of university leaders; there was a personality clash with the style of the chief executive of the agency, who was seen as wishing to impose a draconian regime of inspection on the model of that introduced in primary and secondary schools. It was, however, mainly the consideration of cost, together with the evidence of the Teaching Quality Assessments that virtually all university courses are being taught and conducted in a satisfactory manner, that persuaded the universities to argue that it would now be possible for there to be a "light touch" regime of quality assurance. Although this view was initially resisted by a number of ministers and officials in the Department for Education and Science, the then Secretary of State, David Blunkett, announced in the spring of 2001 that he had accepted that the regime would change. After lengthy discussions, it was agreed that in future the Quality Assurance Agency would focus on the institutional processes for quality assurance, through a process of "institutional audit", although the auditors would be able to "drill down" to look at processes as they had been applied in a small number of academic and other areas. Only if the audit appeared to be finding evidence of a major failure would there be assessment of individual departments on the model of Teaching Quality Assessment. This new method of institutional assessment has been introduced only recently, in 2004, and it is too early to tell how effective and efficient it will be; early signs are that it is unlikely to be very much cheaper than the system that it has replaced and that, as happened with previous methods, the requirements for the production of evidence are onerous.

One oddity of the process of TQA, and indeed the entire work of the Quality Assurance Agency, is that it has exercised no influence on the levels of funding of teaching or on the funds given to any individual university or college for teaching. This is entirely unlike the assessment of research, which is considered below. Participation in the work of the QAA, through TQA or other processes, is a condition of grant by the funding councils; in other words, if a university decided – as some have threatened – to refuse to receive an assessment or audit visit, it would be open to the funding council to refuse to give it any more funds for teaching. This power arises from the duty imposed by statute on the funding councils to inspect the quality of provision of the teaching that they fund. The power has never been exercised, although there have been discussions between the funding councils and the universities concerned about the very few cases where provision was judged to be unsatisfactory.

The problem of linking levels of funding to assessments of quality is a real one, which illustrates some of the real difficulties of operating a fair regulatory regime. It is, first, important to recognise that the Teaching Quality Assessments were based on a judgement of whether the courses being assessed were "fit for purpose". In other words, the assessors had to have regard to whether the course was a highly academic one, intended to reflect advanced knowledge in a specialised discipline, or an applied course, intended to produce graduates equipped to work in a particular vocation or industry. This simplified the task of assessment, since it was not necessary for the assessors to attempt to compare the quality of provision in a course in *Literae Humaniores* (Ancient History and Philosophy) at the University of Oxford with that in Golf Course Management at the University of Birmingham.[15] But the judgment of whether a course is "fit for purpose" does not lead easily to a decision as to how much the state should provide for it; such a decision has to be made

---

15. These two universities are both members of the Russell Group, the group of (self-selected) elite universities. But these distinctions between types of courses can be replicated both within and between all the other UK universities.

primarily on the basis of how much it costs to teach, on the implicit assumption that a university will not provide a course if no one wants to study it.

It would, of course, have been possible for the funding councils to base their funding decisions on the 24-point scale produced by the Teaching Quality Assessments. One difficulty with doing so is that it would have encountered the bitter resistance of the Quality Assurance Agency, which steadfastly resisted the use of the 24-point scale for any purpose, correctly pointing out the statistical innumeracy involved in adding together six ordinal scales representing entirely different and incommensurate aspects of provision. But a more fundamental difficulty lay in answering the question: should funding reward the strong and penalise the weak, or should it attempt to help the weak to rectify their problems? To take a concrete example, one aspect of the Teaching Quality Assessment was the quality of the university's library and other learning resources. One university, Oxford, has had about 600 years to establish its library, aided by the fact that it is by statute a copyright library, entitled to a free copy of every book published in the UK. Another university, London Metropolitan, has had to build up its library by purchase, from inadequate funds, over only a few decades. It is inevitable that Oxford should receive a higher rating, but not clear that the funding council should therefore simply give it more money, thereby worsening the disparity which is largely a matter of history. Even in cases where provision was judged to be inadequate, it is not necessarily in the interests of the students undertaking the course to withdraw funding, since that is likely to make matters worse. For all these reasons, the funding councils have insisted on Teaching Quality Assessment but then largely ignored its results, instead funding a student in a given subject equally at all universities where the subject is taught.[16] In one sense, as critics of the system have pointed out, this is implicitly making the assumption – which is unlikely to be correct – that teaching quality is the same across all the 160 or more universities and colleges which make up the UK higher education system.

This is all the more surprising since exactly the reverse assumption is made in determining funding for research. In that area – accounting for about half of the funding currently allocated to teaching – funding is based on an increasingly selective and rigorous system of assessment which makes fine distinctions between levels of quality and allocates large sums of money on that basis.

Until the 1980s, it was assumed that all university teachers would also be engaged in research.[17] Universities were funded accordingly. No attempt was made by the funding bodies to control the use of these funds and, even within the universities, research remained to a large extent a personal activity, not part of a departmental

---

16. For the purposes of funding, all subjects are assigned to one of four subject bands, with clinical medicine receiving the highest funding and a range of subjects in the arts and humanities the lowest. The whole system for funding of teaching in English universities and colleges is currently (2004) under review.

17. It was, of course, recognised that some might, late in their careers, no longer be undertaking original research, but it was assumed that such people would be balanced by younger academics who were devoting most of their time to research.

plan, unless it relied on the purchase or use of very expensive equipment.[18] During the 1970s and 1980s, however, the growth of the university system, and with it the growth of the number of university teachers, made it increasingly expensive to make the assumption that all of them would receive support to do research. It also became increasingly unrealistic to assume that the research being done by all those university teachers was of equally high quality and, therefore, equally worth the expenditure of public money.[19]

These considerations led, in the late 1980s, to the beginnings of what became known as the Research Assessment Exercise (RAE), still the largest and most comprehensive assessment of research quality undertaken anywhere in the world, although a number of other countries have since emulated the UK.[20] There have been numerous changes of detail since the first RAE, but its principles remain unchanged. The assessment is made by panels of peers, other academics in the subjects concerned, including – in the more recent RAEs – international experts in the subject; the latter have the duty of making sure that claims to "international excellence" are correct. Such claims are important, because the assessment is designed to grade research along a scale which ranges from internationally excellent through nationally important to, essentially, worthless.[21] The panels consider research output, in their own disciplinary area, over the previous years – the exact length of time varying between science and arts subjects. In recent years, academics have been allowed to submit no more than four of their articles, books or other published material (including works of art in relevant subjects) for assessment by the panels.

The grade agreed for a department (or, formally, a unit of assessment) represents the overall quality of the research of its members. This grade is then converted to a steeply ascending scale in which "internationally excellent" research is ranked as worth over three times as much as "nationally important" research.[22] Finally, the

---

18. Today, as in the 1970s, universities actually benefit from two sources of funds for research, known as the "dual support" system. The funding councils (under the aegis of the Department for Education and Science) provide core funding intended to provide for university research infrastructure and allocated at the discretion of the university. The research councils (under the aegis of the Office of Science and Technology, part of the Department for Trade and Industry) provide funds for individual projects, allocated on the basis of research proposals from individual researchers (or groups of them); these funds have to be spent on the project for which they were allocated.

19. It is interesting that there was no public questioning of an equally questionable assumption that all the research topics were of equal value. Thus, while the research councils adopted an increasingly discriminating policy, directing funding towards areas thought to be of particular public benefit, the funding councils continued to assume that it was equally important to fund theology and biotechnology (though at very different levels of funding).

20. It is notable that this does not include the United States. This is because there is no equivalent in the USA of the core funding provided by the funding councils as their part of the dual support system. Instead, federal government support for research, through such agencies as the National Science Foundation, is provided on a project basis, in which the assessment of quality is made by prior peer review, with the funding including a substantial overhead which is paid to the university concerned.

21. At present, it is departments rather than individuals which are graded. The next RAE, in 2008, will move in the direction of individual grading, although such judgments will be confidential and the only public result will continue to be a score for the department concerned.

22. The exact funding weights are: grades 1, 2, 3b and 3a – zero weighting and therefore unfunded at present; grade 4 – weight 1; grade 5 – weight 2.793; grade 5* – weight 3.357 (HEFCE, 2003, p. 19) Different methods were used to allocate funding in Scotland, Wales and Northern Ireland. It is worth noting that 80% of the researchers whose work was assessed were in departments receiving one of the three top grades. To a large extent, therefore, universities chose not to enter departments whose predicted grades were less than 4.

scaled grade is multiplied by an assessment of the average cost of research in a given subject area and by a range of "volume" indicators, which have changed over time, but the principal factor in which is the number of "research-active staff" submitted for assessment. This feature of the RAE has been criticised on the grounds that a department can choose to submit only a part of its staff for assessment, hoping to increase its score for quality even at the expense of reducing its overall income. This can sometimes be worthwhile, particularly for departments with relatively few excellent researchers, because the "headline result" which appears in newspaper league tables and can be quoted in publicity can be considered to be worth more than any foregone income.

The RAE is a massive exercise. It involved, in 1996, the assessment by 60 panels of four pieces of published research for each of over 50000 academics, together with supporting statements about the research environment in 3000 departments. The 2001 exercise was on a similar scale. The result was and will be used to allocate £5 billion of public money for research between 2003 and 2008 after the RAE. The approximate cost of the 1996 review (to the funding councils and to the institutions) was £37.5 million, or about 0.8% of the research funds allocated as a result of the exercise (HEFCE, 2000, p. 23); it is likely that the 2001 review had similar costs. The results not only make a crucial difference to the income of many universities, but also are extremely important in determining the reputation of universities and departments. The university receives the aggregation of sums allocated to all its departments, and can in theory then distribute the total as it wishes, but the grades and sums which follow them are widely known and universities therefore have limited freedom to diverge significantly, in their own internal allocations, from the results of the RAE.

Initial reaction by academics to the RAE was, as with the initial reaction to Teaching Quality Assessment which followed some years later, largely hostile. This hostility has moderated somewhat over time, perhaps because the exercise has become familiar; in addition – with a few exceptions – the assessments are generally regarded as having been made carefully and fairly. The only exception to this is the view, which has been expressed about all the exercises, that they have not given proper weight to applied research, nor to interdisciplinary work that does not fit neatly into traditional academic disciplines. Another reason for the acceptance, albeit grudging, of the RAE may be that academics are well used to making judgments of the research output of their peers and therefore found the exercise intrinsically easier to accept than similar judgements of their teaching, for which there is no agreed methodology or set of standards. Research remains a fundamental, probably in fact the fundamental, criterion for appointment and promotion within the academic profession, so judgments on research excellence are made routinely within departments and between universities.

The RAE has undoubtedly encouraged researchers to plan their work more effectively and to disseminate it, through publication, as quickly and effectively as possible. Because the income which results has become so important to universities and departments, the exercise has encouraged them to plan research much more explicitly than in the past and to demand evidence from academic staff of their progress on research and the prospects for publications which can be submitted for assessment. So important is the income that there have been a number of cases in which departments which received a low grade have been reorganised or even closed, particularly when those departments were at the same time finding it difficult to attract students and therefore funds for teaching; this has been a particular problem in a number of areas of science and engineering.

It is possible, although the argument is very difficult to prove or disprove, that the RAE has increased the quantity of research which has been produced more than the quality of that research. The number of publications by an individual or by members of a department does not form part of the evidence used, since the emphasis is on the four best publications by each individual within the assessment period. There is, therefore, no particular pressure to maximise the number of publications. However, the need to produce those four publications within a set period and then to secure their publication does put a premium on speedy research and writing. In addition, it puts pressure on journals to secure a rapid turn-round from submission to publication; this is particularly acute in the subjects – many of the sciences and economics – in which there is a recognised hierarchy of journals and intense competition to secure publication in what are now sometimes called 5* journals; this echoes the 5* grade awarded in the RAE to the departments demonstrating international excellence. While speed is no bad thing in itself, it is possible that speed has been secured at the expense of full consideration and reflection.

The importance of the outcomes of the RAE to a number of universities has been exacerbated by the trend, over the past twenty years, to intensify the selectivity of funding which results from the assessment. In recent years, particularly following the most recent assessment in 2001, the government has insisted that the English funding council should allocate funds very selectively, increasing the steepness of the gradient relating grade to funding and removing funding entirely from the lower grades. This has had the result, justified in terms of the need to compete internationally by focusing funds on the most excellent departments and researchers, that 75% of the funds allocated have gone to only 25 universities, from the 160 universities and colleges in the English system. This policy has led, as mentioned above, to the closure of departments, particularly in what might be called the "middle rank" universities, without the strengths in research of the elite universities in the so-called Russell Group. It has had less effect on the new universities, the former polytechnics, if only because they have always received smaller research grants and therefore had less to lose.

Before considering the overall impact of regulation on UK higher education in recent years, it is important to mention two final aspects. The first is that of the regulation of the provision of information about UK universities and their courses. While the assessment of teaching and research fits into one particular motive for the rise in regulation identified above – that of the declining trust in the professional and the requirement that his or her quality should be tested – the requirements for the provision of information fit best another motive: that of providing for the needs of the consumer or customer.

The system evolved by the Quality Assurance Agency was always influenced by the twin demands of assessment, presumably in the interests of improvement, and of the provision of information. Indeed, at times the influence of one motive had a major effect on the means of achieving the other. For example, it would have been much cheaper to achieve the objectives of Teaching Quality Assessment by assessing a sample of departments, perhaps at short notice, rather than through the laborious and time-consuming assessment of every department in every university and college. But once it had been determined that one object was to provide consistent and objective evidence and information about each and every course in each and every university, there was no alternative but to assess each course. This then determined that, in the interests of equity and comparability, the same method should be used for each and every assessment.

The fact that the proposed new system of institutional review, now being introduced, would not provide similar information about each course was one of the main objections raised, by officials and by the then chief executive of the Quality Assurance Agency, to the proposal to cease Teaching Quality Assessment. As a result, the government decided that universities and colleges would, in future, have to provide an expanded range of what is now called Teaching Quality Information (TQI), which would, to some degree, replace the information which could have been derived from TQA. It will include, for example, a brief report of the conclusions of external examiners. These are academics from another university who are employed, in relation to each course, to assure the quality of the examination and assessment process; they are required to report to the vice-chancellor, the executive head of the university, and to certify that the standards applied at a particular examination were equivalent to those applied throughout UK higher education. TQI will also include information about the courses themselves, the results of assessments and examinations and the initial employment of the students who have taken the course. There are, it is believed, about 50 000 courses at bachelor level offered in UK higher education and this information will have to be provided for all of them and, moreover, revised annually to keep them up to date. It remains to be seen how this enormous corpus of information is used by parents, prospective students and employers.

The final aspect of the developing regulatory system in the UK is in some ways of particular interest, since it illustrates a form of "regulation without regulation". Alternative descriptions would be "regulation by naming and shaming" or "regulation by league table". This form of regulation has been employed in dealing with the contentious topic of which students should attend which universities. Both government and the universities are committed to "widening participation", that is to ensuring that talented students from disadvantaged groups – from the working classes, from ethnic minorities or with disabilities – are encouraged to attend university; confusingly, a further and related meaning of "widening participation" is that talented students from disadvantaged backgrounds should be admitted fairly to the "best" universities, such as Oxford and Cambridge, where there is the greatest competition for places. The difficulty of regulation as applied to this topic is that it is an article of faith, subscribed to by government, universities and members of parliament, that government should never intervene in the decisions made by universities as to which students they should admit. It is not entirely clear why this should have become such a fetish, but it is one; it leads to such "hair-splitting" as the argument that government may intervene so as to encourage students to apply to university, but not interfere in any way with the process by which their applications are considered.

The tactic adopted by government – through the funding councils – in these circumstances is to publish the aggregate results of admissions decisions relating to students from different disadvantaged groups. The hope is thereby to encourage universities – where they do not seem to be admitting as many students from disadvantaged backgrounds as other similar universities – to alter their processes to achieve a better result. This is essentially "regulation by naming and shaming" since the funding council has absolutely no power to achieve the desired result by any other means.[23] The published tables recognise that there is a wide range of universities and that, for reasons of history or location, they attract different mixtures of students. Each university is therefore assigned a "benchmark", calculated from the average performance of itself and other similar universities, against which its performance is compared.[24] Universities which perform badly against their benchmark are, presumably, shamed into taking action to rectify the position. Similar statistics are also published about the number of students who fail to complete their courses, about the average length of time that students take to complete, and about the income universities earn from industrial contracts (see, for example, HEFCE, 2002).

To summarise, the last twenty years have seen a major extension of regulation or quasi-regulation within the UK higher education system. This regulation has taken a surprising (and confusing) number of different forms. As a whole, however, whether through the actions of government or the funding councils, using financial levers, or through the actions of the universities themselves in establishing – in an act initially of self-defence – the Quality Assurance Agency, there has been a very significant increase in the degree of external scrutiny of what are still theoretically independent and autonomous institutions. This has not only affected university governors and managers, it has had a major effect on the working lives of hundreds of thousands of academic and administrative staff. Academics have been tested and judged as never before; as a result, many of them have felt that their professional expertise has been devalued, that they are no longer trusted or valued,

---

23. This situation is about to change; as a result of legislation in 2004 for the introduction, from 2006, of variable fees for undergraduate courses, an Office for Fair Access (OFFA) has been established. Universities which wish to charge fees above the current level of £1 100 per annum will have to submit, to OFFA, a plan for widening participation. This will have to specify the actions which the university intends to take and how it will use some of the extra funds for this purpose. But, once again, the government has been obliged to promise and to include in the law the proviso that OFFA will not be concerned with individual admissions decisions.

24. The "benchmarks" are widely misunderstood and regarded, by people who should know better, as targets which a university should try to attain. They cannot be targets, since they are (in essence) averages and it is impossible for every university in a particular group of universities to be at or above an average level of attainment.

and that their lives have become pressured and stressed in a way that they could not have conceived of when they first entered the academic profession.

It is intriguing, in the light of this description of what is undoubtedly the attitude of most academics, that Moran (2003) sees the recent history of UK higher education as a prime example of what he calls "regulatory capture". That is, he considers that the universities have successfully defused the impact of regulation, in particular that of the RAE, by ensuring that it serves the ends of the old club elite which it was designed to challenge. As he puts it (2003, p. 141):

> "The story of the changed regulation of higher education and research funding in some respects echoes the history of the transformed quasi-government of the NHS (National Health Service): there is a similar draining away of professional authority, the invasion of enclosed policy communities by the central state, and a new institutional architecture designed to achieve greater central control. But in this domain the response of the regulated has been to capture the new regulatory world. It is this experience of regulatory capture that makes the case of higher education funding and research illuminating. An additional substantive importance is that higher education is one of the few parts of the welfare state that saw serious expansion in scale in the 1980s and 1990s."

In other words, to Moran the case of higher education represents a failure of the regulatory state. This failure has been in spite of the RAE which, as he says (2003, p. 142) "has shown an increasingly impressive capacity to inspect and judge individuals – something rarely achieved in other parts of the new regulatory state". Together with Teaching Quality Assessment, the new systems are "impressive in ... [their] ability to descend to the level of micro-management". Moran admits that (2003, p. 142):

> "these developments have undoubtedly had radical consequences within institutions. They have unleashed fierce struggles between different interests both within and between classes of institutions and have greatly increased levels of formal measurement and hierarchical control within universities ... The ferocity of these struggles means that the age of hyper-innovation continues, typified by the instability of key parts of the evaluative regime."

However, Moran continues, the RAE provides "a striking illustration" of regulatory capture. This is because (2003, pp. 142-143):

> "The system has from the beginning been dominated by the principles of peer review. This assertion of the primacy of core "scholarly" values has proved the key to capture, for it has created one of the critical conditions always needed for regulatory capture: the expertise to make regulatory judgements being controlled by the regulated. The primacy of the principle of peer review has meant that the panels performing the evaluations have been dominated not only by academics, but also by academics drawn from the 'old' universities; the detailed criteria, in turn, have been specified by these peer-dominated panels; and the outcomes, unsurprisingly, have then overwhelmingly favoured units from the old universities. ... The rules privileged scholarly work and the outcome was unsurprising: complete domination of the top rankings by the institutions of the old elite."

Moreover, he continues, this dominance was reinforced by the concurrent changes to the allocation of research funds by the other part of the dual support system, the research councils; these, once again, allowed the traditionally dominant institutions to strengthen their hold over resources (2003: 144).

In a conclusion which is also worth quoting in full, Moran (2003, p. 144) accepts that:

> "This assertion of control over both processes and outcomes is not the result of any improper mode of capture. It is essentially the result of a successful strategy of ideological construction by traditional academic elites. The critical move has been to establish the primacy of traditional scholarly values in the various evaluation processes. It is striking how feeble have been the efforts by carriers of alternative evaluative ideologies, such as business interests and the managers of the economy in the core executive, in asserting alternatives, like the contribution of research to national economic efficiency or business profitability. The analytical significance of the higher education case is that it shows capture to depend critically on fashioning and defending a regulatory ideology alternative to that of high modernism."

Moran is clearly right in concluding that neither research nor Teaching Quality Assessment has had any significant effect in upsetting the established hierarchy of esteem among the universities of the UK. But this conclusion is, in the correct sense of the word, superficial. That is, it ignores the changes that have taken place below the surface; these include the greater attention to the purposes and methods of teaching and learning, the concentration on planning research, both at the project and the departmental level and, above all, the acceptance that academics and university staff in general are not above criticism and are required to justify their existence and their salaries to the public who pay for them. This latter point is likely to achieve greater and greater significance as student fees become a more important part of the funding of British universities. These changes have altered the whole character of academic life as a profession, just at the time when a renewed emphasis on the role of the university towards society and the economy is changing perceptions of the purposes of higher education. Moran has failed to recognise these changes and their implications for the future regulation of higher education, the topic to which this paper now turns.

The basis of regulation in higher education: knights or knaves, queens or pawns

Up to this point, this paper has been largely descriptive and historical, rather than normative. From now on, it seeks to consider explicitly the question of by what means, and to what extent, higher education should be regulated, in the interests of society as a whole. Similarly, the previous sections of the paper have been about the United Kingdom and its recent experiences and experiments with regulation; the focus now turns to Europe as a whole and to the European universities as they come closer together through the Bologna Process.

To aid the discussion, the paper seeks to employ, for analytical and heuristic purposes, a "theory of public service motivation" advanced by Julian Le Grand in *Motivation, agency and public policy: of knights and knaves, pawns and queens* (2003). Le Grand is a distinguished social scientist, the Richard Titmuss Professor of Social Policy at the London School of Economics, who has since writing the book become the Prime Minister's principal adviser on health issues. He begins his book with a quotation from an essay entitled *On the independency of parliament* by the great eighteenth-century Scottish philosopher and political theorist, David Hume (reprinted 1875):

> "In contriving any system of government, and fixing the several checks and controls of the constitution, every man ought to be supposed a knave and to have no other end, in all his actions, than private interest. By this interest, we must govern him and, by means of it, notwithstanding his insatiable avarice and ambition, co-operate to the public good."

Le Grand points out that our assumptions about the individual motivation of those who work in the public services such as health and education (2003, p. 2):

> "will determine the way that public policies are constructed. So, for instance, a policy instrument designed on the assumption that people are motivated primarily by their own self-interest – that they are, in the words of David Hume ..., knaves – would be quite different from one constructed on the assumption that people are predominantly public-spirited or altruistic: that they are what we might term, in contrast to knaves, knights."

Furthermore, public policy design has to take account of the behaviour and motivation of individuals who use public services, since (2003, p. 2):

> "a policy that took no account of individuals' capacity for independent action – one that treated those working in the public sector or those who received its benefits as passive victims of circumstance, or pawns – would be different from one that treated workers or recipients as active agents, that is, not as the least powerful piece on the chess board, the pawn, but as the most powerful, the queen."

As Le Grand points out, belief – at least in the western democracies such as the UK – in one or other extreme of these two pairs of possible views of human motivation and behaviour correspond, at least in large measure, to the preconceptions of two ideological groups, which may be called the social democrats and the neo-liberals. The former emphasise the importance and benefits of collective action, while the latter extol the benefits of market mechanisms. In terms of action, the election in 1979 of the Conservative government under Margaret Thatcher marks the transition in the UK from one set of assumptions to the other, but, as Le Grand observes, this was merely one example of changes in social policy in other countries such as Sweden, the Netherlands, Belgium and, of course, the United States (2003, p. 10). He effectively documents, in a variety of contexts, the effect of different assumptions – sometimes unstated – about motivation and individual agency in the design of welfare and education policies, before turning to policy prescriptions in a number of different fields.

Le Grand does not discuss the case of higher education, although he does discuss education at primary and secondary level as well as the provision of healthcare. But his analysis provides a very useful framework within which to consider the increase of regulation in higher education. This requires, however, some consideration of an issue which Le Grand does not discuss at any length, perhaps because he thinks the answer to be obvious. The issue can be posed as: what are we trying to achieve? Having discussed this issue, the paper will go on to consider, within Le Grand's framework, the implicit and explicit motives of staff in universities and the assumptions underlying the recent actions of governments and regulators. It will then consider the role of students and the wider public who use the services of universities. The final section of the paper will then put forward some principles for the design of regulatory systems in higher education.

What are we trying to achieve?

The question, "what are we trying to achieve?", has two possible meanings in this context. First, what are the objectives of the higher education system? Second, what are the objectives of regulation of that system?

The major difficulty in answering the first meaning of the question, which applies to individuals and their motivation as well as to universities or colleges, is that higher education institutions undertake a very wide range of tasks and that, indeed, the range is widening rather than narrowing. Richard Lambert, former editor of the *Financial Times* in the UK, was commissioned recently by the British Government to survey links between the universities and industry. He was astonished to discover, in the course of his enquiry (2004) how wide-ranging such links already were. New governors of universities in the UK, appointed from other sectors of the economy, are frequently equally astonished at the multiplicity of tasks that a university fulfils and the multiplicity of funding sources which pay for them. Universities are expected to undertake teaching and research, both funded partly or wholly by the state, to provide fee-paying courses for individuals or companies, to undertake contract research for companies, to support the growth of small and medium-size enterprises (SMEs), to contribute to local and regional regeneration, to provide museums, art galleries and other cultural and sporting amenities for their towns, cities and regions and to lend their staff to support a whole variety of other charitable and governmental initiatives and institutions. Even within the university, they are expected to provide catering and residential accommodation, counselling services, financial advice, help with finding accommodation, sports facilities, cultural and leisure facilities and to give advice and support on careers and employment opportunities as well as keeping in touch, over many years, with their alumni. This is all on top of the core functions of research and teaching and the provision of services such as libraries and computing facilities. Many universities support start-up companies or provide services to help local businesses. There is some variation in such provision between different European countries, but the trend towards greater engagement with business and industry, and with local and regional communities and economies, is clear across the continent.

It follows that university staff are likely, in the course of their careers, to be engaged in many of these activities. In addition, many of them would – correctly – assign a high priority to their contribution to their own subject and to the advancement of knowledge within it, on a national or international scale. Such work is based within a particular higher education institution, in which the staff member is employed, and the institution may well give it financial and other support, but part of the benefit accrues to other individuals and institutions across the world and is, in a real sense, undertaken for that reason.

The typical university has thus accrued, been given or acquired, a multiplicity of tasks. It is often difficult, because the nature of the task may be loose or ill-defined – for example, "to assist regional regeneration" – to determine whether or not a particular task is being done well and even more difficult to judge – except by the most impressionistic of criteria – whether the university is performing well as a whole. There is also an obvious danger that a policy instrument or regulatory framework designed to improve performance in one area will have perverse consequences in other areas. It is arguable, at least, that the Research Assessment Exercise in the UK increased the attention paid to producing research outputs but that this occurred in some universities at the expense of attention to teaching.

The answer to the question "what are we trying to achieve?" is therefore difficult to give when the question is applied to the university as a whole or even to many individual staff within it, who may at any one time be performing a wide range of roles. But the answer to the question "what are we trying to achieve by a regulatory system?" is also problematic. Presumably a regulatory, or legislative, framework for a university system should be designed to maximise the productivity of that system, subject to budgetary constraints and to the wish at least to maintain, and if possible to increase, the quality of the output that is produced. In other words, even a regulatory system which is devised primarily to increase accountability for the use of public funds, or to provide more information to parents or consumers, should pass the test that it is a good investment of time, money and effort by university staff, because it has produced a measurable improvement in the service offered. But what is a good investment?

It sometimes seems that, to some advocates of regulatory systems, there is no limit to the expenditure, the investment, that should be made in order to achieve an improvement in service. The prime example of this tendency is advocacy of improvements to health and safety, where it is argued by some – often university health and safety staff, encouraged by national agencies for health and safety – that there should be no limit to the expenditure undertaken to reduce to zero the risk of an accident occurring. This argument implies that the value of a human life, or even of the impairment caused by a less-than-fatal accident, is infinite. Similarly, some advocates of the provision of access for those with disabilities argue that expenditure for this purpose must be undertaken, regardless of its cost or of the number likely to make use of the provision, because access on equal terms is a right. It therefore becomes, in this view, an absolute duty to abide by a regulation, irrespective of its cost.

While these are extreme views, they are certainly not unknown. A milder answer to the question "what is a good investment?" or "how much should we spend on an improvement in quality/access/research output?" is that the investment should be justifiable in economic terms, achieving or being predicted to achieve a return at least equivalent to the long-term discount rate, adding to the net present value of the asset or activity concerned. This gives a standard against which a regulatory system can be judged – although there seem to be few if any examples of such a judgment – which is possibly more precise than the weakest answer to the question "what are we trying to achieve?" which is: to make things better.

The question of the costs of regulation is discussed further below. But, whichever standard for investment is applied, a regulatory system – as Le Grand emphasises – has to be designed to work with the raw material – the people – of the system in question. Should university staff be seen as knights or knaves? What is their view of themselves? What is the view of outsiders and, particularly, governments and regulators?

Knights or knaves: the view from inside

In the second chapter of his book, Le Grand (2003, pp. 23-38) surveys a wide range of literature on the topic of the motivation of public servants and, more generally, on those people who give to charity in ways which supplement or replace public services. He concludes that (2003, p. 38):

> "There are three key conclusions. The first and most important – although perhaps the least surprising – is that altruistic behaviour exists. People can behave as knights, and indeed frequently do so, even in situations where their actions are diametrically opposed to those that would further their self-interest. Moreover, those motivations appear to be prevalent among providers in the public sector, although interacting in complex ways with more self-centred motivations.

> Second, there are, at least in principle, different kinds of knights, motivated by different considerations. In particular, there are act-irrelevant knights, motivated by compassion or feelings of injustice but not necessarily by the need to perform knightly acts themselves. And there are act-relevant knights, individuals in part motivated by the same considerations as the act-irrelevant knights, but also motivated by the need to perform the helping acts themselves. This may in turn be motivated by 'warm-glow' feelings, by feelings involving the alleviation of guilt, or by feelings of duty.

> Third, the evidence suggests that much altruistic behaviour is of the act-relevant kind. This is of great importance for policy design ..."

University staff, and particularly academic staff, definitely see themselves as knights. Histories of the universities trace their origins to medieval monastic foundations, in which selfless scholars, immune to the attractions of a worldly existence, pursued their calling of instructing the young and advancing knowledge of their subject. Even though this image sometimes became tarnished, as in the colleges of Oxford and Cambridge in the eighteenth century, when worldly pleasures certainly took precedence over scholarly pursuits, the image of the selfless seeker after truth, devoted to his subject and his students, is still strongly held, at least as a model to which scholars and academics should aspire.

There is also substantial market evidence. Levels of academic pay, never generous by the standards of occupations demanding similar levels of skill or experience, have fallen substantially in real terms in recent years in most developed economies; they have fallen even further in relative terms, as income inequality has increased in countries such as the United Kingdom and the United States. The general under-investment in universities and their infrastructure, across the whole developed world, during a period when university enrolments have increased, have left university staff working in outdated and overcrowded facilities which would not be tolerated in most other service industries such as banks or retail stores. Yet academic work – outside relatively few shortage areas such as information technology or medicine – continues to be highly prized and job advertisements in subjects in the humanities and many social sciences continue to attract large numbers of applicants. The selflessness of many members of university staffs is also demonstrated by their failure, in most circumstances, to take action in support of their own incomes or conditions of service in ways which might harm their students. Trade union organisers in universities have found it almost impossible to persuade academics, and even administrative staff who have less contact with students, to take prolonged industrial action; more typical is the academic who stays at home on the day of a strike, doing some research, and then re-arranges the seminar so as not to inconvenience his class.

Further evidence can be found in the hours of work of many academic staff. The "transparency exercise", recently undertaken in UK universities as part of an attempt to establish a firm basis for establishing the costs of university activity, found that academics frequently claimed to be working for sixty or more hours per week, much of it on research but also undertaking teaching preparation and marking or other forms of assessment. It is in fact difficult to explain the generally rising productivity of academic and other university staff – in the sense that student numbers in many countries have doubled, while staff numbers have remained static – without taking account of such long hours.[25]

There can be little doubt, in addition, about the strong allegiance felt by most academics towards their subject and their research area. It is, in fact, a common complaint of rectors or vice-chancellors in many countries that their staff feel little loyalty to the institution in which they are working, by comparison to their loyalty to their academic subject. Academics will refer to themselves first as "historian" or "physicist", and only secondarily mention their university. This extra-institutional allegiance is also signalled by a very common usage among academics; if asked "how is your own work progressing?" they will assume, correctly, that the question is about their research. Their "work" of other kinds for the university is of lesser importance and there is in fact a very clear order of importance accorded to work: research is most important, supervision of research students next, teaching undergraduates next and "administration" very definitely last.

Last, academics in particular accord great importance to being considered to be "professionals" and to participating in the collegiate decision-making structures of their institutions. They resent being given orders and feel that they should be trusted to get on with doing their jobs in ways which reflect their knightly motives and their adherence to scholarly values. They have, it sometimes seems, an

---

25. It has, of course, sometimes been argued that the achievement of such productivity gains merely shows that academics and other university staff were, in the past, grossly underemployed or inefficient and that the increase in student numbers merely forced universities to achieve the same standards of efficiency as other parts of the economy.

insatiable appetite for consultation and discussion; the process of arriving at a decision can often be given an importance greater than the ultimate decision itself. Thus university management methods have to incorporate, in response to these claims to professionalism on the part of staff, a strong element of persuasion, even in cases such as the new universities of the UK where a strong managerial culture has developed. In other parts of the UK system, and in many other European countries, academic democracy remains a very strong aspect of university life, one which is much prized and defended and, in parts of eastern Europe, seen by university staff and others as a model for society as a whole.

In all these ways, it seems reasonable to conclude that university staff show strong elements of knightly behaviour. However, in Le Grand's terminology, their knightly deeds are act-relevant. That is, they derive satisfaction, and perhaps are therefore prepared to forego income and other benefits, from the act of teaching and research; they are not entirely disinterested knights, contributing to charitable purposes in some far-flung part of the world. At the very least, however, they exhibit strong allegiance to the pursuit of truth and knowledge, and to its transmission to the young through the processes of teaching and learning, and a strong sense of the behaviour acceptable to a professional.

It is, of course, possible to interpret the behaviour of academics in entirely different ways. Academics can be ferociously competitive, for example in seeking to be the first to publish a particular finding or, at seminars, in demonstrating the superiority of their intellects or knowledge. This has even led, in a number of celebrated cases, to the fabrication of evidence and research findings. Academics can also be competitive on behalf of their students, in ways which are not in any sense disinterested but which suggest that they see successful students as a credit to themselves. In their research activity, they clearly derive a great deal of psychic satisfaction – and sometimes monetary gain – from the act of discovery, the feeling that they are the first person in the world to think a particular thought, discover a particular text or artefact or write down a particular theorem. In addition, it is clear that academics, like other professionals, can be ingenious and determined in defence of their own privileges and ways of working.[26] In such a view, academics and other university staff are knavish in many ways, but adept at concealing their knavish attitudes behind a façade of knightly rhetoric. As was discussed above, Moran (2003) sees the research assessment exercise in the UK as an example of "regulatory capture" precisely because of the success of the elite universities in emphasising a particular form of assessment based on scholarly peer review, although he is careful not to accuse anyone of bad faith in this respect.

Other examples of behaviour by academics do tarnish the knightly image. There have been a number of well-reported incidents of academics seeking sexual or financial favours from students and allegations of corruption more generally in the award of degrees. One argument for the extension of quality assurance to doctoral degrees has also been that there is too much opportunity for corruption under the

---

26. Every academic readily recognises, in his colleagues if not in himself, the academic politician so beautifully described by F.M. Cornford in *Microcosmographia academica* (Johnson, 1994).

current examining arrangements in a number of countries, where the supervisor of the doctoral student is directly involved in the award of the degree.

Nevertheless, and probably with some justice, the self-image of academics and of other university staff definitely contains a very strong element of knightly behaviour, linked in their minds to professional status, a regard for truth in research and care for their students. How far is this self-image accepted by others outside "the academy" and used in the design and operation of regulatory systems?

Knights or knaves: the view from outside

The most obvious indicator of the attitude of outsiders to the workings of universities and the behaviour of academics lies in the development of quality assurance systems throughout Europe and, to different degrees, in other parts of the world. One motive for the introduction of explicit quality assurance methods is to provide comparability between the standards applied in different countries, so as to facilitate mobility through the Socrates/Erasmus programmes of the European Union. But although this motive has received substantial attention through the Bologna Process, it cannot alone account for the growth of quality assurance agencies and the emphasis on quality assurance processes throughout Europe. It seems clear that, throughout Europe, governments and ministries of education are questioning whether universities can be trusted to guarantee the quality of the degrees that they are awarding.[27]

Part of the reason for these questions lies in the very success of the universities in expanding their student numbers and their role within society and the economy. When universities were small institutions, catering to an elite group of students and largely devoted to replicating themselves by producing graduates who would then enter university or school teaching, together with a small number of privileged occupations such as the church or the senior civil service, society and government could afford to let them regulate themselves. Now, however, when close to 50% of cohorts of young people are entering universities in many European countries, education has become a major political issue. Moreover, the fact that graduates are now entering a much wider range of occupations than used to be the case, and that those graduates come from a much larger number and range of universities and colleges, has increased the pressure for explicit means of assessing and guaranteeing quality and for comparisons between universities. It is no coincidence that university league tables based on indicators of university output and quality are popular in many countries. This also accounts for the recent discussion,

---

27. Concern about quality assurance is being expressed beyond Europe. The *Times Higher Education Supplement* reported (13 August 2004, p. 11) that "The Bush administration and Republicans in the US Congress want university accreditation reports – mostly confidential – to be made available to students and their parents. For more than a century, no one has monitored university quality except associations of the universities themselves, in a secretive accreditation process that is largely independent of the Government ... The controversy over the accrediting process has ignited a debate about the question of how universities, whose tuition fees are rocketing and graduating rates dropping, should be regulated."

stimulated by the Netherlands Government, about the development of a typology of university institutions.

Essentially, the growth of quality assurance agencies or similar bodies in so many different countries signals that society has lost confidence in the ability of the universities to regulate themselves and to guarantee the quality of what they do. The universities have lost the privileges of the elite – the ability to say to the rest of society: "trust us" – and now and in the future will have to justify themselves and what they do. This is a symptom, though much more widely spread, of what Moran (2003) identifies as the collapse of the "club culture", by which supposedly democratic societies were actually ruled by tacit alliances of the privileged, of which university staff were certainly a part. In this sense, the growth of quality assurance suggests that university staff were considered, by the rest of society, as remiss knights, not doing their jobs properly, even if not as knaves.

There is little doubt that, in the UK, such attitudes to the need for explicit, and independent, guarantees of quality in teaching were encouraged – in a perfect example of the perverse consequences of regulation – by the system of research assessment which preceded the system of Teaching Quality Assessment by some years. The argument ran as follows. The universities receive money for teaching according to the numbers of students, which are heavily controlled. Their only chance of gaining extra resources lay with a good performance on the research assessment exercise. Therefore they put all their efforts into research and neglected teaching. Therefore they must be held to account by external inspection of their quality of teaching.

In fact, again in the UK, the introduction of the Research Assessment Exercise also signalled a lack of trust in the use of the research funds given to universities by the funding councils. It will be recalled that, until the introduction of the RAE, it had been assumed that all university teachers would, together with their teaching, be undertaking research and that this should be paid for – in the pre-1992 universities – by the state. The RAE, although described from the outset as merely a means of allocating research funding, in fact incorporated the view that, while perhaps all university teachers should be doing research, many of them were not doing so and many more were not doing it very well. Therefore it was necessary, the argument ran, to cease to fund those who were not "research-active" and to discriminate on grounds of quality between the others. Over time, this led to the denial – explicitly in the UK Government White Paper in 2003 – of the importance of the link between teaching and research which lay at the basis of the Humboldtian system and which had been an article of faith in the universities for many years.

In the space of twenty years, therefore, in the UK and in a number of other European countries, external and governmental opinion has moved from a general acceptance of the quality of university teaching and research and of the ability of universities and their staffs to regulate themselves, towards a demand that universities should submit to external verification of their core activities of teaching and research. It is difficult to see this as other than a lack of trust, a judgment that university staffs were, at least, errant knights.

Indeed, it is arguable that one aspect of the public view of academics is that they are best seen as incompetent knaves. This arises in part from the public depiction, in many Hollywood films and in television series such as *Brideshead Revisited* or *Inspector Morse,* of academics as inhabiting a wonderland of beautiful buildings, filled with effete undergraduates; the academics spend much of their time eating and drinking while engaging in clever word-play. While these images derive from out-of-date impressions of a few elite universities, academics in general are seen – probably rightly – as enjoying the immense privilege of controlling their own lives, working as and when, and on what subjects they choose. In this view, the poor pay of academics – seen above as market evidence of their knightly status – becomes instead either a sign of incompetence on their part or as more than compensated by their favourable working conditions. If academics complain, as they frequently do, about the decline in their conditions, this is viewed as "whingeing" in view of the privileges which they still retain and, in the view of some, abuse. On this view, they need to be regulated to force them to do their jobs.

Nothing is ever simple and, just at the time that external regulation of quality in teaching and research was gaining momentum in the 1980s and 1990s, another series of changes in governmental attitudes took place which might, at first, seem to be contradictory. These were the moves, in a number of countries, to give greater independence and autonomy to universities which had hitherto been closely controlled by the state. Presumably, it could be argued, states would not cede their powers to institutions which they felt could not be trusted.

However, it is important to examine the motives behind the granting of increased autonomy. In Austria, for example, the ties between the state and the universities have been loosened, but the novel feature of the reforms has been the introduction of university boards, with a membership drawn both from the state and from independents such as business people, together with an elected rector. Thus the reform is loosening the direct control of the state, but not ceding that control to the traditional collegium of academics, rather to an enhanced managerial control. This had also been the model followed in the statutes of the new universities in the UK.

A further motive behind increased autonomy has been to enhance competition. This motive lies squarely within the concepts of the new public management, that institutions need to be empowered to compete and that this will, in itself, enhance the quality of whatever it is that they are doing. In one sense, therefore, the emphasis on competition and differentiation – universities "playing to their strengths" as it was put in the UK Government White Paper – is designed, if not to turn university staff themselves into knaves, certainly to ensure that their universities behave like knaves, pursuing their own interest and self-advantage at the expense of others. UK ministers have explicitly envisaged, and accepted, that this process might lead to the collapse and closure of individual universities, but that this would be acceptable if it led to an overall improvement through the effects of competition and consumer choice.

In parenthesis, this view gives rise to an interesting question about Le Grand's model. He is concerned throughout his book with individual motivation. But it is at least possible that there could be knavish institutions, perhaps led by knavish rectors or vice-chancellors, who pursued their individual competitive advantage, while their staffs remained imbued with knightly motives, caring for their students and their research and protecting them against the depredations of their knavish leaders. Certainly, in the UK case, the government – and some vice-chancellors – believe fervently in the virtues of competition, which is difficult to reconcile with knightly behaviour. Meanwhile other vice-chancellors preach the benefits of collaboration, for example so that universities can work together to help a local economy. Finally, members of university staff forge research collaboration with staff in supposedly rival and competitive institutions.[28]

Leaving this aside, the whole tenor of government attitudes to higher education, in a number of different countries, seems to be that university staff are either indolent – perhaps a hangover from days gone by – or at least could be made to behave better if they were treated as knaves. Thus they have to be inspected and graded, subject to audit and innumerable accountability procedures which imply that they cannot be trusted, and meanwhile encouraged to compete. Even if the ethos of university staff is one that rejects the primacy of market mechanisms, they must be forced to behave as if the market rules.

Queens or pawns: the role of students

Le Grand rightly emphasises that the design of regulatory systems depends not only on the motivation of providers but also on the role of consumers. As he points out, one of the main features of the reform of public services which has occurred in the UK in recent years is the empowerment of consumers, who have been turned in his words from pawns to queens. No longer are they the passive recipients of the decisions of experts – be they doctors or teachers; they can now play a role in determining the nature and level of the service that they receive. Le Grand makes it wholly clear that he sympathises with this change.

Students have long played a role within higher education that is significantly different from that of a passive recipient of a service, a pawn in the hands of their teachers. The students in Plato's Academy played a vital role in questioning their teacher and the same tradition imbued the medieval universities, even if some accounts of the behaviour of students suggests that scholarly modesty was at times far from their minds. There certainly were periods, as in the doldrums of Oxford

---

28. Le Grand does briefly consider (2003, pp. 62-64) the possible role of non-profit organisations in the delivery of public services. As he points out, the main distinction between a for-profit and a non-profit organisation, in this context, lies not so much in the motivation of the employees as in the fact that a non-profit organisation does not have to distribute a profit to shareholders. But he rightly shows that this does not mean that the managers of a non-profit organisation are motivated by altruism. Nor, he might have added, can one assume – in the light of recent scandals such as Enron – that the managers of for-profit organisations feel any real responsibility to shareholders.
29. An interesting survival of this practice is the requirement that trainee barristers (advocates in the higher courts) in England should eat a certain number of dinners in an Inn of Court, an association of barristers, before being allowed to practise.

and Cambridge in the eighteenth century, when students appear to have done little study, merely putting in obligatory attendance for a minimum period before being awarded their degree.[29] But there were also periods when, in some countries, the students were close to being in charge of the university, employing their teachers. This diversity of historical practice continued in the twentieth century, with students in the UK having a relatively subordinate role as compared with students in countries affected by the troubles of 1968. In almost all cases, student representatives play a role in governing councils or their equivalent, but this role varies from an equality with representatives of the staff and of the management or rectorate, on the one hand, to the membership by one student within a Board of Governors of twenty-five or more. Nevertheless, almost all universities make provision for some student representation on course boards or their equivalent, as well as on committees concerned with aspects of particular interest to students, such as welfare services. In many universities, finally, student unions have considerable power and influence. It is because of these multifarious ways in which students take part in university life, sometimes in full partnership with staff, that most academics resist the notion that students should be described (or thought of) as consumers or customers.

Differences in the formal power accorded to students do not necessarily match closely to the actual role of students in the learning process. Thus some universities accord considerable power to students in formal university bodies, but rely on pedagogic methods which accord little power to students, regarding them as passive recipients of knowledge disseminated to large lecture audiences. Others, such as Oxford and Cambridge, accord little power or influence to student representatives but make use of pedagogic methods which require students, in ones or twos, to discuss or argue with a tutor on a weekly basis. Similarly, pedagogic methods range from the use of a single textbook, perhaps written by the lecturer, with little or no required written work, through to the production of a weekly essay based on substantial research in primary and secondary materials.

Despite these differences, sometimes between and sometimes within higher education systems in different European countries, it would be difficult to see many examples of students being viewed entirely as passive consumers, as pawns in Le Grand's terminology. Even if to different degrees, all universities regard their role as to develop a critical ability in their students, to foster independent thought and to help to shape future functioning members of democratic societies. While a teacher may occasionally react badly to his or her ideas being questioned by a student, most will welcome such signs of critical thought. In recent years, the advent of the Internet has greatly expanded the capacity of students to access information from a wide variety of sources and, in general, universities have welcomed this and adapted their pedagogic methods to take advantage of this fact.[30]

---

30. Some have had more difficulty with the role of the Internet in encouraging plagiarism, but this is actually a minor disadvantage of a technological innovation which, like all such, can be used for evil as well as for good.

155

Even if few students can be viewed as pawns, there do remain questions about the amount of information to which they are given access, for example about the courses available at a particular university. Even more contentiously, there are signs of the rise of "consumer power" in universities in the sense of students arguing that they have not received a service for which they have paid.

In the UK, as was described above, the latest agreement between the universities and government in the field of quality control incorporates, together with audit of institutions, the requirement on them to provide a large volume of Teaching Quality Information (TQI). The Internet has made it possible to do this, but it remains an open question as to who will seek to use this information, which will be very bulky indeed; even only 50 pieces of data about each UK undergraduate course, of which there are 50 000, amounts to a database of 2.5 million items. It is unclear whether, again, parents – who appear to be playing a greater and greater role in their child's choice of course – will use this information, or whether it will similarly be used by employers seeking information about the courses that prospective employees have taken. If the government's hopes are justified, and at the time of writing it has still not been possible to reach full agreement on the data to be made available, then one can imagine that this experiment may be extended on a European scale.

Much more contentious is the issue of the amount of information to which students should be entitled about the academic decisions, for example the grades awarded, which affect them individually or collectively. This intersects with the question of whether students have "got what they paid for" since naturally students who are satisfied on the latter point are unlikely to be unhappy about a grade. The UK has, within the past year, seen legal action taken against a university on the basis that the course did not match the description given of it; in another case, a group of students have taken legal action because a course did not, as they allege was promised, give exemption from professional examinations. These are, for the moment, isolated examples, but they do suggest that consumerism is gaining momentum in higher education and that universities are unlikely to be able to get away with claiming that students are not contractually entitled to a service and are, instead, partners in an academic enterprise. Universities have, so far, been able to avoid legal challenge to "academic" decisions, such as an examination mark, but this may not remain possible. It will be interesting to see whether student behaviour, in this respect, is altered by the advent of (or increase in) tuition fees in a number of European countries. Experience in the United States, and in countries such as the UK where fees have been charged for some courses for many years, does not suggest that there is likely to be a flood of litigation, but time will tell.

All in all, it would seem that students – and other users of services provided by universities, such as industrial companies – are already much closer, in Le Grand's terminology, to queens rather than pawns. Where does that lead in the design of appropriate regulatory systems?

Regulatory systems for European higher education

In *Motivation, agency and public policy* (2003), Julian Le Grand follows his discussion of motivation and agency by considering appropriate forms of regulation in primary and secondary education and in the health service in the UK. He concludes his discussion of agency – of the behaviour of consumers – by asserting the importance of considering the consumers of public services to be queens rather than pawns; they need to be empowered to play a full role in the design and operation of public services and the regulatory systems set up for these purposes.

Le Grand's conclusion about the motivation of public servants is more complex (2003, p. 67):

> "The evidence concerning the relationship between financial rewards and the supply of public services suggests that there may be reward thresholds above and below which behaviour is rather different. Below the lower threshold, financial rewards may be viewed as reinforcing or crowding-in supply, since they signify social approval of the sacrifice the individual is making in pursuing his or her activities. Extra payments above that threshold, however, erode the magnitude of the sacrifice that he or she is making, and thereby partly erode the motivation for the act. Supply is crowded out. However, as payments increase further, another threshold is reached where the relative price effect begins to dominate the crowding-out effect and supply increases again.

> If policy-makers know where the thresholds are for an individual or a group of individuals, it is relatively easy to design a payment system that elicits the supply of the activity that we want (although the impact of any payment system on quality as well as quantity has to be borne in mind). If we do not know the underlying motivational structure, then the best strategy is likely to be the adoption of robust incentive structures: ones designed to align knightly and knavish motivations and to appeal to both the knight and the knave. Although these may be difficult to design, it is not impossible to do so ..."

In the case of higher education, the discussion above has concluded that students and other consumers of higher education services can unambiguously be assumed to be queens rather than pawns. As with the other public services considered by Le Grand, the position with academics and other university staff is more ambiguous; there are strong arguments for considering them to be knights rather than knaves, but also strong arguments for recognising that some of their behaviour is knavish and that they are certainly not immune to normal incentive structures.

However, the importance of the self-image of university staff as knightly and disinterested seekers after truth, professional in their ethics and their approach to their job, should not be underestimated. It suggests that any regulatory system that does not recognise, and try to build upon, that self-image will be resisted and may well be subverted to the point where it fails to succeed. It is essential to design regulatory systems in this light.

Regulatory systems in higher education have to take account, also, of general principles and good practice. In the UK, the experience of designing such systems over the past two decades has been to some extent codified. The government has established a Better Regulation Task Force, composed of independent men and women from business and the public services, to seek good practice and to comment on particular regulations. The task force has published a set of principles for good regulation (BRTF, 2002). Regulatory systems should be:

- *"Proportionate:* Regulators should only intervene when necessary. Remedies should be appropriate to the risks posed, and costs identified and minimised.

- *Accountable:* Regulators must be able to justify decisions, and be subject to public scrutiny.

- *Consistent:* Government rules and standards must be joined up and implemented fairly

- *Transparent:* Regulators should be open, and keep regulations simple and user friendly

- *Targeted:* Regulation should be focused on the problem, and minimise side effects."

The task force has also conducted a special enquiry into the regulation of higher education (BRTF, 2002). They concluded that the current system in the UK did not meet these principles and that the sector was over-regulated, in particular because of the many different demands for accountability and information from different regulators. In addition, they concurred with the National Audit Office, the government agency which inspects and audits all public bodies, that universities were a "low-risk activity" and that this should be taken fully into account in the design of regulatory systems.

All this suggests that the regulation of higher education should be based on trust that the behaviour of academic and other staff will be professional – knights – and that the "consumers" of university services will be active and participative – queens. In the light of the account, given above, of the development of regulation, this is a challenging conclusion; it flies in the face of much of the motivation for the introduction of a regulatory system, the breakdown of trust in university staff and the systems which they administer.

Some may find the conclusion that we should trust university staff to be unacceptable. At the least, however, audit and other regulatory systems should exert a "light touch"; this will recognise that the vast majority of behaviour in higher education is excellent or at least satisfactory and that heavy-handed regulatory systems are unlikely, therefore, to meet the task force's principle of proportionality. It is always important to remember that the expenditure of about £1 billion on the Teaching Quality Assessments of every UK academic department concluded that 98% of the provision was satisfactory or excellent. This was a clear example of regulatory overkill.

This leads to another aspect of proportionality, that of the cost of regulation. When, some five years ago, the UK higher education system attempted to cost the regulatory regime which was then current, it was the first public service in the UK to do so. It emerged at the time that the costs were approximately equivalent to 2% of the total expenditure of the system; unfortunately, no one at the time was able to say whether this was too large, too small, or about right. There are certainly some advocates of regulation, particularly in the field of quality control, who do not believe that there should be any limit on expenditure in this area; we should, on this view, spend whatever is needed, just as we should on health and safety. It is to be hoped that saner counsels will prevail; on one view, every euro spent on regulation is a euro not spent on teaching, learning and research and this opportunity cost has to be recognised.

What then should be the methods of regulation in higher education, recognising that they will differ according to the activity being regulated, that their cost must be limited and that they will rely at least to some degree on trusting university staff?

First, the financial and other affairs of universities should be regulated and audited in exactly the same way, and to the same standards, as other large institutions in the private sector. That is, independent auditors should assure themselves – and give assurance to government and other grant-giving bodies – that there is no evidence of fraud and that the accounts of universities are clear and transparent.

Second, independent auditors should assure themselves that funds are being properly applied to the purposes for which they were granted. It is important to recognise, however, that this is an additional requirement imposed on institutions receiving funds – above that imposed on most private-sector organisations – and that it must therefore be applied with sensitivity and in ways which do not stifle activity and overburden the institution concerned. It will normally be sufficient – since the risks of misuse of public funds appear to be low – to cover this aspect of the work of universities by intermittent sample surveys and certainly not to inspect every aspect of activity each year.

Third, in the field of quality assurance, the primary responsibility for providing and demonstrating high quality must lie with the university itself and external agencies should seek to bolster this responsibility rather than undermine it. A very few examples of corruption aside, university staff take great pride in delivering a professional service and in assessing their students fairly. They should be left to get on with this job, provided that they accept external scrutiny by other academics – from their own or other institutions – and that they expose their methods to the scrutiny of students and others – such as parents and employers – with a legitimate interest. If this is done, and assured by regular but infrequent institutional audit, then there is absolutely no need for external course accreditation or universal Teaching Quality Assessment.

Fourth, in the field of research, the allocation of funds should continue to rely on peer review but should be based on the prospective funding of projects (on the evidence of a plan, regular monitoring and the production of a final report) rather than on funding on the basis of past performance. This does not denote lack of trust but merely good practice in planning and execution of research projects. Research and teaching should continue to be seen as essential contributors to each other, but this does not preclude the need for each to be planned and carried out effectively.

Fifth, regulatory and financial systems should ensure that academic and other staff in universities are sufficiently well paid, and have sufficiently good working conditions, to attract well-qualified applicants to work in universities. Where universities are autonomous and can seek their own funds, this can be left to the market, but it does imply that it may be necessary – because the market will be different in respect of different academic subjects – to reward academics differentially; systems which paid every academic equally cannot survive the transition to a mass higher education system. In systems where governments retain financial control, they will have to recognise the imperatives of the market. Above all, knightly behaviour by university staff should be recognised and celebrated, but not exploited.

Sixth, the principles of good regulation, and the low risks attaching to universities, imply that subsidiarity should be the guiding principle. That is, it is a mistake to seek solutions at a European level when the problems are being effectively addressed at a national, regional or institutional level. There may, of course, be examples where countries or institutions fall below an acceptable standard, but these are likely to be exceptions to be treated by the combined action of peers, rather than by an overarching system imposed on all institutions by external authority such as national governments or the European Union.

Seventh, students should be further empowered to influence institutions towards greater transparency in making academic and other decisions. They should be given the information that they need to choose a course and then participate effectively in teaching and learning. They should also, despite the difficulties in practice, be expected to participate in the governance of institutions and in the monitoring of activity.

Conclusion

The transition from provision to regulation in the higher education systems of Europe is throwing up a fascinating set of challenges in the design of new systems. This paper has sought to identify these challenges and to tease out the assumptions about human behaviour, in particular of university staff and students, which are crucial to the design of systems that will work and that will not be excessively burdensome or expensive. Its central message is that regulatory systems must proceed on a basis of trust – of the professionalism of university staff and the effective participation of students – unless they are to be bureaucratic, inefficient and even counterproductive.

The paper has not been able to consider all the implications of the move from provision to regulation. In particular, there has been little discussion of the changes that will be required in the governance of universities. This is the subject of study by another working group of the Council of Europe and will be the topic of another similar conference.

There are, of course, no easy answers to the question of how to design effective regulatory systems. The central lesson of Julian Le Grand's analysis of knights or knaves, queens or pawns, and of this paper, is that we must take account of human behaviour, human motivation and history. Pride in a good job done, pride in professionalism, pride in helping students to learn, are all good emotions, but also fragile ones. It would be a disaster for higher education if obtrusive regulation were to destroy them.

References

BRTF (Better Regulation Task Force), *Higher education: easing the burden,* London, 2002.

Floud, R. and Johnson, P. (eds), *The Cambridge economic history of modern Britain,* Cambridge University Press, Cambridge, 2004.

Hannah, L., "A failed experiment: the state ownership of industry", in Floud, R. and Johnson, P., (eds), *The Cambridge economic history of modern Britain,* Cambridge University Press, Cambridge, 2004, Vol. III, pp. 84-111.

HEFCE (Higher Education Funding Council for England), *Review of research,* HEFCE, Bristol, 2000/37.

HEFCE (Higher Education Funding Council for England), *Performance indicators in higher education in the UK,* HEFCE, Bristol, 2002/52.

HEFCE (Higher Education Funding Council for England), *Funding higher education in England,* HEFCE, Bristol, 2003/29.

Johnson, G., *University politics: F.M. Cornford's Cambridge and his advice to the young academic politician,* containing the complete text of Cornford's "Microcosmographia academica", Cambridge University Press, Cambridge, 1994.

Lambert, R., *Lambert review of business-university collaboration,* HM Treasury, London, 2004.

Le Grand, J., *Motivation, agency and public policy: of knights and knaves, pawns and queens,* Oxford University Press, Oxford, 2003.

Moran, M., *The British regulatory state: high modernism and hyper-innovation,* Oxford University Press, Oxford, 2003.

O'Hara, K., *Trust: from Socrates to Spin,* Icon Books, Cambridge, 2004.

O'Neill, O., *A question of trust: the BBC Reith Lectures 2002,* Cambridge University Press, Cambridge, 2002.

Power, M., *The audit society: rituals of verification,* Oxford University Press, Oxford, 1997.

Public responsibility for research and access to research results

Jaak Aaviksoo

Introduction

Since ancient times knowledge has been considered to be a public good freely available to all members of the community through education. The only, however substantial, barrier to the general availability was due to restricted access to education for a big majority of the population. The saying *scientia est potentia* reflects the importance given to knowledge in those days. At the same time the advancement of knowledge was more a matter of individual (noble) motivation and commitment than a community effort. The same was largely true throughout the Middle Ages with the exception of the scholarly (and scholastic) activities supported by the Church. A major shift in this pattern was brought about by the Enlightenment. Since then, the advancement of knowledge has been gradually perceived as the universal source of human progress and thus considered both a public good and a public responsibility. Making knowledge accessible to everybody through education, and the advancement of knowledge a publicly acknowledged noble mission of the educated, prepared the ground for the industrial revolution and, later, the Knowledge Society as we know it today. At the same time, knowledge production still remained largely driven by the curiosity of the academics until Napoleon established the *Grandes écoles* and later the Humboldtian concept of a research university was born. By this means knowledge was not only recognised as a public good but also as a national asset to build an economically and militarily strong nation state. State-funded research was born in parallel with national universities. Science and scholarship in the service of truth acquired the first features of research in the service of stakeholders.

While knowledge was always somewhat "spiritual", know-how was very "material". It was always considered to be proprietary – a private good – and subject to secrecy. Generations of craftsmen and industries made their living and fortune on carefully guarded know-how until governments introduced the patenting mechanisms to offer legal protection of what we today call intellectual property rights. Know-how has been considered not only a private good but an unquestionable commercial asset and legal protection has been provided to afford its use for economic profit.

The worlds of knowledge and know-how, scientist-scholars and inventors-engineers hardly overlapped. It may be disputed when these worlds started to come closer to each other but one of the milestones is clearly the famous report by Vannevar Bush,

Science: the endless frontier. The report was clearly influenced by the reflections on the role of research and related military innovations – German V-missiles, British radar and, last but not least, the American atomic bomb – in the outcomes of the Second World War. It laid down the principles of organisation of public basic and applied research to the benefit of national security as well as national economy. These principles are still valid and a good proof of this is the ongoing discussion around the establishment of the European Research Council following the model of the National Science Foundation proposed by Vannevar Bush in 1947.

The last two decades have seen an unprecedented growth in the impact of research, technological development and innovation on economic growth and social development. Progress in chemical and electrical engineering, basic research breakthroughs in physics resulting in modern semiconductor and optoelectronic devices and the resultant information revolution, and most recently the progress in biotechnologies, leaves no doubt about research and technological innovation becoming the most important factor of economic growth and social development. In accordance with these developments, national spending on research and development has steadily grown over the past two decades and reached about 3% of GDP in the United States and 2% in the EU, of which 1% is public spending in both cases.

The emergence of the knowledge economy and society, however, has thoroughly changed the relationship between basic and applied research, science and technology, and consequently, between knowledge and know-how – it is no longer possible to differentiate between these two, at least not in an unambiguous way. The increased inter-relatedness of research and technological development has in turn mixed public and private interests and responsibilities. At the same time the process of globalisation and resultant international competition has increased the pressures on national governments to reduce the costs of labour and capital and to lower corporate tax levels, which in turn reduce possible public spending on research as well as (higher) education. To get a more comprehensive picture we have to take into account the pressures on individual researchers and public research institutions, including universities, to generate more income from commercialisation of their research results. It becomes more and more evident that the historical framework of doing research based on good academic and corporate practice is becoming obsolete together with the corresponding national policies and, possibly, legislation.

All this calls for a serious reconsideration of the balance between public and private interests, rights and responsibilities. This in turn impacts on a wide spectrum of public policies: from research and development (R&D), intellectual property rights (IPR) and education to public health and security. In the following report we are going to touch upon a few issues related to public responsibility for research and access to research results.

Public responsibility for research

Research as a public good

Economists have a number of theoretical arguments in support of the public good character of research and its results – knowledge as well as know-how. This means that when left to market forces alone, society tends to under-invest in R&D thus slowing down economic growth. It is therefore a public responsibility to facilitate more research by either funding it or carrying it out itself and, in addition, by creating incentives for the private sector to invest more in research. The latter is done through various tax incentives and by protecting proprietary rights to research results such as by establishing patent offices.

Right to education

One of the basic human rights is the right to education. We understand education as a generally free and publicly facilitated access to the global wealth of knowledge humankind has created through practical experience and research. If this free access to the body of human knowledge is limited, we are effectively stripped of the right to education. It is, of course, true that education is essentially also a private good but at least on the level of compulsory education it is delivered as a public service. Furthermore, even on the level of higher education it is unthinkable that the students would have to buy, in addition to paying tuition fees to the universities, the content from proprietary sources. Contemporary education, especially at university level, entails research education, that is, access to research (facilities) is a prerequisite of quality education. We may conclude that extensive privatisation of research and commodification of its results threatens the right to education and calls for some intervention.

Security risks

It is evident that scientific research may bring about discoveries that threaten public security on local as well as global scales adding the high-tech terrorism threat to the present security risks. With the present terrorist practices at hand we have to be extremely cautious and control, and possibly limit, private research in potentially dangerous domains at the global level. It is also a security concern in the case of "rogue" or failed states and asks for international effort for an effective containment and possibly elimination of these threats.

Ethical risks

A serious ethical concern is related to the limits to free research into potentially dangerous areas such as stem cells or human cloning. Is a public ban on this research a solution or rather an increased threat through moving the unwelcome research into closed private laboratories or other, potentially dangerous, states? It is a public responsibility to reduce these risks to a minimum.

Reputation and credibility

The reputation and credibility of science and scientists relies heavily on two principles – openness and impartiality. The principle of verification lies at the very heart of the scientific method – every scientific result has to be accessible for unlimited verification and public scrutiny before it establishes itself as a reliable result. Inability to guarantee that access reduces the reliability of the results and decreases the general credibility of science. The same results from the lack of impartiality which is easily incurred by accepting private funding in a combination with limited publication of the results. There is a great danger that as a result of uncontrolled and unlimited privatisation of research science at large loses its public credibility and therefore fails to fulfil its mission as an objective and impartial source of reliable information, especially in the face of serious threats to the public interest such as global warming, genetic manipulations or nuclear energy.

Motivation and temptation

Science is about serving the truth. It is therefore of the utmost importance that scientists are subject to transparent and unquestionable motivation patterns that leave as little room as possible to undue temptations. It is a public as well as private responsibility to create such working conditions for the employed researchers that they can freely engage in the pursuit of truth without being forced or tempted to compromise. It is clear that no research is safe from fraud but evidence shows that it occurs more often when motivation schemes are unbalanced with too high an emphasis on personal return coupled with proprietary secrecy and no public scrutiny. It is a public responsibility to create motivation schemes that uncompromisingly award academic excellence as established by peer-review evaluations.

Critical thinking and autonomy

An indispensable part of scientific culture is the culture of critical thinking and freedom of expression. Critical thinking and freedom of expression provide for the sustainability of reliable research through continuous challenging of the (academic) establishment. In order to be able to do that, research and researchers need sufficient autonomy from all stakeholders. This autonomy must be a public concern and clearly guaranteed by appropriate legislation not only in the case of public but even more so in the case of private research.

Researcher training

In order to meet the increasing demand for research output, a growing number of new researchers is needed. The training of new researchers is first and foremost a public responsibility and is carried out in (public) universities by increasing their capacity for Ph.D. training through the establishment of (international) graduate schools, development of centres of excellence coupled to (international) academic mobility and other instruments. Taking into account the (potential) interest of private research in researcher training the possibilities of various public-private partnership schemes must be explored.

Access to research results

As a crude approximation, research output can be classified as public or proprietary. The problem of access to research results clearly has different aspects in the two cases and they will be analysed separately. It must, however, be mentioned that the most complicated problems arise in the case of mixed public-private research projects. In the present report we are only able to indicate some of the problems to be solved in the latter case.

Access to public research results

It is a long established understanding that the results of any publicly funded research must be made available to the public, as a rule by publishing them in an academic journal. Over the last decade there has been a growing discontent in the academic community with the policies of the major publishing companies who charge academic libraries and other subscribers disproportionately high subscription rates, thereby limiting free access to the results of public research. The conflict is further aggravated by the fact that the publishers effectively expropriate the research results from the researchers and/or respective research institutions by requiring the transfer of the copyright to the publisher. As a result, free dissemination of research results is seriously hindered and made dependent on the marketing policies of the major publishers developed in order to maximise their profits. This conflict has forced the academic community to look for alternative publishing channels, first of all by using modern information and communication technologies. In recent years several initiatives have been launched to move to what is called "open access publishing". One of the first efforts was undertaken by the Scholarly Publishing and Academic Resources Coalition SPARC®, launched in 1998, whose "agenda focuses on enhancing broad and cost-effective access to peer-reviewed scholarship".[31] In February 2002 the Budapest Open Access Initiative[32] was signed and by today it has collected 3 718 signatories. In June 2003 the Bethesda Statement on Open Access Publishing[33] was signed and in October 2003 the Max-Planck Society initiated the Berlin Declaration on Open Access to Knowledge in the Sciences and Humanities.[34] This last document clearly defines the open access contribution.

"Open access contributions must satisfy two conditions:

– the author(s) and right holder(s) of such contributions grant(s) to all users a free, irrevocable, worldwide right of access to, and a license to copy, use, distribute, transmit and display the work publicly and to make and distribute derivative works, in any digital medium for any responsible purpose, subject to proper attribution of authorship (community standards will continue to provide the mechanism for enforcement of proper attribution and responsible use of the published work, as they do now), as well as the right to make small numbers of printed copies for their personal use.

– a complete version of the work and all supplemental materials, including a copy of the permission as stated above, in an appropriate standard electronic format is deposited (and thus published) in at least one online repository using suitable technical standards (such as the Open Archive definitions) that is supported and maintained by an academic institution, scholarly society, government agency, or other well-established organisation that seeks to enable open access, unrestricted distribution, inter-operability, and long-term archiving."

31. http://www.arl.org/sparc/about/index.html
32. http://www.soros.org/openaccess/read.shtml
33. http://www.earlham.edu/~peters/fos/bethesda.htm
34. http://www.zim.mpg.de/openaccess-berlin/signatories.html

It seems that the open access effort is gaining momentum. It is widely supported by the academic community and is waiting for a corresponding managerial commitment to break the ice.

Access to proprietary research results. Corporate research is carried out in order to compete in the markets by innovating and thereby securing profitability, and it is only natural that the research results are considered corporate property. For centuries the patenting system has been in place to achieve two somewhat conflicting goals: to protect the proprietary interests of the patent holder and to make public and disseminate the results of proprietary research. It may be said that the patent system has functioned well by providing the necessary protection of intellectual property rights on one hand and facilitating access to the entailed information on the other hand. The number of patent applications is growing in all three major systems – Europe, the United States and Japan. At the same time an increasing number of questions are being asked concerning the foundations of the patenting institution and its implementation and ability to adapt to changing environments. The most fundamental question is: "Does the patent system favour more research and a more efficient use of research results in society at large?" At present there is no evidence-based answer to this question and so different arguments are produced both pro and contra the patent institution. One of the most recent and thorough pieces of research into the patent system was carried out by the US National Academies and published in the book *A patent system for the 21st century*.[35] It says, "We do not know if the benefits of more and stronger patents extend very far beyond a few manufacturing industries such as pharmaceuticals, chemicals, and medical devices. It is even less clear that patents induce additional research and development investment in the service industries and service functions of the manufacturing economy." At a meeting of the OECD Committee for Scientific and Technological Policy at Ministerial Level, the final communiqué says, "Patenting has accelerated rapidly in the past decade, with the number of patent applications filed in Europe, Japan and the United States increasing by 40% between 1992 and 2002, from 600000 to 850000 per year. The effects of such patenting on incentives to innovate, on the diffusion of scientific and technical knowledge and on competition remain unclear and vary across industry sectors and technological fields."[36] It may be concluded that the overall usefulness of the patent system needs further study by experts such as economists, scientists and engineers in different disciplines, inventors, business managers and legal scholars. It may be added that there is also a strong voice against intellectual property altogether (see Martin, *Against intellectual property*[37] and references therein). A similar appeal has been made by "Scientists for Global Responsibility" at the meeting "Knowledge – Common Heritage, Not Private Property".[38]

Between public and proprietary

The recent changes in the status of public universities and other public research organisations allowing them to engage more and more in revenue-generating

35. http://www.nap.edu/books/0309089107/html/
36. http://www.oecd.org/document/0,2340,en_2649_34487_25998799_1_1_1_1,00.html
37. http://www.uow.edu.au/arts/sts/bmartin/pubs/95psa.html
38. http://www.sgr.org.uk/SciencePolicy/Knowledge10Nov.html

activities in co-operation with private enterprises has created grey zones of semi-public/semi-private research. Since 1980, when American public universities were allowed to file patent applications, there has been an increasing number of patent applications by public universities in both the United States and Europe. Since it is hardly possible to trace with which funds the invention was developed there is a possibility that publicly funded research will no longer be available to the public for free use but will become proprietary. With increasing financial pressures on universities, this becomes more and more of a real perspective. And the other way around – it has been taken for granted that universities and other public entities may use patented know-how in their academic endeavours. With the increased mixing of private and public interests in the universities they may not be treated in the same way in the future. As a conclusion we may say that the present situation with intellectual property rights is far from normal and encompasses serious risks for the universities.

It is evident that in the emerging knowledge economy, research, technological development and innovation ask for an ever-increasing share of the national income. It is also evident that public spending alone cannot meet the economically and socially grounded need for research expenditure and that private interest may yield a more cost-efficient return of the research effort. Therefore, a balanced private-public partnership has to be established, including public support of private research; only, however, while bearing in mind the aforementioned risks that call for sensible public control of the whole research organisation and a far-reaching revision of intellectual property rights. Inability to do so may well result in conflicts and court cases.

In addition to the general and financial questions discussed above, there are several ethical issues that need to be addressed. The most important one is to what extent private knowledge may be used for (unlimited) private profit, as for instance in the case of vaccines and drugs to fight such diseases as Aids.

Conclusion

The recent global trends have raised a number of questions concerning increased public responsibility for research and research results, which entail both huge public and private benefits but may also pose serious threats to the public interest. It is evident that we need a more thorough public debate of these issues to avoid unexpected outcomes of the privately driven knowledge economy and public discontent with misuse of the new knowledge. These threats call for stronger public control of research organisation at the national but also international level. This in turn is impossible without strong and competent public research institutions, which are open establishments and reasonably independent of major private interests. In the present situation these institutions are first of all major public universities, which have to be charged with an additional mission of openly and critically monitoring (inter)national research for any possible threats to the public interest. This mission can only be carried out in the case of sufficient public funding to allow for necessary independence and competence. It is only by this means that knowledge may be advanced without risk of harm to society at large.

Equal opportunities in open and diversified systems of higher education

Júlio Pedrosa de Jesús

Summary

When Europe is aiming at having the most competitive knowledge-based economy, opening and widening the opportunities to complete higher education are fundamental goals to consider. However, the opening of higher education is also a question of building citizenship and strengthening democratic development, which implies the consideration of equal opportunities for all those prepared and interested as a major policy and strategic issue.

The developments which led to a change from elite to mass provision of higher education studies started in the United States in the 1960s and have been energetically pursued in various European countries. These changes will be discussed taking into consideration that, in Europe, higher education has moved from elite institutions to diversified mass systems in processes which were, usually, driven mainly by economic factors and through the addition of new sectors to existing well-established universities.

I have also taken the view that we do not know enough about these developments and that we need to know more about the place that social justice and gender and other equity questions have had in the processes of change observed in higher education. It is also considered a need for Europe to study more widely, and in depth, the higher education systems and the equity policies and actions all across the United States and Canada, instead of concentrating attention only on specific aspects of the smallest part of such systems, the research universities, as has been the case in the most common approaches.

The responsibility for equal opportunities has to be considered at governmental, institutional and operational level for distinct and related matters. Although there is no question that governments and institutions have given some attention to gender, ethnic minorities and low-income groups in grant and loan programmes, access policies, regulations and mission statements, for example, I am calling for more research-based and reliable information on policy formation and implementation, on the effects and barriers, on the structures and responsibility framework.

If the success of the Bologna Process and of the development of the European Areas of Higher Education and Research are, indeed, to be considered of great importance for all Europeans, all persons and entities concerned have to reaffirm their commitment to stimulate and support, in their respective countries and at

European level, a thorough debate about the development of higher education systems for the future.

Social cohesion and inclusion policies have to be properly considered, implemented and monitored continuously at all levels of public responsibility. In fact, the results achieved in these instances are of the utmost importance when devising equity policies for higher education. I would also suggest that higher education institutions can be partners of research and educational projects and programmes aiming at building equal opportunity policies and actions at other levels of education.

Finally, it is considered that, although there is a need for deeper analysis of the achievements and drawbacks of the American system for provision of open higher education, it seems that diversified and differentiated systems of higher education can handle the equal opportunities issues better than unified models. In fact, there is evidence that the specific groups mentioned above now have a higher level of representation than in the corresponding societies. However, there is also evidence of a distribution between sectors, institutions and courses which deserves more research and attention.

All this means that implementing the proclamation of strengthening social cohesion and reducing social and gender inequalities at both national and European level as a central and important political goal requires all possible efforts to have the equal opportunities issues at the heart of the European higher education agenda.

Introduction

Higher education and research development have been considered of fundamental importance for promoting development based on knowledge and innovation. This means that the goal expressed in the EU Lisbon Strategy, of having in Europe the most competitive knowledge-based economy, requires higher education provision to all those interested and prepared. In fact, the idea of opening higher education to increasing numbers of students has been a continuing trend in developed countries over the past forty years, leading to a change from elite to mass provision of higher education studies. This movement started in the United States in the 1960s and has been observed in various European countries, with distinct timings but similar motivations and policies. These developments have stimulated novel and challenging access issues (Williams, 1997; Chevaillier, 2002), as well as turning equal opportunities (Neal, 1998) into a question that has to be considered in policy making and implementation.

Open and mass higher education means having much more diversified candidates and students in the age-group 18-21, including some groups (economically disadvantaged, women, ethnic minorities and disabled) which were excluded from higher education in the past, as well as providing learning through life opportunities to the adult population. Credit accumulation and transfer, modularisation and accreditation of prior learning are, certainly, issues connected with creating opportunities for some of the new publics aiming to enter universities.

The development of the Bologna Process, in particular the Berlin conference of 2003, raised the issue of lifelong learning with reference to important matters related to equal opportunities, as is the case of offering education and training to new and diversified publics. The communiqué of the Conference of Ministers responsible for Higher Education, who met in Berlin on 19 September 2003, addresses these issues in the following terms: "Ministers underline the important contribution of higher education in making lifelong learning a reality ... They stress the need to improve opportunities for all citizens, in accordance with their aspirations and abilities, to follow the lifelong learning paths into and within higher education."

In the United States, opening higher education to all led to a differentiation of the systems and institutions that has persisted over the past forty years. I believe that the discussion of the role of universities in the Europe of knowledge has to address together the issues of opening and widening the access, of equity and of diversification and differentiation in higher education. A diversified higher education system raises the question of the distribution of different groups within the system (Bastedo and Gumport, 2003), but here, again, the American experience of forty years of opening access and a diversified system deserves close attention and study.

No discussion on equity can be separated from that of public responsibility in higher education. This is more justified when Europe is being seen as "the last bastion in the world of fully (or almost fully) tax-supported higher education" (Johnstone, 2004) and when ministers in the Berlin conference reaffirm their position that higher education is a public good and a public responsibility. This means that it is appropriate to look at how national and European policies on higher education confirm that option and to discuss directly related questions.

Political and institutional entities have to consider that both the systems and the institutions face novel challenges as concerns finance, equity, accessibility, curriculum development and learning conditions to deal with a large and diversified population of candidates and students. The Council of Europe initiative of bringing these issues to the higher education agenda is a major contribution for the future of universities in Europe.

Developments in higher education in Europe

Any debate on equity issues in higher education requires careful consideration of the developments observed in higher education during the last forty years. In fact, although the Bologna Process, the European Higher Education Area and the European Research Area seem to dominate the agenda in many European countries, little attention is given to the routes that led to the present systems and, more fundamentally, to the question of the kinds of system and institution that will better serve our future.

Looking first to what changes are more closely associated with opening and widening the provision of higher education, we can note the creation of the polytechnics sector in the United Kingdom in the 1960s, following the Robbins

Report, which argued in favour of expanding entrance by defending the principle that "courses of higher education should be available for all those who are qualified by ability and attainment to pursue them and who wish to do so" (Robbins, 1963, pp. 7-8, as cited in Neal, 1998, p. 20). Measures towards a similar kind of diversification were observed in other European countries, at different times (Austria, Finland, Italy, Germany, the Netherlands, Norway, Portugal), showing that the unification of the British system, in 1992, has not been a general trend. This movement is associated with a tendency towards including all post-secondary education and training in higher education, through the creation of binary systems. It seems also to be the case that, in most countries (Braun and Merrien, 1999) these changes came as reactions to the demand for more higher education places and for higher level training of the workforce. The general response was to add new sectors to existing university systems and not to devise strategic policies aiming at providing novel, forward-looking, higher education systems and institutions.

A second important trend to be considered has to do with the systematic appeal for more responsiveness of higher education institutions to the needs of economic development, both through research and training. That this was seriously considered in the development of the new sectors can be seen in the main missions they were given, with great emphasis on shorter and more applied degree programmes, regional development and industrial co-operation. The emphasis given today to technology transfer associated with scientific research and the programmes specifically designed to promote co-operation of universities with enterprises are also important signals that most of the recent changes in higher education continue to have economic factors as the driving force.

The third development has to do with the increase in size of higher education systems and the corresponding dimensions of the state budgets dedicated to this public service. This gave impetus and a good reason for concern with efficiency, accountability, quality and assessment.

These developments are important for characterising the context and changes which have to be present in our discussion. A context associated with models of expansion influenced by the needs of economic development and by the increase in demand and changes which added new sectors to the existing, usually old and well-established, universities. These changes were responsive or reactive, rather than proactive and planning for new and future roles for higher education in Europe.

It does not come as a surprise that such an expansion, through an "adding to the universities option", resulted in inconsistencies, academic and research drifts, insufficient or inadequate answers and a lot of frustration for almost all concerned (candidates to higher education, students, employers of graduates, politicians, academics, institutional leaders). In contrast, the most successful case in the American policies for opening access to higher education, the Master Plan adopted in California in the 1960s, that resulted from a careful consideration of the requirements associated with an open access policy, has recently been evaluated and considered still as a valuable diversified and differentiated system.

One can say, then, that an equal opportunities policy does not usually come as a clear political priority, stated, planned and implemented at different levels of responsibility. In fact, as far as I know, research on equity, although scarce, shows how necessary it is to give a distinct relevance and attention to the widening of higher education to all, as well as paying attention to specific social groups in higher education governance.

Equal opportunities issues and challenges

Higher education systems in European countries are the result of diverse histories, contexts and development processes. However, they share the common feature of being associated with state provision and of usually being a highly regarded and very valuable public service paid for by taxpayers. In this context we may ask why the issue of equity has not been raised more strongly in statements about the European Higher Education Area, in the Bologna Declaration or in any of the communications from ministers' meetings on its follow-up process. In fact, one should ask if there is adequate awareness, information and research-based knowledge about how different and specific groups of citizens (economically disadvantaged, women, ethnic minorities, disabled), who in the past have been excluded from higher education, are now present in mass higher education systems, as entrants, as graduates and as professionals.

In a recent work dedicated to the equal opportunities question in the United Kingdom, Neal (1998, p. 116) considered that in that country two main questions should be raised:

– what can we do to address the issue of inequality?

– how can we make equal opportunities policies and anti-racist initiatives work?

The same author continues by considering that "one aspect of 'looking forward' will be concerned with identifying and suggesting ways in which equal opportunities policies, their formulations and their implementation, can be genuine attempts to address issues of (in)equality and social justice".

I am arguing here that one good reason for the low priority given to the equal opportunity issues and to other fundamental questions can be found in those features of the changing of higher education in Europe. And I will take this point of view to defend the idea that equity should be treated together with a new approach and forward-looking vision for higher education missions, goals, systems and institutions; systems and institutions designed, planned and implemented to promote citizenship, social as well as economic development, with open entrance and provision of higher education aimed at responding to new goals and publics.

This is to say that I consider it an urgent need that we, in Europe, open a debate about the nature and goals of our systems and institutions of higher education. In other words, that we ask if our countries are equipped to provide higher education for all those prepared and interested, guaranteeing equal opportunities for the different social groups and individuals. I believe that by opening this debate we can give a major contribution to "consolidating and enriching the European citizenship" (Bologna Declaration, 1999, p. 1) and to "strengthening social cohesion and reducing social and gender inequalities both at national and European level [reaffirming] the position that higher education is a public good and a public responsibility" (Berlin Communiqué, 2003, p. 1).

I am inclined to consider that, without discussing the achievements, the constraints and the inconsistencies associated with the development of mass higher education provision in Europe, those goals will be difficult to achieve and limited in their potential results. In fact, not only should such a debate be stimulated, but also it should be accompanied by urgent measures to increase the level of knowledge of the American experience of diversified and differentiated systems, and of the results of their equal opportunities policies and actions. One should pay attention to the fact that the European countries have not followed the American pattern of devising integrated policies and systems for open higher education provision. This option, added to the fact that the results and achievements of the United States' experience are very poorly and partially understood, reinforces the idea that a thorough analysis and debate should be promoted now, taking as central issues the nature and missions of the systems and institutions, equal opportunities and student diversity.

Indeed, if Europe is seen as "the last bastion in the world of fully (or almost fully) tax-supported higher education" (Johnstone, 2004) and our ministers reaffirm "the position that higher education is a public good and a public responsibility" (Berlin Communiqué, 2003, p. 1), there is very good reason to consider the equity issues at the top of higher education agendas at three main levels of responsibility:

– government/parliament, for provision of policies and legal, financial and regulation frameworks, at a macro level;

– institutional governance, where national and European policies have to be harmonised and translated into policies, strategies and actions;

– structures, units and programmes or projects where the day-to-day action happens.

However, since the information and knowledge about the equal opportunities issues in our own systems, in Europe, seem to be very scarce, we need more investment in research-based knowledge and in reliable information about the equity issues in each European country. But it is also a responsibility of governments to be aware of the new and very distinct conditions in which institutions work today. In fact, the experience gained from mass systems shows that, nowadays, institutions have more and highly diversified candidates and students, requiring quite distinct approaches from those adopted for the much more homogeneous and highly selected publics of the past. This trend will be more and more the rule as the widening of European higher education to part-time and diverse students tends to increase. It is, certainly, the responsibility of the institutions and their staff to be prepared to provide adequate answers to this new reality, to work and succeed with the students they have and not to dream about imagined, but not real, students. It is also the institutions' responsibility to devise policies, strategies and actions to give those "real students" the conditions they need to make the best of their own abilities, skills and knowledge.

Of course, students' competences, skills, levels of knowledge and personal projects are very much conditioned by their previous schooling and by their cultural, social and economic backgrounds. A close and careful attention and consideration of these crucial contextual factors cannot be ignored in their higher education paths, at the different levels of responsibility. Governments have to realise the importance of continuing to evaluate the results of policies specifically implemented to deal with social injustices and their relation with the equity issues in education. In fact, when social cohesion is a central aim in the European Union, and education and training is so important in economic policies, it is appropriate to call for a greater attention to equity in education, at all levels, and for the corresponding action at the political level. Higher education institutions, funding agencies and researchers, on the other hand, should be asked to provide their own contribution to the creation of knowledge that will help to design and implement more effective policies to build social justice in education, at all levels.

Final remarks

I started by saying that there are enough good reasons to consider that the equal opportunities issue is an important dimension in the future of higher education in Europe, and that it would be appropriate to offer a few contextual factors for consideration. Among other developments of higher education to be taken into account we call attention to the model most countries have used for expansion of their systems, for the strong appeal to economic considerations and involvement and for the importance given to efficiency, accountability and quality assessment.

I have also argued that we do not know enough, and need to know more, about the role that social justice, gender and other equity questions have had in the processes of change in higher education and that they are having today. It is also considered to be important for Europe to study more widely, and in depth, the higher education systems, equity policies and actions, across all the USA and Canada, instead of concentrating our attention only on specific aspects of the smallest part of such systems, the research universities, as has been the case in the past and present approaches.

The responsibility for equal opportunities has to be considered at governmental, institutional and operational level for distinct and related matters. Although there is no question that governments and institutions have given some attention to minority and low-income groups in grant and loan programmes, access policies, regulations and mission statements, for example, I am calling for more research-based and reliable information on policy formation and implementation, on effects and barriers and on structures and the responsibility framework.

Inclusion policies planned and implemented by governmental and social entities for other levels of education are extremely important in the building of conditions for equity in higher education. Institutions and researchers can contribute if

177

involved as partners in specific education and research programmes aimed at understanding and reinforcing the capacity for social justice at large.

Although there is a need for deeper analysis of the achievements and drawbacks of the United States' system for provision of open higher education, it seems that diversified and differentiated systems of higher education can handle the equal opportunities issues better than unified models. In fact, there is evidence that the specific groups mentioned above have now achieved a higher level of representation than in the corresponding societies. However, there is also evidence of a distribution between sectors, institutions and courses which deserves more research and attention.

I can only conclude by saying that, if strengthening social cohesion and reducing social and gender inequalities at both national and European level is a proclaimed central and important political goal, we have to make all possible efforts to have the equal opportunities issues at the heart of the European higher education agenda.

References

Bastedo, M.N. and Gumport, P.J., "Access to what? Mission differentiation and academic stratification in US public higher education", *Higher Education,* Vol. 46, 2003, pp. 341-359.

Berlin Communiqué, *Realising the European Higher Education Area,* adopted by European ministers of education on 19 September 2003.

Bologna Declaration, *The European Higher Education Area. Joint Declaration of the European Ministers of Education,* 19 June 1999.

Braun, D. and Merrien, F.-X. (eds), *Towards a new model of governance for universities? A comparative view,* Kingsley Jessica, London, 1999.

Chevaillier, T., "Higher education and its clients: institutional responses to changes in demand and in environment", *Higher Education,* Vol. 33, 2002, pp. 303-308, Special Issue.

Commission of the European Communities, *The role of universities in the Europe of knowledge,* COM(2003)58, CEC, Brussels, 2003.

Johnstone, D.B., "Cost-sharing and equity in higher education: implications of income contingent loans", in Amaral, A., Dill, D., Jongbloed, B. and Teixeira, P. (eds), *Markets in higher education: rhetoric or reality?,* Kluwer Academic Publishers, 2004, pp. 1-13.

Neal, S., *The making of equal opportunities policies in universities,* SRHE and Open University Press, Buckingham, 1998.

Williams, J. (ed.), *Negotiating access to higher education – The discourse of selectivity and equity,* Society for Research into Higher Education and Open University Press, Buckingham, 1997.

Financing higher education:
the economics of options, trade-offs and dilemmas

Carlo Salerno

Introduction

There is growing concern that European higher education is running headlong into financial crisis ("Pay or decay", *Economist*, 2004). Greater competition for increasingly scarce public funding, the impending brain drain to the west stemming from an ever-widening gap in overall funding and the steadily rising costs of teaching and doing science are forcing parliaments from London to Budapest to seriously rethink how they currently fund their higher education systems. One has to look no further than England's passionate debates about top-up fees, Germany's public higher education crisis (Wessel, 2003) or the European Commission's call[39] for member states to nearly double aggregate R&D investment by 2010 to see that rhetoric is indeed moving towards reality.

The current debates about financing higher education are tenuous because they directly threaten European countries' age-old tradition of providing individuals with a higher education at very little or no consumer cost, yet it is important to not lose sight of the fact that the state is and will likely remain for some time higher education's dominant benefactor. Policy makers' efforts at promoting cost efficiency and enhancing educational quality have given rise to a diverse and sometimes quite elaborate array of funding systems as well as internal steering mechanisms. Who should bear the responsibility is certainly a key concern, but so is the extent to which the structures that are already in place work for or against the broader goals and objectives underlying different national systems. In this paper I look at how economic theory can be used to help explain the mixed modes of higher education financing in place today. As we will see later, the dilemmas and trade-offs that come with pursuing different options do much to explain the complexity and controversy behind the more general debate.

Mapping public funding

While there are a number of rationales for public investment in higher education (for instance, paternalism or political inculcation), the justification usually invoked by economists is that society reaps part of the benefits. Individuals receive substantial private returns, primarily through higher salaries, and the public

---

39. *More research for Europe: towards 3% of GDP*, communication from the European Commission, 2002.

derives social returns (at least in principle) in the form of less crime, a healthier population, and a more productive workforce. Adhering to the maxim that "he who benefits pays", what emerges is a mixed public/private financing scheme where students pay tuition to cover their private benefits and governments provide higher education institutions with additional financial support, mainly through annual appropriations, as a way to publicly subsidise the social benefits.[40]

The ways in which governments actually channel public funding to higher education is nevertheless much more complex than simply providing individual institutions with a bag of money and the variety of mechanisms used reflects a wide range of political, social and economic motives. Direct appropriations may provide institutions with equal subsidies for all students in all programmes or it may be overly generous to certain academic programmes in order to achieve specific economic objectives like redressing manpower shortages in key areas of the national and/or regional labour markets. Indirect funding channels like financial aid may be means-tested with the goal of rectifying distributional inequities or they can be merit-based to try and ensure that the brightest individuals have the means to exploit their potential. And while private providers normally do not receive direct government support, they often procure substantial indirect funding since their students are generally eligible[41] for the same or similar financial aid packages and tax abatements that students at public institutions receive (Jongbloed and Salerno, 2002). Indeed most funding regimes tend to incorporate all of these different options and more, leading to sometimes very complicated systems.

A useful way to coalesce this diversity is by evaluating public funding systems along two dimensions (Jongbloed and Koelman, 2000):

– the extent to which governments seek to directly manage higher education institutions' operations;

– the extent to which funding is predicated on meeting different objectives.

The first is a more formal way of asking how centralised or decentralised authority is in the national higher education system. Market-driven sectors provide institutions with considerable latitude to use public funding as they see fit and are apparent in their institutions' autonomy when it comes to how funding is procured and spent: unrestricted block grant appropriations (for both research and education activities), the ability to hire faculty at market wages and freedom to set tuition fees are three particularly illustrative examples. As one moves further in the direction of centralisation, government oversight and regulation intensifies: first

---

40. I oversimplify here only for illustrative purposes. Externalities, unobservable product quality and information asymmetries between consumers and producers are all believed to explain the rise and dominance of non-profits in markets for "welfare" goods like health or higher education and research (Barr, 2001), yet so is altruism and hence donative revenues (Hansmann, 1980) in the form of private philanthropy are equally important. However, while this aspect is a dominant feature of American higher education it is of little use for characterising the current state of European higher education funding systems.

41. The primary condition in most national systems for students at private institutions to receive indirect subsidies is that the provider in question be officially recognised by the government.

towards government steering and eventually towards government control. Faculty members become civil servants and government line-item appropriations separate everything from large and small capital purchases to individual institutions' staff allocations and salaries. Institutions with surpluses in any given line-item usually cannot carry funds over to other categories and the excess funding goes back to the state.

The second dimension considers the criteria on which appropriated funds are allocated to meet different goals and objectives. At one end are systems that heavily employ input-based criteria; here meeting objectives is predicated on ensuring that the necessary resources are made available. Output- or performance-based measures exist at the other extreme, where funding is tied instead to the results or end product. Between the two extremes lie the more common mixed systems where allocation mechanisms are based on mixed measures.

These ideas are captured graphically in Figure 1. Quadrant one (top left) is where one would expect to find the more traditional type of funding/budgeting. Here centralised systems usually allocate funding based on annual requests (activity plans; budget proposals) submitted to budgetary authorities. This is sometimes referred to as negotiated funding. While central level planning dictates allocations in principle, in practice the various line-item budgets are often based on the previous year's allocation. Separate budget items then are negotiated between representatives of educational institutions and the relevant funding authorities (that is, education ministries or national funding councils). Annual changes (usually increases) for any given line-item are treated on an institution-by-institution basis and often rely on cost projections. Typical appropriation categories include staff salaries, material requirements, building maintenance costs and investment. These are determined by referring to norms with respect to indicators like unit costs (or unit cost increases) or capacity (for example, the number of students funded). The German and French systems still retain many of these characteristics.

Figure 1. Mapping public funding regimes

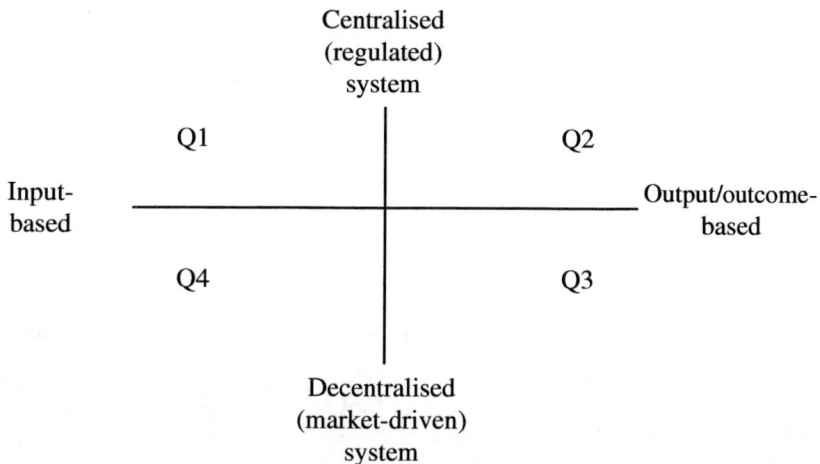

Quadrant two (top right) is still a centralised system but now the criteria on which funding is allocated are based more on the outputs achieved rather than inputs required. The criteria employed vary but output measures may include graduation rates or the number of credits (weighted number of passed courses) accumulated by an institutions' students in different academic fields. A good example for this quadrant is Denmark's taximeter model or Sweden's funding scheme, which both allocate funds to institutions based on a mix of enrollment numbers and credits passed. This is also the case in the Netherlands, where funding is based on both the number of first-year students and the number of master's degrees conferred (see Jongbloed and Vossensteyn, 2002). The Research Assessment Exercise (RAE) that is done in the United Kingdom would also fit here.

Quadrant three (lower right) characterises market-oriented systems whose key feature is higher education institutions that essentially compete for a given supply of graduates or research activities on price by submitting tenders to national funding agencies. Competition is encouraged and applies not only to education activities but also to research (usually through some type of national research council). Contracts are established between funding agencies and higher education institutions with the latter agreeing to deliver graduates for targeted labour market needs or research outputs targeted at strengthening the innovative capacity of the country. Importantly, institutions receive core funding only after they have met the agreed upon criteria, which may involve the types and qualifications of students admitted to the higher education institution, the (maximum) level of tuition fees (if any) charged by the institution, and the commitment made by the higher education institution towards its students in the instruction and teaching processes.

The last quadrant (lower left) is probably the most progressive and the one where much of the current debate about the implementation of voucher systems is taking place. Basically an institution's core funding here is tied heavily to consumer preferences. For education, students receive vouchers that can be traded for educational services at the institution of their choice and which can be used within fairly flexible parameters.[42] Institutions must monitor the quality of their teaching and their supply of courses, because unattractive programmes will not receive sufficient funding. A more blended system may involve a part voucher/part differentiated course fee arrangement. Tuition levels may be regulated by the government but flexible pricing is expected to make students pay attention to the quality of the service they get from the higher education institution. The only real difference between research here and that done in quadrant three is the greater emphasis on basic research.

Funding system trends

Surveying the funding mechanisms in place across OECD states, governments in a number of countries have increasingly attempted to separate support for teaching

---

42. Flexible here means that such vouchers are good for a certain period of time and can only be redeemed by enrolling in programmes supplied through a given number of accredited or recognised providers.

and research by providing block (lump-sum) funding for each activity – covering the day-to-day running costs. There has also been a move away from negotiated line-item funding (quadrant one behaviour) and instead towards outcome-based and formula-driven schemes that are more typical of quadrant two. One can also observe the tendency to replace block funding for research with competitive funding mechanisms (Q4), or performance-based funding mechanisms (Q3). The extent to which such moves have taken place naturally varies across countries. For example, in some systems universities have greater access to additional funding for specific initiatives.[43] In all cases though, the allocation of block grants or targeted funds still tends to be tied to specific quality and accountability requirements. A summary of international shifts in system-wide funding mechanisms can be likened to a clockwise movement of systems in quadrants one through three towards quadrants two through four.

Options for higher education financing

In debates about higher education funding the crucial question really is how to strike the "right" balance between what types of objectives the system wishes to achieve and the socio-political culture of who "owns" higher education. For many, this debate centres on the balance between public and private investments in higher education but in reality it is much broader and broaches more practical questions like the extent to which funding can or should be supply-driven versus demand-driven or whether it should be input-oriented or performance-based. Funding mechanisms and more general financing options need to meet multiple goals and still be flexible enough to accommodate emerging trends like greater flows of international students and the widespread, yet poorly understood, adoption of information and communications technology.

The discussion until now points to three overarching aspects to system-level funding: (1) market versus government steering, and with respect to the market point, (2) demand versus (3) supply orientation. These form the basis for the taxonomy of higher education financing options that is presented in Table 1. The different columns are built around which actors take the lead in shaping the nature of universities: students, higher education institutions or the government. The rows are grouped by each option's basic philosophy as well as how public and private financing mechanisms come to bear. The correspondence between what is here and that presented in Figure 1 is loose but evident. The demand-driven option fits somewhat roughly over quadrants four and three, the supply-side option over quadrants two and three and the government-oriented option over quadrants one and two.

---

43. The United Kingdom has done a lot in this area. In general, special funding may exist for programmes increasing the participation of certain target groups, specific skills areas, postgraduate training, setting up research infrastructure, public-private research partnerships, or specific strategic research in "areas of excellence".

Table 1. Three options for funding higher education

	Market-oriented		Government-oriented
Steering philosophy	Demand-driven Freedom of choice/ customer-oriented	Supply-driven Providers choose	Government chooses which programmes to fund based on macro-efficiency and other criteria
	Encourage mix of publicly funded and non-funded providers Government's role is to organise and oversee quality control	Encourage mix of publicly funded and non-funded providers Encourage competition on the basis of prices and quality of services offered	Protection of socially relevant programmes
Public funding method	Voucher-style system (Applicable only to government-approved programmes)	Contract funding (tenders) – all providers can compete for contracts Suppliers have freedom to choose how funding is internally allocated	Formula funding based on input and output measures
Private funding method	Fees partly covered by vouchers	Top-up fees	Uniform fees (if any) for publicly funded programmes
Tuition fees	Differentiated fee schedules Fees determined by providers	Fee levels depend on mixture of competition and providers' strategies Fees also determined by quality programme length	Non-recognised providers charge differential fees
Student support	Grant plus loan combination for both cost of living and tuition Government-backed loans and scholarships Extra entitlements for disadvantaged students	Providers supply student support packages based on merit and need Government-backed loans and scholarships Providers offer loan schemes subsidised through private banks	Government-backed loans and scholarships

Source: adapted from Jongbloed and Vossensteyn, 2002.

Discussion

Both Figure 1 and Table 1 lay out useful frameworks for thinking about financing higher education but each should be approached and interpreted with a good deal of caution. In practice the lines between concepts like demand- and supply-driven or centralised and decentralised are much fuzzier than they are presented here and no system really fits precisely into any one category. That said, what is presented can be very useful as a basis for thinking about the economic trade-offs and dilemmas that come with currently operating in or possibly shifting towards different financing options.

Though the demand-driven option offers individuals the greatest amount of choice and leverage in the market for higher education, several important factors come into play. First, information asymmetry makes it difficult for consumers and producers to contract on quality (Glaeser and Schleifer, 2001; Weisbrod, 1988). Now colleges and universities are believed to form as non-profits in order to mitigate "shirking" but this does not fully resolve the non-contractible quality problem; because individuals cannot accurately value the education product they purchase until long after it has been consumed (Winston, 1999), they still must base their college-going decisions on market signals of quality. Unfortunately, the available evidence suggests that even though considerable effort is put into providing prospective students with the necessary information, their final decisions often rest on remarkably poor and/or incomplete information (James et al., 1999). Second, a system where students dictate what a degree programme is and what courses are relevant only exacerbates the quality/signalling problems, which makes it far more difficult to officially recognise programmes or monitor quality. Third, a strongly demand-driven scheme runs the joint risk of promoting macroeconomic inefficiency[44] and forcing culturally important but financially weak programmes to close. In this regard, a government-oriented approach may have the downside of limiting choice but it has the benefit of helping to ensure that public funding meets the public's needs and that enrolments in programmes that may be key to the nation's economy (such as secondary education or civil engineering) or its cultural identity (for example, native languages) do not get crowded out by potentially misguided consumer choices.

If prices (tuition fees) act as one signal of institutional (or programme) quality then the use of uniform tuition rates typical of government-oriented schemes also generates information asymmetry by making it more difficult for students to properly discriminate between institutions or programmes. Governments tend to view losses in market functionality that come with fixing (or not imposing) tuition fees as a reasonable trade-off to rectifying market failures associated with distributional inequities and promoting access. This is a perfectly rational justification except that there is very little empirical evidence to convincingly suggest that

---

44. A good example of this can be found in Uganda where the government funding scheme subsidises the top 10% of students but does not regulate which programmes they enrol in. The problem they currently face is a dearth of science and technology graduates that could stimulate the economy and a glut of graduates with degrees in the humanities.

demand for higher education is elastic. Moreover, setting low or no tuition fees may help to correct one form of distributional inequity (by helping to ensure that students from lower-income families are not priced out of the education market) yet it creates another by subsidising students in expensive physical and biological sciences programmes to a greater extent than those in social sciences or humanities fields (Salerno, 2004).

Low or no tuition fees also create the government failure that Wolf (1993) describes as the disjunction between who pays the cost and who receives the goods. When the consumer's revenue does not fully cover the producer's costs and some third party (government) ends up subsidising the difference, such a practice also runs the risk of promoting waste as students have little incentive to fully take advantage of the resources that institutions place at their disposal. This is a classic moral hazard problem. Since students control education production, excessive government subsidies act as an incentive for students to under-utilise institutions' resources.[45] Unfortunately, neither the government nor the institutions can know to what extent waste has occurred until after the fact. The main implication is that both the government and institutions could have put those resources to more productive use in other markets, such as academic research.

Supply- and demand-driven systems also encourage a mix of public and private providers to promote competition, innovation and efficiency. This has gone further in the sense that some governments are even raising the issue of letting all institutions operate on a level playing field (that is, private providers should have the same privileges and access to public funding as public providers). Regulations on the conditions attached to public funding, student support and accreditation are at stake here. In many systems, private providers can and do receive public subsidies for education as was briefly mentioned earlier, usually through indirect channels like government-backed student loans or general tax abatements. There is good reason to consider such an option: a number of systems informally exploit their private sectors to accommodate unmet demand rather than make short-term investments in the public system.[46] Ironically though, the trade-off that comes with creating a more open higher education market-place by incorporating private providers into the national system or providing them with public funding is that it also requires more government oversight in terms of quality control. Since the authority to award degrees is granted by the state, governments generally do not allow private higher education providers to operate unless they meet minimum standards that are usually imposed on public providers. This issue has taken on new meaning particularly with non-recognised providers (either from other countries or from within) increasingly dotting southern European countries' education landscapes (Kokosalakis, 1999).

---

45. One has to look no further than the many students that rarely enter university libraries, but play online computer games in university computing laboratories, or fail to visit their professors' offices outside of class to get additional help, for examples of students wasting institutional resources.

46. Portugal has taken this approach in the past (Teixeira et al., 2004) and in Germany there is concern that *Länder* are providing overly generous subsidies to private (recognised) providers while both national and international attention focuses on how inadequately funded their public sector is (HRK, 2004).

At the institutional level, block-grant funding (at least on the education side) is increasingly becoming the preferred mode as system planners argue greater institutional autonomy will in return promote transparency and enhance efficiency because those who use the resources are in the best position to determine how they should be employed. Yet policy shifts like this are often undertaken specifically because public funding is usually scarce and hence little investment is made in the structures necessary for its success. Institution managers in previously centralised systems have never had to manage their own funding and without retraining, this is liable to produce short-run mismanagement and likely have the effect of increasing the flow of waste rather than stemming it. Then there is the more theoretical problem of higher education institutions as non-profits. If one is to believe that institutions behave like physicians' co-operatives (Pauly and Redisch, 1973) then block-grant funding will not work unless it is tied to outcomes rather than inputs. The classic argument is that universities in such funding systems will cross-subsidise research with education funds because faculty members prefer research to education and the nature of producing or transferring knowledge is too difficult for thirdparties to effectively monitor (James, 1990; James and Neuberger, 1981).

On the topic of injecting more private money into higher education one should observe that students, their parents and private businesses are more inclined to spend money on universities when they have the feeling that their demands are met more closely. The chances for this to happen are far greater in a deregulated system that allows institutions and students or institutions and businesses to work more closely together and decide on programme content or research directions without government interference. The two market options in Table 1 are thus natural candidates for generating more funding from the private sector. Demand-driven systems could feasibly encourage private contributions that can be combined with voucher-style systems to pay for tailor-made courses. Similarly, a supply-driven structure would likely encourage institutions with strong teaching and research profiles to seek closer collaboration with private business in order to enhance the quality of degree programmes, secure much-needed research funding and offer student support packages to students that study in particular fields.

Conclusion

In sum, students' interests are arguably best served by the demand-driven option, particularly since it is capable of addressing the growing interest in lifelong learning. Institutions enjoy a much more stable operating environment in the supply-driven option and would enjoy considerable autonomy to balance stakeholders' needs with their expertise in how to meet them. This option also provides the most fertile environment for industry/university partnerships to rise and thrive, even if research agendas were to become more applied and less basic as a result. Society naturally stands to gain the most in the government-oriented option, where the supply of graduates in important fields like health, teacher training, and other public services can be effectively monitored and regulated by means of a planned and accountable system of publicly supported programmes. Of course, the ability to implement any particular funding option depends heavily on the extent to which funding is even available. This, in fact, is the crisis currently facing many European higher education systems and what has prompted so much discussion about greater private investment both from individuals and from industry.

Perhaps the main point to be taken away from all of this is that the sometimes strange characteristics of higher education markets do not lend themselves nicely to textbook economics principles. Each of the financing options presented above gives rise to dilemmas and trade-offs that suggest none is effective in isolation. Policy makers and planners may not directly factor the economic concerns I address here into their system-level decision making, but the fact that many financing systems possess a mix of market- and government-oriented mechanisms strongly suggests that tacit understanding of these issues does exist. A better understanding of these trade-offs then can do much to explain current predicaments and also provide a useful guide for pursuing alternative financing schemes.

References

Barr, N., *The welfare state as piggy bank: information, risk, uncertainty, and the role of the state,* Oxford University Press, Oxford, 2001.

Glaeser, E. and Schleifer, A., "Not-for-profit entrepreneurs", *Journal of Public Economics,* Vol. 81, No.1, 2001, pp. 99-115.

Hansmann, H., "The rationale for exempting non-profit organisations from corporate income taxation", *Yale Law Journal,* Vol. 91, 1980, pp. 54-100.

HRK (Hochschulrektorenconferenz), "HRK calls for priority support for higher education institutions – The backbone of the higher education and research system has been neglected for far too long", press release, 2 February 2004.

James, E., "Decision processes and priorities in higher education", in Hoenack, S.A. and Collins, E.I. (eds), *The economics of American universities,* State University of New York Press, Buffalo, 1990, pp. 77-106.

James, R., Baldwin, G. and McInnis, C., "Which university? The factors influencing the choices of prospective undergraduates", Australian Department of Education, Training and Skills (DEST) Evaluation and Investigations Programme Document 99/3, 1999, available at: http://www.dest.gov.au/archive/highered/eip-pubs/99-3/whichuni.pdf

James, E. and Neuberger, E., "The university department as a non-profit labor co-operative", *Public Choice,* Vol. 36, 1981, pp. 585-612.

Jongbloed, B.W.A. and Koelman, K., "Vouchers for higher education? A survey of the literature", study commissioned by the Hong Kong University Grants Committee, CHEPS, Enschede, 2000.

Jongbloed, B.W.A. and Salerno, C.S., "Funding and recognition: a comparative study of funded versus non-funded higher education in eight countries", *Beleidsgerichte Studies Hoger onderw. & Wetensch. onderzoek,* Vol. 92, Ministerie van Onderwijs, Cultuur en Wetenschap, The Hague, 2002.

Jongbloed, B. and Vossensteyn, H., "Financiering masters: Argumenten en Arrangementen" (Funding masters: arguments and arrangements), Studie in opdracht van de Werkgroep Financiering Masters, Ministerie van OC&W, 2002.

Kokosalakis, N., *Non-official higher education in the European Union,* Gutenberg Publications, Athens, 1999.

Pauly, M. and Redisch, M., "The not-for-profit hospital as a physicians' co-operative", *American Economic Review,* Vol. 63, No. 1, 1973, pp. 87-99.

"Pay or decay", *Economist,* 22 January 2004.

Salerno, C.S., "Rapid expansion and extensive deregulation: the development of markets for higher education in the Netherlands", in Amaral, A., Dill, D., Jongbloed, B. and Teixeira, P. (eds), *Markets in higher education: rhetoric or reality?,* Kluwer, Dordrecht, 2004.

191

Teixeira, P., Rosa, M.J. and Amaral, A., "Is there a higher education market in Portugal?" in Amaral, A., Dill, D., Jongbloed, B. and Teixeira, P. (eds), *Markets in higher education: rhetoric or reality?*, Kluwer, Dordrecht, 2004.

Weisbrod, B.A., *The non-profit economy,* Harvard University Press, Cambridge, 1988.

Wessel, R., "Private colleges make inroads: Europe's public universities lose appeal as overhauls languish", *Wall Street Journal Europe,* 1 December 2003, p. A8.

Winston, G.C., "Subsidies, hierarchy and peers: the awkward economics of higher education", *Journal of Economic Perspectives,* Vol. 13, 1999, pp. 13-36.

Wolf, C., "Markets or governments: choosing between imperfect alternatives", MIT Press, Cambridge, 1993.

New trends and new providers in higher education

Stephen Adam

European higher education has undergone profound changes in the past five years and the nature and pace of this transformation is bound to continue. Obviously, many of the innovations have been associated with the Bologna Process and the creation of the European Higher Education Area. However, we must not forget that this is itself a product of many factors including: globalisation; real/imagined pressures on government expenditure; a desire to modernise antiquated educational systems and practices; mass participation in higher education; the headlong rush for knowledge-based economies, etc.

The traditionally serene higher education sector is finding its agenda crowded with initiatives and buffeted by a multiplying number of unfamiliar challenges that cannot be ignored. The following brief review of "new trends and new providers" seeks to chart broadly what is happening, as well as provide some insights and questions about the implications on the Council of Europe September 2004 conference theme – "Public responsibility for higher education and research". It also attempts to highlight some of the different dimensions that "public responsibility" might encompass – a cascade of responsibilities that might include the citizen, employer, student, institution, local community or ministry as well international organisations.

So what are some of the new trends and new providers and who, if anyone, should assume responsibility for their impact? Are we moving into stormy weather or calm seas? The evidence points to something akin to educational global warming – more turmoil, unsettled government reactions, and even an increase in educational temperatures. The "new trends" manifest themselves at three interconnected levels: (i) local; (ii) national/regional; and (iii) international. This paper will touch on the first, just to note its importance, but will predominantly focus on the national and international dimensions where public responsibility faces its most significant challenges from transnational education. Although no simple definition exists, transnational education refers to education unconfined by national boundaries. According to the Council of Europe/Unesco Code of Good Practice in the Provision of Transnational Education it encompasses:

> "All types of higher education study programmes, or sets of courses of study, or educational services (including those of distance education) in which the learners are located in a country different from the one where the awarding institution is based. Such programmes may belong to the education system of a State different from the State in which it operates, or may operate independently of any national educational system."

Transnational education crosses borders and often bypasses state authority. In so doing, it challenges preconceived notions about the provision of learning, particularly how it should be delivered and by whom.

Local level – Trends impacting on higher education institutions (HEIs)

The trends impacting on higher education institutions at the local level are familiar to most of us and can be grouped into the following four areas, each of which poses different challenges:

– changing educational environment. The role of HEIs and the environment within which they operate is transforming. There are increasing financial pressures, more competition, additional students of different types and requirements, increasing institutional diversity (reflected in the adoption of international and even global educational mission statements) and closer links with industry. The role of the university is being challenged in ways never previously experienced. Even the traditional distinction between private and public education is becoming blurred. Universities and markets are uneasy bedfellows yet their marriage is becoming more common as universities embrace business models. One of the most obvious challenges to local providers is the arrival of transnational education providers that offer alternative educational opportunities. These new realities give rise to a number of obvious questions – how do these challenges affect local and national responsibilities for higher education? How are internal and external responsibilities changing in this new competitive environment?

– increasing institutional autonomy and resultant internal structural reforms. The changing role, size, shape and nature of HEIs are leading to consequential changes in their internal organisation, staffing, administration, autonomy and accountability. There is a growing focus on the responsibility of institutions to improve their internal good governance as well as introduce more efficient organisational structures. Still absent from many institutions are: open meetings; minuted decision taking; fair appointment practices; full public/staff accountability, etc. This challenges us to consider how effective good governance can be developed and maintained, and who has responsibility for this;

– organisation, content and expression of the curricula. Something akin to a paradigm change in the organisation and expression of the curricula is underway. New-style approaches to the expression of the curricula in terms of learning outcomes, credits and the adoption of student-centred learning highlight the role of teaching, learning and assessment. The challenge of new delivery technologies (open/distance, e-learning, etc.) also raises questions about standards, recognition and control. We need to consider whether institutional and national responsibilities are widening, and what this may mean in terms of public responsibility;

– cheating and plagiarism. The advent of new technologies – particularly the Internet – is posing a serious threat to the current processes and nature of the assessment of academic work. We need to be very clear about the responsibilities of the student and the institution in overcoming these problems. Do public responsibilities extend down to students and institutions?

These areas of concern and the questions they raise focus on the local dimension where the trend for increasing local academic autonomy should not imply any diminished role for public responsibility. Quite the opposite, they highlight the need to take such responsibility seriously and ensure that every stakeholder plays a full and active role in the development of open, transparent and accountable educational processes. This should be a hallmark of the European Higher Education Area.

National level – Trends impacting on ministries, competent authorities and agencies responsible for higher education

There is growing evidence that new trends and new providers are having increasingly profound effects at the national level. In particular the following two areas are significant:

– new style frameworks of qualifications;

– borderless education.

The rapid development and adoption of new frameworks of qualifications (some encompassing lifelong learning) by Denmark, Ireland, Hungary and the United Kingdom and the use of external reference points (levels, level indicators, learning outcomes, qualification descriptors, workload and benchmark statements) has profound implications for the relationship between the state, its agencies and higher education institutions. Following the recommendations in the Berlin Communiqué of 2003, the Bologna signatories were encouraged to develop a framework of comparable and compatible qualifications for their higher education systems and undertake to elaborate an overarching framework of qualifications for the European Higher Education Area. These developments will impact on the relationships and processes between the different higher education stakeholders. This raises the matter of the right balance between state "regulation" and institutional autonomy in implementing these new devices. How should public responsibility relate to national frameworks and the emerging overarching European framework of qualifications?

This initiative had its origins in the Danish Seminar on Qualification Structures in the European Higher Education, March 2003. A second Danish "Bologna" seminar is to take place in January 2005 where a Bologna Follow-Up Group (BFUG) working party report will be considered. This will detail some of the characteristics of "new-style" national frameworks[47] of qualifications and their relationship to

47. "New style" national frameworks of qualifications are those that are output-focused and employ levels, level descriptors, qualifications descriptors and learning outcomes. These form external reference points that, *inter alia,* help promote more effective quality assurance systems, support student-centred approaches and facilitate the creation of autonomous, responsible and accountable higher education institutions.

a proposed overarching European framework of qualifications. This initiative has major implications for the recognition of higher education qualifications and the institutions that provide them. Furthermore, new frameworks of qualifications are intimately related with the existence of academically autonomous HEIs and the adoption of outcomes-focused systems, tools and methodologies to express qualifications, levels and level/qualification descriptors. Effective higher educational governance is inconceivable without academic autonomy and the development, for many countries, of a new relationship between the state and universities. The traditionally paternal state-institution relationship for many countries is giving way to a more mature relationship that makes institutions responsible and accountable for the decisions they take as independent institutions.

The collective impact of these developments will be significant as they will play an increasingly important role in the creation of the European Higher Education Area. The provision of external reference points, academic autonomy and new quality assurance regimes are something that all educational providers have to respond to – whether they are public or private providers, national or transnational in origin. Qualifications will be firmly placed in national systems of level and the overarching Bologna cycles.

Borderless education: transnational education (including corporate, for-profit, not-for-profit, franchises and branch campuses) is a growing phenomenon and the advent of new education providers poses significant challenges to traditional patterns of education and the authorities responsible for them. Many countries continue to display a schizophrenic and negative attitude towards imported education whilst heavily promoting the exportation of their own. Transnational education has profound and complex effects on different sectors, cycles and types of education, and public authorities are often confused about how to react.

It is certainly true that transnational education has both positive and negative effects. The negative views usually emphasise the existence of "degree mills" and bogus institutions, which exploit the public with sub-standard institutions that are unregulated, unmonitored and exist outside the control of national education systems. The positive aspects emphasise the benefits of increased learning opportunities (more choice – particularly where existing public provision of education is restricted), the constructive impact of more competition from innovative imported programmes, and access to new markets for educational exporters.

Transnational education should never be regarded per se as an inherently negative or positive phenomenon – rather it is a fact of life that cannot be "un-invented" or abolished. It touches on all dimensions of the current European educational debate engendered by the Bologna Declaration, including matters of recognition, transparency, accreditation, cultural and academic autonomy, convergence and divergence. It has the potential to have both a benign and/or a malign impact and consequently it should not be ignored. The competition it represents can sharpen our domestic education provisions and consequently the quality of educational exports, which in turn, can promote our distinctive European cultures worldwide.

It can also lead to a dumbing-down of qualifications as competitive forces can reduce standards to the lowest common denominator.

The chameleon-like nature of transnational education means it is not amenable to traditional approaches to regulation and too often public authorities are ignoring the problems by allowing "illegal education" to flourish in an uncontrolled manner that leaves the citizen unprotected. Transnational education certainly interacts with traditional education and education systems. The trick will be to devise ways to promote its beneficial aspects and diminish its harmful impacts. One solution being pioneered by a number of countries is to recognise that transnational education has implications for national education systems and domestic quality assurance frameworks. This involves creating more flexible national regulation of imported transnational education providers to allow the possibility of their formal state recognition (accreditation), after a suitably rigorous process of assessment of the foreign provider (for example, in the Slovak Republic the new Higher Education Law of 2002 liberalised the approach to transnational education). This approach has the advantage of encouraging the recognition and regulation of good transnational education and isolation of non-recognised providers about whom public authorities can warn citizens.

All national and international bodies in the European region should adopt a balanced attitude towards transnational education. National and European priorities can complement, rather than stand in opposition to, each other. The potential and actual advantages associated with transnational education are significant and its import and export should be encouraged as a vehicle to improve access, widen participation, enrich the curriculum, and expand choice and flexibility. European involvement will widen the market for European education. National governments and institutions should not adopt a protectionist stance towards transnational education, as this is likely to be ineffective and counterproductive in terms of the development of an internationally competitive European education.

Action is required at every level by national and international higher education stakeholders in Europe. Transnational education impacts on education in far-reaching and significant ways. Inaction on the part of European providers (exporters), students, regulators, receiving countries (importers), and international organisations would harm the development of the European Higher Education Area. This area is essentially a dynamic and competitive higher education zone of excellence that is intended to attract European and non-European students, as well as export our culturally distinctive educational programmes. A protectionist stance would stifle the forces for change, which would particularly harm the modernisation process under way in some central and eastern European states many of whom welcome good quality transnational providers to help supply education that the public provision cannot offer.

Whatever happens, it is important that the position of rogue providers is made as difficult as possible. One important initiative to help this is the forthcoming publication by the ENIC (Council of Europe/Unesco) and NARIC (European

Commission) networks[48] of an overview of questions prospective students and employers should ask of any education providers. This was agreed in the Strasbourg Statement on Recognition Issues in the European Higher Education Area, June 2004. This type of approach illustrates a useful way in which the provision of information can empower the student/learner so that they can be made aware of the pertinent questions to ask any education provider. In addition, public authorities need to adopt a common approach in setting the requirement for the provision of accurate, objective and up-to-date information on higher education options. This should include nationally recognised transnational providers.

Transnational education certainly raises a number of difficult questions including: – How should public authorities fairly treat these new forms of education? Should all education providers be attached to a state so public responsibility can be exercised? What are the public responsibilities of exporters of transnational education? What are the public responsibilities of states receiving transnational education? Can public responsibility for transnational education be better discharged if the transnational providers are given the opportunity for official recognition?

International – Trends impacting on international organisations and institutions

The global educational world is transforming rapidly as states and regions seek to benefit from more aggressive marketing of their education systems in order to attract students and export their programmes. A global education market is being created and the resultant increase in transnational education emphasises recognition issues and the role of international organisations active in this field (Council of Europe, European Commission, Unesco, etc.).

Transnational education raises awkward questions regarding mixed jurisdictions and confused responsibilities. Recently, the World Trade Organization (WTO) General Agreement on Trade in Services (GATS) has disturbed the traditional academic world by questioning hidden subsidies associated with trade in higher education. GATS identifies the following four modes of educational service supply: cross-border supply (virtual universities); consumption abroad (study abroad mobility schemes); commercial presence (branch campus); and movement of persons (teacher mobility). The GATS dimension goes to the heart of the debate about public responsibility for higher education. Education is often regarded as a public good and a service which is largely provided by the state and that citizens have a right to enjoy. However, many states admit they cannot meet public demand in the age of mass higher education. A further complication is that higher education systems increasingly involve a complex mixture of public and private provision. This trend towards the progressive liberalisation of education calls into question the special status of public education provision where unfair competitive advantage may be deemed to exist. Only the future will reveal the precise implication of

---

48. http://www.enic-naric.net

GATS for public and private provision of higher education but there is every chance that there could be severe repercussions for any unfair state support.

Across the globe a number of national codes of good practice associated with the provision of transnational education exist. A notable example of an international code is the Council of Europe/Unesco Code of Good Practice in the Provision of Transnational Education. This elaborates good practice principles for transnational education providers. However, the knowledge and use of such codes is very limited and this raises the question of what roles should international agencies play in relation to public responsibility for transnational education? Are international databases of recognised (approved) transnational providers useful? How can international codes of educational good practice be consistently applied in the international sphere?

In the context of new forms of cross-border higher education provision, a recent joint initiative by OECD and Unesco is to produce guidelines on quality provision in cross-border higher education. This proposal followed a resolution of the general conference of Unesco and the governing board of OECD in 2003. It seeks to strengthen quality assurance, accreditation and recognition of qualifications at both national and international levels through the development of these non-binding international guidelines. It is anticipated that such guidelines would not supersede national regulations but enhance collaboration between sending and receiving countries. Four main policy objectives dictate the guidelines: the need to protect learners from the risks of misinformation; to make qualifications readable and transparent; to make recognition procedures more fair and reliable; and to increase mutual understanding and co-operation between national quality assurance agencies.

These global guidelines, when they are finalised, are likely to be a significant and useful development but their necessary, non-binding nature may limit their impact. This is a real problem as the existence of a plethora of well-crafted recognition tools and international codes of good practice is of little use if they are not implemented. In this context the (currently) forty Bologna states could well have a real opportunity to develop a common approach that ensures a universal adoption of appropriate policy instruments and codes of practice within the European Higher Education Area. Appropriate national authorities need to assume responsibility for the quality assurance of such instruments to ensure they are fully implemented. This sort of action would go a long way to help define the European Higher Education Area and identify some of its core values – what it exactly stands for.

Conclusions

The emerging European Higher Education Area is to be completed in 2010, with its overarching framework of qualifications, new-style national frameworks, transparency tools (Diploma Supplement, etc.), mobility mechanisms and co-ordinated policies for quality, transparency and recognition. This is a new unknown in the global educational mix. Perhaps the main question we all need to consider is what role, if any, does the European Higher Education Area have in relation to the public responsibility for higher education and research – does it change anything? The answer to the last question must be yes! The Bologna Process should lead to a co-ordinated approach to many of the awkward questions raised in this paper. The current reality is that in most states quality assurance and recognition systems are simply not seriously addressing the quality of new education providers whatever their status (private for-profit/not-for-profit or public HEIs exporting and validating programmes of study).

European education is faced with many significant questions. The emerging trends do not inevitably lead to an educational apocalypse but certainly a very different education world is being constructed. Perhaps the most difficult question facing us is: what exactly will it be like to exist within the European Higher Education Area when it is completed in 2010? Are we creating a cut-throat internal competitive market or a common academic space that represents quality education, good governance, shared academic values and a commitment to transparency and fair recognition?

To pursue the economic approach adopted in the literature review by Alain Schoenenberger on higher education and academic research as a public good or a public responsibility, we need to explore what sort of educational market might be created. It is certain to be imperfect and may well involve a complex system of interlocking monopolies. Will the European educational space be self-regulated and if so how will national regulation cope with transnational education that is by definition borderless in nature? A more co-ordinated Bologna approach to transnational education, as importer and exporter, is certainly required. A public debate needs to be instigated between national and international stakeholders in order to develop co-ordinated policies on the implications of transnational education. This can help to define the European Higher Education Area and in a practical way embed the Lisbon Recognition Convention and its associated code of good practice.

It is possible to draw at least three conclusions. Firstly, that new trends and new providers will increasingly have a profound impact at local, national and international levels, challenging us to re-examine our narrow notion of public responsibility from its focus on the role of the state to encompass a series of reciprocal responsibilities by different actors at different levels. The second conclusion is that the whole academic community needs to take a more dominant role, in shaping the newly emerging educational world, as active participants concerned to impart and protect core academic and democratic values. This may also help us develop a more mature understanding of the evolving role of the autonomous university in the twenty-first century. Finally, it is clear that borderless education poses a unique set of challenges that requires a more sophisticated and effective response by states than exists at the moment where most states are commonly failing in their public responsibilities.

References

Adam, S., *Transnational education project report (western Europe),* Confederation of European Rectors' Conferences, 2001.

Adam, S., *Transnational education report (central and eastern Europe),* Swedish National Agency for Higher Education, 2003.

Campbell, C., "Transnational education", in European university of the 21st century, *Cuadernos Europeos de Deusto,* Vol. 29.

Council of Europe/Unesco, *Code of Good Practice in the Provision of Transnational Education,* adopted by the Lisbon Recognition Convention Committee in Riga 2001, Council of Europe/Unesco, 2001, available at: http://www.coe.int

Committee of Vice-Chancellors and College Principals (CVCP),[49] *The business of borderless education,* CVCP, 2000.

ESIB (The National Union of Students in Europe), *ESIB student handbook on transnational education,* ESIB, 2003, available at: http://www.esib.org.

Hrabinská, M., "Transnational education in the Slovak Republic – Threat or challenge," *Higher Education in Europe,* Vol. XXV, No. 3, 2000.

OECD/Unesco, *Quality provision in cross-border higher education (draft guidelines),* OECD/Unesco, 2003, available at: http://www.oecd.org

Rauhvargers, A., "Improving the recognition of qualifications in the framework of the Bologna Process", *European Journal of Education,* Vol. 39, No. 3, 2004, available at: http://www.upf.edu/bolonya/butlletins/2004/octubre/andrejs.pdf

---

49. The CVCP is now known as Universities UK.

The public responsibility of higher education: preparation for the labour market

Guy Haug[50]

The education agenda and economic/social priorities

European higher education has entered a major process of structural change related to the determination of its governments and universities to complete the creation of a coherent, compatible and competitive European Higher Education Area by the year 2010 in the context of the Bologna Process. Yet, this process of change has from the beginning put more emphasis on "qualifications" than on "degrees": the origin and content of the Bologna Declaration is easier to understand if it is read not as an academic document, but rather as an agenda for change in higher education driven by social and economic considerations. Within the EU it has also a strong link to the common European labour market.

It is therefore not surprising that in addition to the structural reforms (Bachelor/Master, ECTS, Diploma Supplement) that are at the core of the Bologna reforms, two objectives have been gaining importance and may now have come to the top of the Bologna agenda: the need to promote the competitiveness and attractiveness of European universities in the world and the need to draw up a European framework of reference for qualifications, that is, an instrument fostering the compatibility and cross-recognition of qualifications, whether for the purpose of further studies/training or access to the labour market.

It is interesting to point out that these two aspects have also become core concerns in recent initiatives taken within the EU's Lisbon Strategy. At the same time as announcing the Union's overall goal to become a leading knowledge-based economy and society, the European Council in 2000 emphasised that this was only possible with deep changes in social and educational systems. The Lisbon Strategy wants to create "more and better jobs" and at the same time to foster social integration and citizenship. This combination of goals underlies the work programme on the objectives of education and training systems ("Education and Training 2010")[51] adopted in 2002. It wants to achieve "enough compatibility to allow citizens to take advantage" of Europe's diversity (instead of being limited by it) and hopes that Europe will once again become "the most-favoured destination of students, scholars and researchers from other world regions".

---

50. The analysis and views expressed in this article are those of the author and are not necessarily shared by the European Commission.
51. All documents on "Education and Training 2010" are available on the Europa server:
http://europa.eu.int/comm/education/policies/2010/et_2010_en.html

These goals are closely related to the emergence of a real European labour market, which is bound to shape a good deal of university offering and functioning in the years ahead. The combination that has existed in some countries between long study times, low graduation rates, high graduate unemployment and a shortage of qualified young people in key areas is unlikely to be accepted by society hence-forward. This adds to the signals showing that educational policy is less and less isolated from its context and is increasingly driven by economic and social issues.

Contributions of Bologna to the debate on "employability"

The Bologna Process has had a strong and positive effect on the debate about the relationship between higher education and professional life, in particular concerning the preparation of graduates for the labour market.[52] It has raised the profile of the issue and increased the awareness that the employability of graduates has become an increasingly important and shared concern all over Europe. A similar acknowledgement can be found in the European Union's "Education and Training 2010" work programme with respect to education/training systems as a whole, even though particular emphasis is placed on vocational education, lifelong learning and, interestingly, higher education.[53]

This has been acknowledged by universities, in particular in their Salamanca Message of 2001 which stated that "European higher education institutions recognise that their students need and demand qualifications which they can use effectively for the purpose of their studies and careers all over Europe" and universities "acknowledged their role and responsibility in this regard".

On the government side, the meetings in Prague and Berlin gave ministers an opportunity to put a number of issues at the centre of attention. In Prague they stressed the importance of lifelong learning and formally acknowledged that citizens must be in a position to use their qualifications, competencies and skills effectively throughout Europe. They called for the first time for the development of a common framework of qualifications (and for coherent quality assurance/accreditation mechanisms as a means to build up such a framework). They also called for "modules, courses and curricula which are 'European' by their content, orientation or organisation, in particular those leading to joint degrees". In Berlin little more was added about employability issues, but ministers underlined the importance of improving the understanding and acceptance of the new qualifications, including through reinforced dialogue between higher education and employers, and the need for different orientations and various profiles of qualifications, in order to accommodate the diversity of needs, including labour market needs. At the more operational level they called (again) for a framework of

---

52. This section is largely based on material gathered for the *Trends II* and to a lesser extent on the *Trends III* reports (both documents are available from the Bergen website: www.bologna-bergen2005.no

53. *Communication on the role of universities in the Europe of knowledge* (February 2003) and *Joint interim report on the implementation of "Education and Training 2010"* (February 2004). Both documents are available on the Europa server (cf. above, note 51).

comparable and compatible qualifications, adding that such qualifications should be described in terms of workload, level, learning outcomes, competencies and profile. For the first time, they specifically wondered whether and how shorter qualifications "may be linked to the first cycle of qualification", that is, the bachelor level. Yet, among the various bodies involved in the follow-up work for the next two years (until the ministerial meeting in Bergen in 2005) there is still no involvement of employers or industry.

At EU level the most important development within the Lisbon Strategy is the call for a European framework of reference for qualifications encompassing vocational education and training and higher education. Hence, the need to set in place this crucial instrument is now a core part of both the Bologna agenda (as expressed by ministers in Berlin) and the EU's Lisbon Strategy.

As a clear illustration of its "crystallisation" function, the Bologna Declaration's intention to promote the employability of graduates on the European labour market has been widely endorsed at national level because it has been seen as underpinning national plans aimed at enhancing employability. Such plans have emerged in member states for different types of reason:

– in several countries employability has been a long-standing backbone of the national higher education policy and the Bologna Declaration is naturally seen as reinforcing national efforts;

– in countries where bachelor-type qualifications have confirmed acceptance on the labour market the main emphasis seems to be not so much on employment in general (graduate unemployment tends to be low), but rather on the adjustments to specific market needs, especially in view of growing skills and labour shortages;

– in new member states, the Bologna Declaration's emphasis on employability has met other, convergent, calls for reform related to the preparation for the European labour market, well before the end of the transition phase;

– in several countries the attention paid to employability and links with industry in the Bologna Process has been seen as a welcome support provided to efforts aimed at curbing high graduate unemployment rates.

These various reasons explain why in most countries the acknowledgment that employability needs to be fostered seems to be a powerful source of change and reform in higher education. In the EU context, this trend has been further reinforced thanks to the strong (yet not exclusive) emphasis on growth and employment provided by the Lisbon Strategy and its impact on national agendas in education and training (mainly through the thirteen European objectives set out in "Education and Training 2010").

These developments point in the same direction as the Bologna Process, whose impact can be found mainly in three areas:

– the most visible aspect is that the declaration created a broad debate about employability after a first (bachelor-type) degree. There are still reminders that higher education is not only for professional purposes and there is still some concern in the university sector that first degrees should not be geared too narrowly to short-term needs on the labour market. But on the whole the move is clearly towards a stronger attention to employment prospects and the acquisition of core, or transversal, skills. The few qualification frameworks that have emerged at national level are strongly "outcome-based" and qualifications are mostly defined in terms of skills/competencies acquired by graduates. The debate underlined that both academic and professional bachelor degrees need to be "relevant" (although not in exactly the same way). In several countries new legislation made relevance to the labour market a key factor for the authorisation (or "accreditation") of new programmes or made the collaboration with professional bodies compulsory in the development of new curricula. This is sometimes combined with specific efforts to promote first-degree graduates on the labour market, for instance by adjusting the statutes/laws regulating access to the civil service or to regulated professions;

– the second impact of the Bologna Declaration's interest in employability is that it provided new impetus for the further development of the college/polytechnic sector and for its creation in a few more countries. In nearly all countries with a binary system the declaration re-opened a debate on the respective roles of various types of higher education institutions and on the profile of their degrees. This debate has been especially intense in countries where a strong college/polytechnic sector provides a relatively high proportion of graduates with qualifications geared towards access to the labour market after two, three or four years. In these countries the need for a shift towards "employability" in the university sector is clearly not felt in the same way as in those where higher education is mostly or exclusively found at universities. This new impetus for professional higher education has also led to the creation or extension of a binary system in several countries, for instance through the creation of professional degrees at bachelor and in some countries also at master's level;

– finally, the Bologna Declaration has played an important role in drawing attention to the increasingly European dimension of the issue of employability. In most countries the widening of the European dimension in higher education qualifications is seen mainly in conjunction with the development of the EU programmes for co-operation and mobility (Socrates, Leonardo). The *Trends III* report observed a strong link between mobility and employability. In the wake of the Prague Communiqué there is also renewed attention given to the setting up of joint, integrated or double-degree courses in several countries. A number of countries have created special funding possibilities for such courses or promote the development of courses with a "European" orientation taught in English and designed for national and foreign students alike. The continuous development of European summer courses in a wide spectrum of disciplines and specialisation areas, run by a single institution or jointly by higher education networks such as Universities from the Capitals of Europe (UNICA) or the European Consortium of Innovative Universities (ECIU), should also be noted in this regard. Within the EU context the series of directives on professional recognition are important tools for employability in Europe. They are under review and the Commission has put forward a proposal to replace them by a single directive on professional recognition. This would have happened anyway, but at the same time it underpins the labour market objectives of the Bologna Process.

Lessons learnt and suggestions for policy development

The above developments within the Bologna Process may be interpreted as signals of fundamental change in European higher education in its interface with the labour market dimension. This section will try to identify the main lessons learnt for future policy development:

– higher education is ever more integrated with economic policies as a key factor of competitiveness. This refers both to the ability of graduates to compete successfully in the European labour market and to that of universities and national systems to compete worldwide in view of the globalisation of technologies and markets;

– employability is a key aspect that should be taken into account, along with others, when higher education institutions design or renovate curricula and learning methods. This is in full agreement with the best tradition of universities, who have for centuries educated (and indeed "trained") lawyers, doctors, church executives, researchers and top civil servants and allowed them to earn a living while at the same time serving the community and acting as citizens. The main change is not with reference to the essence of the mission of universities, but only to the much greater number and diversity of economic and social positions requiring higher education in modern, knowledge-based economies and societies. This also implies that there is no fundamental contradiction between employability and the development of the humanistic, social and citizenship aspects of higher education;

– the relevance of higher education should be assessed with reference to the European, rather than just the national, labour market. Although the Bologna Process extends to the whole of Europe, this is of course particularly true with respect to EU countries, where the Bologna Process and the implementation of the Lisbon goals reinforce each other, particularly with respect to aspects of higher education related to employability;

– employability should be assessed with regard to all possible forms of professional occupation on the European labour market, including self-employment (in other words, employability is not limited to the possibilities of working as an employee for an employer);

– employability should always be understood as sustainable employability rather than as a mere preparation for the immediate or short-term needs of the labour market. The term was forged in France as *employabilité durable* and there is an ever clearer understanding that it refers not only to high level, long or academic courses, but also to more vocational ones;

– all initial and lifelong leaning courses should pay attention to employability, but there are various ways in which higher education qualifications can be "relevant to the labour market", depending on their level and main orientation. The European Higher Education Area needs to be coherent but diverse in all respects, including with regard to employability;

– the design of a coherent European framework of qualifications serving as a common reference based on trustworthy quality assurance or accreditation mechanisms is the major challenge for the next stages of both the Bologna Process and the Lisbon Strategy.

References

This chapter is largely based on material gathered for the *Trends II* and to a lesser extent on the *Trends III* report (both documents are available from the Bergen website: www.bologna-bergen2005.no

All documents on "Education and Training 2010" are available on the Europa server: http://europa.eu.int/comm/education/policies/2010/et_2010_en.html

Communication on the role of universities in the Europe of knowledge (February 2003) and *Joint interim report on the implementation of "Education and Training 2010"* (February 2004). Both documents are available on the Europa server (cf. preceding reference).

The public responsibility for information on higher education

Johan Almqvist and Martina Vukasović

Within the transfer from the information-based to the knowledge-based society, the focus on mere acquiring of information has been shifted to the adequate use of reliable and up-to-date information. With the exponential growth of information potential, primarily through the Internet and use of electronic communication, obtaining information is no longer a problem. On the contrary, one often feels lost in the jungle of all kinds of information: necessary and unnecessary; relevant and trivial; targeted and general; trustworthy and of suspicious reliability. It is as if one actually needs guides to go into that jungle and find whatever one is looking for and find one's way out again. The question then becomes: how to find the guides, how to choose the most skilled ones and who is responsible for providing them?

All relevant stakeholders, ranging from the education ministers of states party to the Bologna Process to the umbrella organisations of higher education institutions and student unions, see higher education as a public good and a public responsibility. The understanding of these terms may vary, but it is a common belief that society in general and government in particular have a substantial role to play in creating the possibilities for provision and quality assurance of higher education. Therefore, there is also a substantial public responsibility for information on higher education.

However, in analysing the nature and scope of this responsibility, one of the questions that needs to be addressed is what kind of information on higher education we are referring to. Is it the information that is available or the information that is needed? How do the two correspond to each other? Closely related to this is the question of which target groups are using information on higher education: what sort of information do they need and who is responsible for providing it to them? And is it only a question of provision as such or there is more to it?

Information on higher education – What does it mean?

The answer to the question given in the subheading varies greatly with the respondent. Diverse groups are using information on higher education – students, sometimes their parents, higher education institutions, governments and ministries, employers, society in general – to name but a few. This question cannot be answered without interlinking the target groups with the purpose of the sought information: choosing a study programme, finding potential employees or employment, planning national development strategies or state budgets. We will attempt at this point to establish a matrix of target groups and purposes to define what sort of information on higher education is necessary, whether it is already available and who is responsible for its provision.

Target groups or potential users of information can generally be grouped in the following categories:

- students – prospective, current and graduate, as individuals as well as student organisations and those working to protect and promote student rights and student interests;
- higher education institutions – both domestic and foreign;
- governments – both national (including regional and local) and foreign;
- employers (both small-scale, "direct" employers and large companies);
- society in general.

Even a first glance at these five target groups leads to an understanding that they require very different types of information.

Prospective students are interested in the content of the study programmes, the skills and knowledge they are likely to acquire if they follow the programmes, the requirements for entering a programme (both in terms of academic and financial requirements) as well as the possibilities for further employment. Current students would focus on additional aspects such as completion of studies and counselling services, while graduates will concentrate on the possibilities for further education or employment. An individual student is probably not very interested either in the structure of the whole higher education system (unless this is his/her specific subject area), or in when the legislation framework was changed last, or in how much the state invested in higher education over the past five years. However, student organisations are likely to, or at least should, participate in the reform of higher education, which also includes legislation change and investment and development planning; thus, they need information on these matters.

Higher education institutions require information on the needs of the labour market and society to construct their programmes and to meet the expectations and needs of the general public. They also need information on possibilities for mobility and international co-operation, which also implies information about other higher education systems and programmes at other institutions. Furthermore, to be able to fully participate in the decision-making process at the regional, national, European and international level, they need wider information on the entire educational system as well as funding, development and planning in general.

Governments and ministries responsible for higher education (should) create development strategies on the basis of reliable information on the needs of the labour market; possibilities within the existing higher education institutions and potential needs for new and different providers of higher education; and expectations and competencies of prospective students and the expectations the general public has when it comes to higher education. Furthermore, any development and reform of higher education also includes a system-wide analysis of the efficiency and effectiveness of higher education systems, both in terms of employability and use of material (including financial) resources and in terms of meeting the needs of the community and the advancement of society's knowledge base.

Higher education institutions from abroad, as well as foreign governments, need information on higher education primarily on the system and institution level, particularly for co-operation, mobility and recognition purposes. Individual higher education institutions from abroad would also need particular information on specific programmes and courses, again for co-operation, mobility and recognition purposes.

Employers are another seemingly coherent target group. They are, of course, primarily interested in the competencies and skills graduates have after completing their higher education, which implies information both on the structure and content of courses, but also information on quality assurance procedures at programme, institutional and national level. However, it may be argued that small or medium-sized enterprises will most likely limit themselves to this kind of information, while large companies and multinational investors (especially in transition economies) may also seek information on the higher education system as a whole, development strategies, and the relationship between higher education and the economy, not only in terms of funding higher education but more on how higher education can return this investment.

As for society in general, although its need for information on higher education may not be that prominent, society at large should have information on the overall role of higher education in society, all of the possible benefits communities have from higher education, what has been achieved, and not least how taxpayers' money has been put to use. In this respect, higher education institutions and governments are accountable to society and should justify the investment and support given as well as providing information on institutions' work and achievements.

To sum up, we present the following matrix:

	Purpose	Level
Individual students	– entry – progression and completion – mobility – recognition – employment	– course/programme level – institution level – system level (primarily on recognition issues or student welfare)
Student organisations	– protection and promotion of student rights and interests	– all levels (depending on where the organisation is working)
Higher education institutions	– development of study programmes and institution as a whole – planning, funding purposes – international co-operation (including student and staff mobility – quality assurance and recognition	– course/programme level – institution level – system level – transversal information (for example, relevance of courses for the labour market and the economy of the region/country) – international level

Governments	development of: – the education system (funding, reforms, recognition, mobility, quality assurance and accreditation) – the economy (relationship between higher education and the labour market, use of research in development) – society in general	– institution and course/ programme level – system level – transversal information – international level
Foreign stakeholders (HEIs from abroad or foreign governments)	– co-operation – mobility and recognition	– course/programme level (primarily HEIs from abroad) – institution and system level (both foreign HEIs and governments) – transversal information
Employers (small to mid-size)	– finding suitable employees	– course/programme level – institution level – system level (if from abroad)
Employers (large scale)	– finding suitable employees – investment and development	– course/programme level – institution level – system level – transversal information
Society in general	– accountability of HEIs to society – assessing relevance of higher education to society in general (in terms of economic but also social and cultural development)	– institution level – system level – transversal information

What is "good" information on higher education?

Although the structure, content and usage of information on higher education vary greatly from group to group, some underlying principles of information (should) exist.

Principles of "good" information

Availability, accessibility and relevance

"Information should be made available" is a worn-out, rather empty request, especially when information is all around us. However, as we said before, availability of information is not limited to asking whether there is a place/medium where certain information is published but rather if this place is available and accessible to those concerned. The development of the Internet contributed to a significant improvement in this respect and facilitated (as well as decreased the costs of) publishing information; however, it has to be remembered that the Internet and computer technology are not accessible to everyone and that alternative methods of publishing must be explored. In some cases, this does mean going a step back in time and using plain old printed materials. In other cases, it implies certain adjustments to accommodate disabled persons, for instance.

Furthermore, the question of availability and accessibility also pertains to whether information is presented in a way that is understandable to those concerned: an individual student interested in student welfare schemes may not (and should not be expected to) understand legislation related to the issue or statistical data on student grants and loans which may be used by a ministry of finance. What he/she needs is a straightforward explanation of the rules and procedures related to grants and loans, deadlines for application, etc., and this is what should be made available to the student.

The question of terminology is closely related to the issue of understandable information. In the framework of the Bologna Process in particular, we see different understandings of certain terms which often lead to misunderstanding and confusion. A simple example is that of the different meaning people with different backgrounds (both professional and personal) attach to terms such as degree, diploma, first/second cycle, qualification, and certificate. It is usually only those professionally involved with these issues who would be able to explain the differences in these terms, and even this explanation may vary depending on the language and country in question. Therefore, any provider of information should take into account these possible differences and provide a glossary that would help users to understand the full meaning of the data given.

The question of accessibility and availability is closely related to that of relevance. The issue of relevance has two aspects:

– any information provided has to be relevant for the user;
– no relevant information should be withheld.

This may seem like another worn-out request, or something that goes without saying. However, experience shows that sometimes important information can be withheld on purpose or buried and hidden in clusters of – bluntly speaking – rubbish. Of course, the demand for relevance means that users have to know what information is relevant for them and what is not, and they have to be able to notice if some important piece of the puzzle is missing. A good example of empowering users of information (primarily individual students) and facilitating searching are the "Questions you should ask" developed by the ENIC and NARIC Networks.[54]

Accuracy and credibility

Information on higher education should be as accurate as possible. A part of the demand for accuracy is the proper use of terminology (or providing glossaries to facilitate understanding) but it also includes providing relevant statistical data where possible. However, this does not mean putting mere numbers wherever one sees a good spot, but providing, if relevant, credible statistical data based on reliable research. And the keywords here are "credible" and "reliable".

---

54. http://www.enic-naric.net

Most of the information on higher education, especially for individual students, is provided by higher education institutions and is related to their own programmes, courses and the quality of education they provide. In times where potential students are being swamped with online advertisements from degree mills and public administrations and employers in several countries have found that many of these fake degrees have gone undetected for a long time, this is of the utmost importance. While not saying that no information provided by higher education institutions is trustworthy, we would like to underscore that there must be a possibility for students and other interested users to check if the information provided by the institution is reliable. This can be done in various ways:

– by student organisations providing their own information on the institution and giving interested users the possibility of comparing the two sets of information;

– by public authorities, either by checking the full set of information (which is often too ambitious and not really necessary) but even better through quality assurance and accreditation procedures in which the whole institution, including its information strategy, would be given a label of trustworthiness – or not.

Good information = quality-assured information

The demand for accuracy and credibility, together with the other principles described earlier, lead us to the following conclusion: all information on higher education must be quality assured. It may even be argued that quality assurance of information on higher education is an integral and very important part of quality assurance of higher education as a whole, at all levels, from individual courses to the system level. On the one hand, an accredited institution with developed internal quality culture and quality assurance mechanisms is likely to transfer the same standards it has in teaching, research and governance to the provision of information. On the other hand, it is the responsibility of public authorities dealing with quality assurance to include the standards and procedures for information provision in the set of standards and procedures of quality assurance of programmes or institutions as a whole. And it is the responsibility of all the relevant stakeholders to continuously monitor and evaluate the attainment of these standards.

Public responsibility for information on higher education and the Bologna Process

Having in mind the complexity of the foreseen European Higher Education Area as well as the processes establishing it, it is of particular interest to address the use of and responsibility for information in a global perspective.

One of the paramount objectives of the Bologna Process, easy mobility of students and staff, relies on information, both regarding various mobility programmes and regarding issues such as recognition, the social dimension of mobility and non-academic obstacles to mobility (administrative, financial and language obstacles). If one looks further, to the European labour market, the need for information is even more evident – not only for employers who need more information to find their way in the diversity of qualifications but also for the potential students and graduates who need information both on the skills and competences (to be) acquired through higher education and on the needs of the labour market.

Information on quality assurance as such, and accreditation, is another aspect of the Bologna Process where availability and credibility of information is crucial. This does not include only the outcomes of the process of quality assurance and accreditation on different levels but also their relation to the recognition of qualifications, funding of higher education, employability, etc. This means that both the institutions themselves and the quality assurance/accreditation agencies have to provide fair and adequate information on their own procedures and standards for quality assurance and accreditation.

Related to both quality assurance and mobility is the issue of recognition of qualifications or study credits. The core problem in recognition is essentially a problem of information – do credentials evaluators and recognition authorities possess sufficient and reliable information to make a fair assessment of a qualification? The answers is more often no than yes. Under the Bologna label, two transparency tools have been adopted to facilitate recognition. One is the Diploma Supplement – developed jointly by the European Commission, the Council of Europe and Unesco/CEPES in the late 1990s – and we would like to welcome the commitment of all Bologna countries to start issuing Diploma Supplements to all of their students from 2005 automatically, in a widely spoken language and free of charge. On the other hand, the introduction of the European Credit Transfer System (ECTS) – even though its purpose is not only to facilitate recognition and ensure transparency – and its development into a credit transfer as well as an accumulation system is yet another aspect where the provision of information is at the heart of the problem. It is the primary responsibility of public authorities, but also of other stakeholders such as student organisations and institutions, to ensure the proper introduction and use of ECTS.

Finally, we come to the qualification frameworks; both national and the overarching European one. It is often argued that qualification frameworks will be the crucial building block of the European Higher Education Area. It might also be an answer to the problem that several objectives of the "structural" dimension of the Bologna Process aim at the provision of information but little thought was given to how that information should be collected, compiled and presented to the various target groups. It is in the development of the national qualification frameworks that the public responsibility for information on higher education is the greatest – both in terms of development of the frameworks (in full co-operation with all relevant stakeholders) and also when it comes to providing accessible, reliable and accurate information on qualifications to all those interested, be they students, the labour market, higher education institutions or society in general.

By way of conclusion

The responsibility for providing accurate, accessible, reliable and relevant information on higher education lies primarily in the hands of public authorities – ministries responsible for higher education but also other public bodies dealing with higher education, such as different national or regional councils, quality assurance agencies, etc. A crucial aspect of this responsibility is ensuring that the different providers of information on higher education abide by the principles of good information we have outlined here. The process of ensuring good information includes both setting the standards and checking if these standards are being met, and developing rules and procedures to protect the victims of deliberate abuse of information (for example, by an institution claiming to be accredited when it is not).

A *laissez-faire* or self-regulation approach from governments and public authorities will not suffice, because the cost of inaccurate information is far too high. For students, in terms of having spent vast amounts of money and, more importantly, years of their lives that they will not get back. For employers, studies show that employing a candidate that does not match the job requirements is a very costly affair. And not least, for the state – hence society at large – in terms of both return on investments in grants, loans and financing of institutions and of missed tax income.

Very importantly, however, this does not absolve higher education institutions, employers or student organisations from the responsibility for the provision of good information; it is only through the joint efforts of all those involved that adequate provision of information to diverse target groups can be secured.

Conclusion and further policy development

The public responsibility for higher education and research – Conclusions and suggestions

Eva Egron-Polak

Introduction

The Council of Europe's Steering Committee for Higher Education and Research (CDESR) is a particularly well-suited forum to discuss and examine public responsibility for higher education and research because it brings together representatives of both public authorities and higher education institutions. The conference, organised to examine the question of public responsibility by the committee, brought together a large number of higher education leaders, representatives of government and of the EU Commission, students and associations. All papers that were presented and discussed were excellent and very rich; the questions they raised and the debate they stimulated were equally so. All references made in this report relate to chapters in this volume.

The issue of public responsibility is a timely one and the stakes are high in debating it at this time, because the conference was part of the Bologna seminars and thus expected to provide input into this process, as it prepares for the next ministerial meeting in Bergen in 2005. For this reason, the report provides a synthesis of the main points of discussion but includes as well the relevant recommendations that participants endorsed and which, taken collectively, were submitted to the Bologna Follow-Up Group as immediate outcomes from this reflection. The discussions were thought provoking, underlining the complexity and interconnectedness of various policies, measures and questions. They made it clear how the topic of public responsibility for higher education and research crystallises so much of the current debate on the changes taking place in higher education at the local, national, regional and global level and the challenges these changes pose for policy makers and for the higher education and research community.

Structure of the general report

The objective was to explore the nature, scope and exercise of public responsibility for higher education and research in today's society and particularly in Europe. It was, and deliberately so, a look only at one side, the public authority side, of the equation and this was clearly recognised and noted. Neither the responsibilities of institutions to society nor the responsibilities of students and other stakeholders were examined, in order to sharpen the focus, but noting that such reflections require equal time and consideration. This is also reflected in the recommendations, where the focus is also exclusively on public authorities' responsibilities or where additional work research and other discussions are needed. Indeed, the list of recommendations that were prepared as an integral part of this report, concludes with the following statement:

> "Building the Knowledge Society that is democratic, inclusive, equitable and competitive is a *shared responsibility* in which an examination of the responsibilities of public authorities must be completed by an analysis of the public responsibility of all other stakeholders. We urge that such corresponding analysis be undertaken as well."

This report is little more than a bird's eye view of the complex and multiple issues that are covered in detail in the various papers. All references in this report are to these authors. The report first quickly sets out the context or the changing landscape in which higher education and research are evolving in Europe. Second, some of the key messages with regard to the rationale and the ways in which public responsibility can be, is or indeed should be exercised are presented. For the most part, these messages are also the source of the final recommendations. While there are areas of consensus concerning the areas of public responsibilities, the means or various instruments for exercising such public responsibility and their impact is a very complex matter. At least three different ways of examining these issues or three distinct frameworks for analysis appear possible. Each could serve to structure the ongoing work and each is summarised. Following this section, the core and additional public responsibilities are presented very briefly before the challenges and outstanding questions are summarised.

Indeed, there are far more questions than answers in these attempts to define the nature and scope of public responsibility and so highlighting some of the risks and areas for further research is also a worthwhile exercise. Such research is needed to understand better each of the different public policy instruments and the interaction between them as well as with other forces which also play a role in higher education and research, including the market.

Finally, as indicated earlier, throughout the report, the main recommendations that were endorsed and some additional suggestions that issued from the discussions are integrated as appropriate. (The complete list of recommendations is also reproduced separately.)

Context

At the present juncture, there is an overwhelming agreement on what structures or most influences the context in which institutions of higher learning and research are evolving today. Some of these features or defining forces are almost universal and affect systems everywhere. Others are specific to Europe. Among those that were brought forth repeatedly, and thus colour the overall approach to the topic of public responsibility, are the following:

– the advent of the Knowledge Society means that higher education and research have become sectors of strategic importance – key to national and regional competitiveness and innovation, a vehicle to build or secure social cohesion and institutions for the embedding of democracy;

- in most of Europe mass higher education is now well and truly established and in the Knowledge Society and even more so in the knowledge-based economy, individual expectations for higher education have risen and are changing, but absolutely not diminishing;

- higher participation rates have not removed inequities based on socioeconomic, racial or ethnic origins of students and significant gaps remain within many countries and between countries in Europe;

- higher education and research performance cannot be analysed using only a national framework for its evaluation, but must rather be viewed in a global context, where increasingly there is a global higher education market;

- higher education must compete for a place on the public agenda with other sectors such as health; competition for scarce resources (from both public and private sources) is also increasing the competition between institutions of higher education and is leading to greater commercialisation and commodification of knowledge;

- growing demand for higher education, less funding for its supply and the availability and capacity of information and communications technologies have contributed to the rise of new providers – national, transnational, public and private, including non- and for-profit and those employing new delivery means;

- new actors, national, regional and even international, both governmental and non-governmental have been added to the higher education landscape and are exerting or expected to exert increasing influence and carry responsibilities on various aspects of higher education and research, such as quality assessment, regulation, information provision, etc.

And, in Europe, in addition or concurrently, the changes and forces that are steering higher education and research are largely influenced by the Bologna Process and the ministers' overarching 2010 goals of establishing the European Higher Education Area and the European Research Area, all linked, especially since the Berlin conference in 2003, to the European Union's objective for Europe to become the most competitive and dynamic knowledge-based economy in the world.

Key messages

The successive ministerial summits and declarations within the Bologna Process, which twice (Prague in 2001 and Berlin in 2003) made specific reference to the idea that "higher education should be considered a public good and is and will remain a public responsibility", provided the overall starting point for the more specific probing for what such statements mean and what such responsibility may entail.

In this rapidly shifting and very complex context, the roles higher education and research are expected to play and the demands that society places on higher education and research are changing. The governance of higher education institutions is hotly debated and the relationship between institutions and the state or the authorities that exercise public responsibility in higher education and research in each country are also in transition. At the same time, demands on the public authorities and on the public purse are also changing and imposing new lower and perhaps upper limits to the scope of public responsibility and bringing new actors to the table.

Nevertheless, there is a clear sense that throughout Europe, the concept of public responsibility is changing and not just in the higher education sector. For some, public responsibility is under threat; for others it is expanding unduly. Under these circumstances, all would agree that an open, ongoing and inclusive debate about the scope, the need for and the limits of public responsibility is essential. Most would also agree that the era in which we live is one in which the creation of knowledge and innovation are of unprecedented importance (Blasi, 2005). It was recommended that

> "in light of their importance in the process of building a Europe of knowledge, higher education and research be viewed as strategic investments rather than as consumers of resources and that public funding must remain a major source of their support".

It must be noted that while the initial discussion and presentations of the topic of public responsibility for higher education took on a very economic tone, especially with the careful examination of the concept of "public good", there was also a great effort to continuously add other dimensions. Nevertheless, a thorough overview of the literature demonstrated the overwhelming presence of economic theory in the examination of this topic and pointed out the paucity of non-economic analysis in this field (Schoenenberger, 2005). It was also underlined that applying the concept of "public good" in the strictest, and purely economic sense, could actually pose a long-term threat to the viability of higher education and research (Weber, 2005). Thus clarity of definitions and in-depth reflection on the various aspects and instruments of public policy and responsibility are essential and need to supersede the expediency of using politically correct terms even if those, as in this case, can serve in favour of the objectives pursued, namely retaining an important role for public authorities and public finance in higher education. It was to reflect these issues that it was recommended that

> "public responsibility for higher education and research be understood as a multi-dimensional concept that includes the establishment and maintenance of the required legal infrastructure, elaboration of policy, provision of funds and the further development of the social dimension, to meet the current and future needs of the Knowledge Society",

and that ministers

> "acknowledge that funding, motivating and stimulating the development of higher education and research is as important a part of public responsibility as the exercise of regulation and control".

Indeed, just as higher education and research play multiple roles in society and in the economy, the nature and scope of public responsibility is complex and has multiple dimensions. It must be underlined though, that these are intrinsically linked. The rationale for public responsibility for higher education and research cannot be divorced from the mission of universities and their responsibilities vis-à-vis students and democratic society as well as the world of work. In this regard, it was recommended that

> "in keeping with the values of democratic and equitable societies, public authorities ensure that higher education institutions, while exercising increased autonomy, can meet society's multiple expectations and fulfil their various purposes, which include personal development of learners, preparation for active citizenship in democratic societies, development and dissemination of advanced knowledge and preparation for the labour market".

It was also repeated that no universal model for defining the nature and scope of public responsibility exists and that local and national conditions will each time colour the way it is exercised (Shishlov, 2005).

There is overwhelming consensus that higher education and research are a key area of public responsibility and even the strictly economic, and therefore only partial, justification is solid: higher education is an investment of strategic importance. However, in the current circumstances of competing priorities vying for public authorities' attention, it becomes urgent to strengthen such justification by finding new ways to quantify what in economic terms are called the "externalities", in other words to quantify the benefits that accrue to society as a whole, and go beyond the private returns on the investment in higher education.

In addition, it was pointed out that increasingly important concepts such as "social capital", which refers to social ties, shared values, etc., form part of a broader objective – social cohesion. These aspects are far more difficult to quantify, yet they are particularly pertinent if the rationale for public intervention in higher education and research is to be based on the contributions made to society's overall well-being (Schoenenberger, 2005). In economic parlance, this leaves the theory of market failure as a primary justification for public investment in higher education. Justifying public responsibility through the failure of market forces seems a less than satisfactory manner in which to demonstrate the importance of this key sector. At the same time, getting at the indirect or social benefits that society and the economy as a whole derive from a strong and independent higher education and research sector is essential to complete the analysis of the rationale for public responsibility.

Yet, this very brief justification for why we need to probe deeper to gain better understanding of the economic and non-economic rationales for public responsibilities in the higher education and research system must not ignore that public policy and public institutions can also fall short of expectations and needs. Thus it is appropriate also to note that government failure and inefficiency in terms of fairness, etc., can exist in higher education and research as well (Weber, 2005).

Frameworks for analysis

Several frameworks may be used to analyse both the scope and the level of public responsibility for higher education. Given the limits of viewing higher education and research from a purely economic perspective, when all the objectives of higher education are considered, it seems clear that whichever framework is adopted, it must also integrate political and social considerations at the very least. Determining the appropriate role or type of involvement of public authorities and assessing the effectiveness of various instruments used to exercise public responsibility needs also to be anchored in shared societal values of democracy, human rights, equity, etc.

In terms of analysing the public responsibility for research, first it must be noted that to some extent research presents a different set of challenges from the learning and teaching aspects of higher education. Nevertheless, there is also perhaps even a stronger rationale for public responsibility in the area of research, with in addition to the social and political considerations, some ethical and security aspects to keep in mind. Furthermore, it can be argued that the very nature of the scientific method of critical and open enquiry defines the space that needs to be occupied by public authorities (Aaviksoo, 2005).

Thus in research, it was recommended that

> "in order for universities in the European Higher Education Area to meet society's requirements for research and respond to the public interest, public authorities must provide adequate funds and, together with the research community, design policies to regulate conditions under which private resources can best be used".

In all of this, however, and despite the need for public authorities to play an important role in creating an environment that is conducive to strong development in research and higher education, it must be underlined that public responsibility is not the same as direct public intervention. Finding appropriate instruments, which can build and not obstruct the creation of such an environment, is often a particularly difficult balancing act between too little and too much control.

Recognising that this is a delicate balancing task, it also requires appropriate conditions at the institutions of higher education. They must have sufficient levels of autonomy and adequate governance structures to set priorities, and make and implement strategic choices. It was therefore recommended that

> "public responsibilities be exercised throughout the European Higher Education Area with due regard for the need of higher education and research institutions and systems to act freely and efficiently in the pursuit of their mission".

The three frameworks that were put forward to facilitate the analysis of the nature and scope of public responsibility can be summarised as follows:

– an instrumental framework, which looks most particularly at the nature of state or public intervention. It highlights the fact that such exercise of public responsibility can be made through legal or policy instruments; through financial supports and various incentives such as tax breaks and investment opportunities, or by the exercise of moral influence through which public authorities can create an environment conducive to public respect and trust in higher education and research (Shishlov, 2005);

– the second framework that can be adopted is based on the level of engagement. This means that specific areas of public responsibility are assessed in terms of those where public responsibility is essential and exclusively exercised by public authorities, aspects where such public responsibility is desirable and rests, for the main part, in the hands of public authorities and third, areas or aspects of higher education and research that do not require the intervention of public authorities and where such intervention is important but optional (Shishlov, 2005; Bergan, 2005);

- the third framework can be called functional and takes, as its starting point, the needs of society. The scope of public responsibility is defined in terms of its purpose. It is exercised to ensure the appropriate quantity of higher education and research available in society; it is necessary to guarantee fair distribution of access to higher education and research, and it ensures the quality of education and research. The concept of quality, when extended to include research, could also include public responsibility to provide vigilance and oversight to protect public safety and uphold ethical considerations (Weber, 2005; Aaviksoo, 2005).

As the concept of public responsibility is likely to continue to evolve, it will become increasingly vital to find means to analyse and to assess how best to define the optimal role of public authorities in a variety of contexts. Each of the frameworks that have been articulated, either explicitly or implicitly, offers a different perspective on this discussion and may bring new insights. Collectively they serve as a solid starting point for ongoing research.

Core responsibilities

The establishment of a clear and favourable policy framework in which higher education and research can adequately develop, and the provision of basic funding to support this development, are the two most obvious aspects of public responsibility. Yet, within each of these broad areas, what should be covered in such a policy framework, how binding it ought to be, what mechanisms it should employ and how far it should extend are all questions open to debate. Similarly, the level of public funding and how it might be supplemented by other fiscal measures and mechanisms, or how best to aid individuals or families to make bigger contributions to the cost of higher education are the kinds of details where, as the saying goes, the devil may still be winning the battle. Nevertheless, these are the domains where public responsibility is of the utmost importance.

These and other considerations of equitable access and objective or disinterested review with regard to quality of learning and research were at the heart of many of the presentations and discussions concerning the core public responsibilities for higher education and research. Noting that decreasing public financial support has already led to an increase in private involvement in both teaching and research, whether through the introduction of or rise in tuition fees or through growing sponsorship of research by industry, it is clear that the number of issues that must be considered when defining the scope of public responsibility has grown. For this reason, it is urgent that whatever approach is taken to redefining the scope and nature of public responsibility in this field, sufficient time is allowed to carefully weigh its short and medium-term impact against all the goals being pursued in the European Higher Education Area.

In terms of research, as alternatives or supplements to public funding are explored, it was recommended that

> "considering the importance and the potential benefits and risks of research, public authorities ensure that adequate and disinterested oversight is developed and that access to research results be broadened, for example by adopting and supporting open access publishing initiatives".

More specifically, looking at the teaching and learning aspects of higher education, a variety of alternatives exist and are being explored and tested around the world to fill the funding gap left by generally declining public finance. In Europe too the search for ways of financing higher education takes place against a background where public authorities are either unwilling or unable to meet the need for expansion. A variety of approaches are possible but ultimately the choice is a political one, which can take the form of institutional or individual subsidies, income contingent repayment schemes, etc. (Salerno, 2005). The key issue that is underlining the debate about funding choices is how to uphold the principles of accessibility and equity, yet retain high-quality higher education. Research and evidence-based policy making and a long-term vision are essential in this regard and it was also recommended that

> "to respond to increased pressure for cost-sharing in higher education, where students and families may be expected to bear a greater share of the direct costs, public authorities stimulate further research and debate on the impact of different instruments such as tuition fees, student grants, bursaries and loans, etc., on aspects such as equality of opportunity, system efficiency, social cohesion, long-term impact on public funding, etc., as a basis for future action".

Additional aspects of public responsibility

In the light of the importance that is assigned to higher education and research as instruments or levers of economic, political and social development in Europe, it is not surprising that the areas of public responsibility appear to be expanding, even as the level of direct support and involvement in terms of funding may, in many cases, be declining. The exact scope of public responsibility varies from country to country, according to history and tradition and the system of government in place. In most countries though, in addition to the core responsibilities mentioned above, some or all of the following areas would also be considered as part of the public responsibility. Indeed, as the process of building the European Higher Education Area progresses, these additional areas appear to be less and less optional.

Employability

Whose responsibility is it to bridge the gaps between higher education and employment? Even if the reply most likely involves both institutions of higher education and public authorities, there are a number of ways in which public authorities have drawn the link between higher education and employability and brought it to the fore during the various stages of the Bologna Process. Perhaps it is most visible from the full acceptance by both the ministers and other actors of the need for a coherent European framework of qualifications that will cover vocational training as well as higher education and their commitment towards a more outcome-based view of qualifications. Such a framework and a competency-based approach to qualifications aim to further facilitate the movement of graduates within the European labour market. They are also expected to bring greater ease and flexibility for movement within and to and from the higher education systems. This issue has been given a high profile in several ways during the process of building the European Higher Education Area and in several ways has become an integral part of public responsibility (Haug, 2005). On the one hand, this requires that higher education institutions address the issue of employability when designing their programmes and fully integrate the lifelong learning mission into their plans. On the other hand, and in support of these developments, it is recommended that

"with the aim of enhancing sustainable employability of graduates in the European labour market, public authorities ensure that appropriate bridges exist between higher education institutions and the world of work; elements of such bridging include a coherent qualifications framework at the national and European levels, transparent mechanisms for recognition of qualifications and quality assurance, two-way information flows between the labour market and higher education, and flexible exit, entry and re-entry opportunities".

Information provision

As the higher education landscape shifts and changes due to structural reforms brought about by the Bologna Process and the diversification of institutions and programmes, a key and growing area of public responsibility is to ensure that learners, employers and others in society are well informed. This public responsibility though has as much to do with the substance of the information – comparability, accuracy and relevance – as with its availability or accessibility. Indeed what is of concern is the quality and the overall legitimacy of information available on systems, programmes and qualifications in higher education offered by all providers, national and transnational, public and private. The most important users of such trustworthy information are the learners, but employers too need to know what they can expect in terms of outcomes and competencies when hiring graduates. It was recommended that

"avoiding burdensome administrative arrangements and seeking greater transparency, public authorities in the European Higher Education Area adopt a common approach in setting the requirements for the provision of accurate, objective and up-to-date information on higher education options, including on transnational education providers, which corresponds to the needs of learners as well as other stakeholders, enabling and empowering each to make informed choices at all stages from entry to employment and including for mobility purposes".

In addition, information that can guide or empower users to ask the right questions and seek appropriate and relevant information is also needed. Finally, ensuring that such data has undergone some kind of objective quality control is also a growing responsibility for public authorities, especially as private and commercial interests are increasingly active in higher education (Almqvist and Vukasović, 2005).

Regulatory mechanism

Linked to making sound choices and knowing what can be expected from graduates is another priority area of public responsibility, namely quality assurance and quality assessment processes in higher education. These remain of the utmost importance when the overall higher education sector is expanding, yet where direct control may be diminishing, new providers are being created or imported and the overall system is becoming both more complex and more prone to change. The processes of quality assessment are an important instrument of regulation and, again, in most countries in Europe and at the regional level, public authorities are examining and debating most appropriate approaches. The United Kingdom, where attention paid to such regulatory mechanisms has perhaps the longest history in Europe, offers some powerful lessons, good practice cases as well as, in the words of Roderick Floud, rich experiences of what to avoid. Overall, the United Kingdom experience suggests quite strongly that such regulation be developed with due regard to a balance between costs and benefits, with due respect for university values and trust in university staff to act as "knights", rather than "knaves", which means trust that they generally act in the best interest of the students and the system. Also, quality assessment and regulation needs to build on internal processes for promoting quality rather than undermining them and any such regulatory mechanisms need to be guided by the principle of subsidiarity (Floud, 2005). Keeping these lessons in mind, it was recommended that

> "public authorities establish, as an essential regulatory mechanism in increasingly diversified higher education systems, cost-effective quality assessment mechanisms that are built on trust, give due regard to internal quality development processes, have the right to independent decision making and abide by agreed-upon principles".

Public responsibility and transnational education

The presence of transnational education providers is not felt to the same extent in all countries of Europe; however, the expansion of what is often also called borderless education is creating new challenges and demands for all stakeholders, including public authorities. It is doing so at the local but also at the regional and international levels. Precisely because of its transnational nature, borderless education requires a co-ordinated European, if not global, response that takes place within a public policy framework. In this area change and innovation is often very rapid and new actors or new alliances are being formed and getting involved in training and education. Both important academic and commercial interests are driving these developments but decision makers, as well as higher education leaders, academics, students and even employers, have far more questions than answers about the benefits and potential risks of a rapid expansion and diversification of ways and providers delivering higher education (Adam, 2005). It is in order to seek some of these responses that it was recommended that "a public debate between national and international stakeholders be promoted in order to develop co-ordinated policies on the implications of transnational education, keeping in mind the Lisbon Recognition Convention and the Unesco/Council of Europe Code of Good Practice in the Provision of Transnational Education as well as the efforts of OECD and Unesco to develop guidelines on quality provision in cross-border education".

Risks, challenges, opportunities and outstanding questions

Even if predominantly and firmly embedded within the public sector, most systems of higher education and research, including those in Europe, are increasingly characterised by a mix of public-private aspects, whether it is in knowledge production, provision or funding. Thus the process of defining public responsibility has become an art of finding the balance within these grey zones and blurred boundaries while seeking the most suitable, acceptable and effective means to obtain the desired ends. In addition to a balancing act, it is also a process of negotiation among multiple stakeholders.

Quite clearly, public funding, even if by no means sufficient or exclusive, is critical for higher education and research within the European Higher Education Area. It is, however, equally important to have laws guaranteeing institutional autonomy, to have firm policies about non-discriminatory access to higher education on the basis of merit, to have clear policies concerning degree structures, to enact enabling tax laws concerning funding of research, to pass laws determining when and how new institutions can be established and to establish transparent rules concerning recognition, accreditation, and quality assessment of institutions of higher education whether they are domestic or foreign. It is in fact the policy environment that can be either conducive or stifling for the growth and sound development of higher education and research. Such a policy environment can exert a critical steering effect at the level of institutions as well as at systemic levels and have important financial implications too. It is more than evident that each policy instrument and the interplay among them require further analysis and discussion.

Furthermore, if the full multiplicity of roles of higher education is factored into the vision of the European Higher Education Area and the collective goals of social cohesion, democracy and equality of opportunity are to be pursued, the policy framework must be widened and expanded. To achieve these far-reaching political goals public authorities need to create conditions and expectations and provide the support for education based on values. Among these, reasserting democracy as an inner value to the university is most important (Zgaga, 2005). Looking at other values for the EHEA, such as inclusiveness and equity, links to many other sectors of public policy – social, health and increasingly immigration policy and others, are required so that concrete ways can be found to remove barriers for all minority groups (Pedrosa de Jesús, 2005).

A vision and proactive measures at all levels of the system will be required, and the European ministers who will meet in Bergen in May 2005 are urged to:

- affirm their commitment to making equal opportunity in higher education a fundamental building block of the European Higher Education Area and to undertake actions that will allow the development of systemic and institutional responses to enable all individuals to realise their full potential and thus contribute to the shaping of a competitive and coherent Europe of Knowledge;

- acknowledge that funding, motivating and stimulating the development of higher education and research is as important a part of public responsibility as the exercise of regulation and control;

- as the basis for the formulation of a coherent and sustainable public policy in Europe, stimulate a comprehensive and in-depth analysis of various approaches that would lead to increased funds for higher education and research, paying particular attention to the requirements of meeting equity, effectiveness and efficiency objectives as well as those of quality and autonomy.

Recognising the funding shifts, how should other policy instruments of public responsibility be adjusted? Who and how will the best policy and regulation infrastructure be designed? How much of a role should rest with public authorities and how much should be left to the market to create the conditions in which autonomous institutions of higher education are empowered and entrepreneurial enough to both compete and co-operate? How can we avoid the worst-case scenario of little public support and over-regulation? What are the best conditions in which institutions can exercise their mission to provide higher education of quality to students and lifelong learners and to undertake research to advance knowledge and improve the quality of life, in a sustainable manner, for all citizens? And what is the best way to assess whether higher education is fulfilling this mission? Finally, how should public authorities regulate these autonomous institutions through accountability and assessment exercises?

What is clearly of universal concern in Europe and elsewhere is that funding and commitment of resources accompany the laws and regulatory mechanisms thus enabling their sound implementation. Goals such as becoming more attractive to the best qualified students and researchers and becoming the most competitive knowledge economy in the world require the commitment of adequate funds and other support in both higher education and research.

As it was pointed out earlier, the stakes are very high for Europe, for public authorities at the national level, for higher education leadership faculty, researchers and students, for employers and for society at large. All countries and the region as a whole need a higher education and research system that meets economic and social targets and helps all individuals achieve their full potential in society. Achieving such goals requires many instruments and levers to work in harmony rather than in contradiction with one another. The very complexity of these issues, though, makes it difficult as often contradictory objectives push and pull the system in different directions. It is almost always a matter of striking the right balance on a shifting continuum. The importance of the issues though requires full and active participation of all stakeholders in the search for a balanced, collective and negotiated response.

So, in conclusion, it is important to recognise that building the Knowledge Society or the Europe of Knowledge, which is democratic, inclusive, equitable and competitive, is a shared responsibility in which an examination of the responsibilities of public authorities must be completed by an analysis of the public responsibility of all other stakeholders.

Recommendations adopted by the conference

The conference recommends that:

1. in light of their importance in the process of building a Europe of Knowledge, higher education and research be viewed as strategic investments rather than as consumers of resources and that public funding must remain a major source of their support;

2. public responsibility for higher education and research be understood as a multidimensional concept that includes the establishment and maintenance of the required legal infrastructure, elaboration of policy, provision of funds and the further development of the social dimension, to meet current and future needs of the Knowledge Society;

3. public responsibilities be exercised throughout the European Higher Education Area with due regard for the need of higher education and research institutions and systems to act freely and efficiently in the pursuit of their mission;

4. in keeping with the values of democratic and equitable societies, public authorities ensure that higher education institutions, while exercising increased autonomy, can meet society's multiple expectations and fulfil their various purposes, which include personal development of learners, preparation for active citizenship in democratic societies, development and dissemination of advanced knowledge and preparation for the labour market;

5. in order for universities in the European Higher Education Area to meet society's requirements for research and respond to the public interest, public authorities must provide adequate funds and, together with the research community, design policies to regulate conditions under which private resources can best be used;

6. considering the importance and the potential benefits and risks of research, public authorities ensure that adequate and disinterested oversight is developed and that access to research results be broadened, for example by adopting and supporting Open Access Publishing initiatives;

7. to respond to increased pressure for cost-sharing in higher education, where students and families may be expected to bear a greater share of the direct costs, public authorities stimulate further research and debate on the impact of different instruments such as tuition fees, student grants, bursaries and loans, etc., on aspects such as equality of opportunity, system efficiency, social cohesion, long-term impact on public funding, etc., as a basis for future action;

8. with the aim of enhancing sustainable employability of graduates in the European labour market, public authorities ensure that appropriate bridges exist between higher education institutions and the world of work; elements of such bridging include a coherent qualifications framework at the national and European levels, transparent mechanisms for recognition of qualifications and quality assurance, two-way information flows between the labour market and higher education, and flexible exit, entry and re-entry opportunities;

9. avoiding burdensome administrative arrangements and seeking greater transparency, public authorities in the European Higher Education Area adopt a common approach in setting the requirements for the provision of accurate, objective and up-to-date information on higher education options, including on transnational education providers, which corresponds to the needs of learners as well as other stakeholders, enabling and empowering each to make informed choices at all stages from entry to employment and including for mobility purposes;

10. public authorities establish, as an essential regulatory mechanism in increasingly diversified higher education systems, cost-effective quality assessment mechanisms that are built on trust, give due regard to internal quality development processes, have the right to independent decision making and abide by agreed-upon principles;

11. a public debate between national and international stakeholders be promoted in order to develop co-ordinated policies on the implications of transnational education, keeping in mind the Lisbon Recognition Convention and the Unesco/Council of Europe Code of Good Practice in the Provision of Transnational Education as well as the efforts of OECD and Unesco to develop guidelines on quality provision in cross-border education;

In particular, the conference recommends that ministers meeting at the Bergen ministerial conference of the Bologna Process, in May 2005:

– affirm their commitment to making equal opportunity in higher education a fundamental building block of the European Higher Education Area and to undertake actions that will allow the development of systemic and institutional responses to enable all individuals to realise their full potential and thus contribute to the shaping of a competitive and coherent Europe of Knowledge;

– acknowledge that funding, motivating and stimulating the development of higher education and research is as important a part of public responsibility as the exercise of regulation and control;

– as the basis for the formulation of a coherent and sustainable public policy in Europe, stimulate a comprehensive and in-depth analysis of various approaches that would lead to increased funds for higher education and research, paying particular attention to the requirement of meeting equity, effectiveness and efficiency objectives as well as those of quality and autonomy.

Building the Knowledge Society that is democratic, inclusive, equitable and competitive is a shared responsibility in which an examination of the responsibilities of public authorities must be completed by an analysis of the public responsibility of all other stakeholders. We urge that such corresponding analysis be undertaken as well.

List of contributors

Editors

Sjur Bergan

Sjur Bergan is Head of the Council of Europe's Department of Higher Education and History Teaching, Secretary to its Steering Committee for Higher Education and Research and a member of the Bologna Follow-Up Group and Board. He is a frequent contributor to the debate on higher education policies in Europe, the author of many articles and editor of *The heritage of European universities* (with Nuria Sanz, 2002), *Recognition issues in the Bologna Process* (2003) and *The university as Res Publica: higher education governance, student participation and the university as a site of citizenship* (2004).

Luc Weber

Educated in the fields of economics and political science, Luc Weber has been Professor of Public Economics at the University of Geneva since 1975. As an economist, he serves as an adviser to the federal as well as to cantonal governments and he has been a member of the Swiss Council of Economic Advisers for three years. Since 1982, Professor Weber has been strongly involved in university management and higher education policy as Vice-Rector and then Rector of the University of Geneva, as well as Chair and, later on, Consul for International Affairs of the Swiss Rectors' Conference. At present, he is Vice-Chair of the Steering Committee for higher education and Research of the Council of Europe and of the International Association of Universities (IAU), as well as a member of the Board of the European University Association. He is also the co-founder of the Glion Colloquium.

Authors

Jaak Aaviksoo

Jaak Aaviksoo has been Rector of the University of Tartu since 1998 and Chairman of the Board of Estonian Rectors' Conference since 2004. He was Minister of Education of Estonia in 1995-97 and before that Vice-Rector of the University of Tartu. He is a physicist and Professor of Optics and Spectroscopy at the University of Tartu. He has been visiting professor and scholar in the Russian Federation, Germany, France and Japan. He is a member of the Estonian Academy of Science, the Academic Council of the President of Estonia and the Board of the European University Association.

Stephen Adam

Stephen Adam is principal lecturer and leader of the undergraduate politics area in the Department of Social and Political Studies at the University of Westminster. He is the author/rapporteur of a number of research projects and studies for the

237

European Commission and other organisations including: the Diploma Supplement Development Project (1999), ECTS Extension Feasibility Project (2000), the Transnational Education Projects – Western and Central/Eastern Europe (2001 and 2003), a background report on *Qualification structures in European higher education* for the first Danish Bologna Seminar on Qualifications Frameworks (2003), and the *Learning outcomes background report* for the Edinburgh "Bologna" seminar (2004). He is currently contributing to the BFUG working group report on qualifications frameworks and is a member of the EC experts group advising on the creation of a European qualifications framework for lifelong learning.

Johan Almqvist

Johan Almqvist is a student of computer science at Lund University and at the University of Oslo. He was the 2004 chairperson of the ESIB – The National Unions of Students in Europe – and has previously served on the executive committee of the ESIB as well as the Swedish National Union of Students (SFS).

Paolo Blasi

Paolo Blasi is Professor of Laboratory Physics at the University of Florence; he was Rector of the University of Florence in 1991-2000, and President of the Italian Rectors' Conference in 1994-95. He is a member of the French Comité national d'évaluation (CNE). His scientific activity has resulted in over eighty publications concerning the properties of the atomic nucleus and reactions between nuclei. Paolo Blasi was awarded the honorary title of Doctor of Humanae Letters by New York University in 1997 and by the University of Arizona in 2003, and awarded the title *Chevalier de l'ordre national de la Légion d'honneur* by the President of the French Republic in 2000.

Eva Egron-Polak

Eva Egron-Polak is Secretary-General of the International Association of Universities (IAU), a Unesco-based non-governmental organisation. With a long experience in international co-operation in higher education, as the head of IAU she is engaged with the most pressing issues in current higher education policy debates globally – internationalisation and intercultural learning, sustainable development and cross-border education, among others. Prior to joining IAU she was Vice-President (International) of the Association of Universities and Colleges of Canada. She was educated in the Czech Republic, Canada and France.

Roderick Floud

Roderick Floud is President of London Metropolitan University and a Board member of the European University Association. He was President of Universities UK from 2001-03. His latest publication is *The Cambridge economic history of modern Britain* and he is a Fellow of the British Academy.

Guy Haug

Guy Haug is a European expert on higher education policy in an international setting. He is currently advising the European Commission (Directorate of Education). Before that he was centrally involved in shaping the Bologna Process as Principal Adviser to the European Association of Universities. Until 1998 he was Director General for Europe of the Council on International Educational Exchange, New York/Paris. He worked for the EU for the inception of the Erasmus, Tempus and Asia-Link programmes. He has co-operated with the Council of Europe, the Nordic Council of Ministers, OECD, Unesco and many NGOs. He holds a master's degree in Law (Strasbourg), an MBA (Ottawa) and a Ph.D. in Political Science (Tübingen).

Júlio Pedrosa de Jesús

Professor Júlio Pedrosa de Jesús has been a full professor at the University of Aveiro since 1988 and his main research interests at present are focused on higher education and science policy and governance. Having devoted thirty years of his career to teaching and research on inorganic and materials chemistry, Professor Pedrosa has been Vice-Rector and Rector of the University of Aveiro, President of the Portuguese Council of Rectors (CRUP) and Minister of Education of Portugal.

Carlo Salerno

Carlo Salerno is a Senior Research Associate at the Center for Higher Education Policy Studies (CHEPS) at the University of Twente in the Netherlands. His research focuses on the economics of higher education with special attention to issues surrounding university productivity and costs as well as the behaviour of institutions as non-profits. Since coming to CHEPS in 2001, he has authored or co-authored a number of monographs and papers in the areas of higher education privatisation, funding, per-student cost estimation and efficiency.

Aleksander Shishlov

Born in 1955 in Leningrad, Aleksander Shishlov graduated from St Petersburg State University's Department of Mathematics (1977) and Department of Law (1994). He holds a Ph.D. in Mathematical Cybernetics (1984). In 1977-90, he was research fellow and head of department in academy research institutes dealing with research and design of control systems for robots and AI systems. Since 1990, he has dealt with public policy and municipal management; from 1990-1993, he was a member of St Petersburg City Council; and from 1995-2003, a member of the State Duma of the Russian Federation and member of the Parliamentary Assembly of the Council of Europe. In 2002-03, as Chair of the State Duma Committee on Education and Science, made important contributions for Russia's accession to the Bologna Process. At present, he is Director for Education Programmes at the St Petersburg Strategy Centre of Humanities and Political Studies.

Martina Vukasović

Martina Vukasović holds a BSc in Astrophysics and has been active as a student representative for six years in Serbia and Europe. She was the Chairperson of the ESIB – The National Unions of Students in Europe – in 2002 and has served on various committees of both ESIB and the Student Union of Serbia. She also worked in the Higher Education and Research Division of the Council of Europe and is presently involved in several activities related to the reform of higher education in Serbia and South-Eastern Europe.

Pavel Zgaga

Pavel Zgaga is a professor at the University of Ljubljana and Director of the Centre for Educational Policy Studies at the Faculty of Education. His research is primarily focused on the philosophy of education and on educational policy, particularly in contemporary issues of internationalisation of higher education. He is former Vice-Minister and Minister of Education of Slovenia, a signee at the Bologna Declaration and currently member of the Bologna Follow-up Group and Board. Pavel Zgaga is closely involved in the development of higher education in South-Eastern Europe.

The Council of Europe Higher Education Series

Series editor: Sjur Bergan

The Council of Europe Higher Education Series, launched in 2004, aims to explore higher education issues of concern to policy makers in ministries, higher education institutions and non-governmental organisations, not least student representatives. Beyond that, the books will be of interest to all those interested in the development and future of higher education in Europe.

The topics covered by the Higher Education Series will reflect the commitment of the Council of Europe to the basic values of democracy, human rights and the rule of law and its belief that education and higher education play a key role in developing the democratic culture without which democratic societies cannot thrive, as well as in developing the skills, knowledge and values that modern, complex societies require.

The volumes in the Council of Europe Higher Education Series will reflect the lively debate on higher education policy currently under way in Europe as well as the Council of Europe's contributions to that debate. Authors will be invited to put forward their own views on the topics selected, and the series will seek to provide a forum for debate rather than outline a set of official positions. Through the topics covered and the views presented, it is hoped that higher education policy makers at all levels will find inspiration and ideas for their own work.

Volumes published in the Council of Europe Higher Education Series:

1. *The university as Res Publica: higher education governance, student participation and the university as a site of citizenship* (2004, editor: Sjur Bergan);

2. *The public responsibility for higher education and research* (2005, editors: Luc Weber and Sjur Bergan).

Other Council of Europe publications on higher education

Recognition issues in the Bologna Process (2003, editor: Sjur Bergan).

Language policies in higher education: invitation to a debate (2002).

The cultural heritage of European universities (2002, editors: Nuria Sanz and Sjur Bergan).

Concepts of democratic citizenship (2000).

The Council of Europe/Unesco Convention on the Recognition of Qualifications concerning Higher Education in the European Region and its explanatory memorandum (1998).

Regional co-operation in higher education (published with the Nordic Council of Ministers as TemaNord 1998:553).

Democracy and governance in higher education (1998, editors: Jan de Groof, Guy Neave and Juraj Švec, published jointly by the Council of Europe and Kluwer Law International).

Relations between state and higher education (1996, editors: R. in't Veld, H.P. Füssel and G. Neave, published jointly by the Council of Europe and Kluwer Law International).

Recognition of higher education qualifications: challenges for the next decade (1996).

Sales agents for publications of the Council of Europe
Agents de vente des publications du Conseil de l'Europe

BELGIUM/BELGIQUE
La Librairie européenne SA
Rue de l'Orme 1
1040 BRUXELLES
Tel.: (32) 2 231 04 35
Fax: (32) 2 735 08 60
E-mail:mail@libeurop.be
http://www.libeurop.be

Jean de Lannoy
202, avenue du Roi
B-1190 BRUXELLES
Tel.: (32) 2 538 4308
Fax: (32) 2 538 0841
E-mail: jean.de.lannoy@euronet.be
http://www.jean-de-lannoy.be

CANADA
Renouf Publishing Company Limited
5369 Chemin Canotek Road
CDN-OTTAWA, Ontario, K1J 9J3
Tel.: (1) 613 745 2665
Fax: (1) 613 745 7660
E-mail: order.dept@renoufbooks.com
http://www.renoufbooks.com

CZECH REPUBLIC/
RÉPUBLIQUE TCHÈQUE
Suweco Cz Dovoz Tisku Praha
Ceskomoravska 21
CZ-18021 PRAHA 9
Tel.: (420) 2 660 35 364
Fax: (420) 2 683 30 42
E-mail: import@suweco.cz

DENMARK/DANEMARK
GAD Direct
Fiolstaede 31-33
DK-1171 COPENHAGEN K
Tel.: (45) 33 13 72 33
Fax: (45) 33 12 54 94
E-mail: info@gaddirect.dk

FINLAND/FINLANDE
Akateeminen Kirjakauppa
Keskuskatu 1, PO Box 218
FIN-00381 HELSINKI
Tel.: (358) 9 121 41
Fax: (358) 9 121 4450
E-mail: akatilaus@stockmann.fi
http://www.akatilaus.akateeminen.com

FRANCE
La Documentation française
(Diffusion/Vente France entière)
124, rue H. Barbusse
F-93308 AUBERVILLIERS Cedex
Tel.: (33) 01 40 15 70 00
Fax: (33) 01 40 15 68 00
E-mail: commandes.vel@ladocfrancaise.gouv.fr
http://www.ladocfrancaise.gouv.fr

Librairie Kléber (Vente Strasbourg)
Palais de l'Europe
F-67075 STRASBOURG Cedex
Fax: (33) 03 88 52 91 21
E-mail: librairie.kleber@coe.int

GERMANY/ALLEMAGNE
AUSTRIA/AUTRICHE
August Bebel Allee 6
Am Hofgarten 10
D-53175 BONN
Tel.: (49) 2 28 94 90 20
Fax: (49) 2 28 94 90 222
E-mail: bestellung@uno-verlag.de
http://www.uno-verlag.de

GREECE/GRÈCE
Librairie Kauffmann
28, rue Stadiou
GR-ATHINAI 10564
Tel.: (30) 1 32 22 160
Fax: (30) 1 32 30 320
E-mail: ord@otenet.gr

HUNGARY/HONGRIE
Euro Info Service
Hungexpo Europa Kozpont ter 1
H-1101 BUDAPEST
Tel.: (361) 264 8270
Fax: (361) 264 8271
E-mail: euroinfo@euroinfo.hu
http://www.euroinfo.hu

ITALY/ITALIE
Libreria Commissionaria Sansoni
Via Duca di Calabria 1/1, CP 552
I-50125 FIRENZE
Tel.: (39) 556 4831
Fax: (39) 556 41257
E-mail: licosa@licosa.com
http://www.licosa.com

NETHERLANDS/PAYS-BAS
De Lindeboom Internationale Publikaties
PO Box 202, MA de Ruyterstraat 20 A
NL-7480 AE HAAKSBERGEN
Tel.: (31) 53 574 0004
Fax: (31) 53 572 9296
E-mail: books@delindeboom.com
http://www.delindeboom.com

NORWAY/NORVÈGE
Akademika, A/S Universitetsbokhandel
PO Box 84, Blindern
N-0314 OSLO
Tel.: (47) 22 85 30 30
Fax: (47) 23 12 24 20

POLAND/POLOGNE
Głowna Ksiegarnia Naukowa
im. B. Prusa
Krakowskie Przedmiescie 7
PL-00-068 WARSZAWA
Tel.: (48) 29 22 66
Fax: (48) 22 26 64 49
E-mail: inter@internews.com.pl
http://www.internews.com.pl

PORTUGAL
Livraria Portugal
Rua do Carmo, 70
P-1200 LISBOA
Tel.: (351) 13 47 49 82
Fax: (351) 13 47 02 64
E-mail: liv.portugal@mail.telepac.pt

SPAIN/ESPAGNE
Mundi-Prensa Libros SA
Castelló 37
E-28001 MADRID
Tel.: (34) 914 36 37 00
Fax: (34) 915 75 39 98
E-mail: libreria@mundiprensa.es
http://www.mundiprensa.com

SWITZERLAND/SUISSE
Adeco – Van Diermen
Chemin du Lacuez 41
CH-1807 BLONAY
Tel.: (41) 21 943 26 73
Fax: (41) 21 943 36 05
E-mail: info@adeco.org

UNITED KINGDOM/ROYAUME-UNI
TSO (formerly HMSO)
51 Nine Elms Lane
GB-LONDON SW8 5DR
Tel.: (44) 207 873 8372
Fax: (44) 207 873 8200
E-mail: customer.services@theso.co.uk
http://www.the-stationery-office.co.uk
http://www.itsofficial.net

UNITED STATES and CANADA/
ÉTATS-UNIS et CANADA
Manhattan Publishing Company
2036 Albany Post Road
CROTON-ON-HUDSON,
NY 10520, USA
Tel.: (1) 914 271 5194
Fax: (1) 914 271 5856
E-mail: Info@manhattanpublishing.com
http://www.manhattanpublishing.com

Council of Europe Publishing/Editions du Conseil de l'Europe
F-67075 Strasbourg Cedex
Tel.: (33) 03 88 41 25 81 – Fax: (33) 03 88 41 39 10 – E-mail: publishing@coe.int – Website: http://book.coe.int